Talk on television

What happens when the audience becomes an active participant in television programmes? Why do ordinary people tell their stories in public? Can rational, critical debate result from such studio discussions? Is any public good served by them or are they simply trashy entertainment which fills the schedules cheaply? Not only is everyday conversation increasingly dependent on television, but more and more people are appearing on television to discuss social and personal issues. *Talk on Television* examines the value and significance of televised public discussion and debate.

The authors analyse a wide range of programmes – including *Donahue*, *Kilroy* and *The Oprah Winfrey Show*, drawing on interviews with both the studio participants and those watching at home. They ask how the media manage audience discussion programmes, and whether the programmes really are providing new 'spaces' for public participation. They find out how audiences interpret the programmes when they appear on the screen themselves, they analyse the contribution made by 'experts', and they unravel the conventions – debate, romance, therapy – which make up the genre. They consider TV's function as a medium of education and information. Finally they discuss the dangers and opportunities the genre holds for audience participation and public debate in the future.

Sonia Livingstone is a Lecturer at the London School of Economics and Political Science. She is the author of *Making Sense of Television* (1990) and, with Peter Lunt, of *Mass Consumption and Personal Identity* (1992), as well as numerous related articles. She is also on the editorial board of *Journal of Communication* and *European Journal of Communication*.
Peter Lunt is a Lecturer in Psychology at University College, London. He is co-author of *Mass Consumption and Personal Identity* and of a series of articles on related topics.

Communication and Society
General Editor: James Curran

Talk on television

Audience participation and public debate

Sonia Livingstone and Peter Lunt

London and New York

First published 1994
by Routledge
11 New Fetter Lane, London EC4P 4EE

Simultaneously published in the USA and Canada
by Routledge
29 West 35th Street, New York, NY 10001

Typeset in 10/12 Times by Megaron, Cardiff
Printed and bound in Great Britain by Clays Ltd, St Ives plc

British Library Cataloguing in Publication Data
A catalogue record for this book is available from the British
Library.

Library of Congress Cataloging in Publication Data
Livingstone, Sonia M.
    Talk on television: audience participation and public debate/
    Sonia Livingstone and Peter Lunt.
    p.cm. – (Communication and society)
    Includes bibliographical references and index.
    1. Talk shows. 2. Television viewers. 3. Television
    broadcasting – Social aspects. I. Lunt, Peter K. (Peter
    Kenneth), 1956–. II. Title. III. Series: Communication
    and society (Routledge (Firm))
    PN1992.8.T3L58 1993
    791.45′6–dc20   93–15440
                                                                   CIP

ISBN 0–415–07737–0 (hbk)
ISBN 0–415–07738–9 (pbk)

We dedicate this book to Joseph and Anna

Contents

Tables

Acknowledgements

The original research reported in this book has been partially supported by funding from the University of Kent at Canterbury, The London School of Economics and Political Science, and University College London, and it has benefited from facilities at Oxford University.

We are grateful to many people for their constructive discussions and stimulating feedback while we were writing this book, including Jay Blumler, Sarah Butterfield, Daniel Dayan, Paul Dickerson, Rob Farr, Peter Jackson, Elihu Katz, Tamar Liebes, Rodney Livingstone, George Myerson, Tom Nossiter, Martin Roiser, Nikolas Rose and Mallory Wober. We also thank Abigail Bilkus, Graham Calvert, Paul Dickerson, Pandora Geddes, Ann Gosling, Ann Milne, Fiona Paton and Mallory Wober for their practical research help. Finally, we wish to thank all those who took part in our interviews and focus group discussions, without whom this book would not have been possible.

Chapter 1

Television talk and talking about television

OVERVIEW OF THE BOOK

In this book we examine the value and significance of public discussion and debate on television. More and more people, members of the general public and so-called experts, are appearing on television and radio to discuss and debate issues of the day. Is any purpose served by these discussions or are they simply entertainment programmes designed to fill the schedules? Why do people go on television and what kinds of discussion and debate result? Why do the broadcast media increasingly offer opportunities for participation and how do they manage the arguments which take place?

We have selected audience discussion programmes for particular attention. As cheap daytime television they are easily dismissed and they have received little critical analysis. However, through these and other forms of participatory or access programming, the broadcast media may be seen to offer new opportunities for the public to debate a wide range of political, social and moral issues on television. The opinions of viewers, participants and critics are divided over these programmes. Is this a new form of public space or forum, part of a media public sphere? Or is this a travesty of real political debate with no 'real' consequences? Do such programmes offer new opportunities to the public to question established power or are the programmes part of a media diversion from the real political and social action? In order to address such questions, we talk to viewers and programme participants in the context of an interdisciplinary analysis which raises questions about the changing role of the mass media in political discussion, participatory democracy and public discourse.

In audience discussion programmes, a studio is filled with invited lay people and experts who discuss a topical question, social problem or matter of human interest under the direction of a programme host. The experts and ordinary people are generally seated together and can each make a contribution if they get the attention or invitation of the host. The host keeps the programme moving and stops particular individuals dominating, roving among the studio audience with a microphone. Often no conclusions are reached but a range of opinions and experiences are discussed, together with the expression of strong and varied emotions. The audience discussion programme draws on several genres – the talk show, open access programming and current and consumer affairs. We ask what it would mean for this genre to match up to its own claims for making a serious contribution to public debate.

For some, it is obvious that the mass media are the only institution which can provide a space for public debate in modern society. Others argue that even if a genuine public sphere is possible, and even if the media can contribute to it positively rather than simply undermining it, then these programmes are not where this will happen. Isn't the audience too small, isn't it just composed of bored housewives, aren't the programmes too trashy and cheap? Surely it's just entertainment, not intended to be taken seriously? People are often confident in their judgements about television's supposed significance or irrelevance. However, the social scientist's concern is that any new form should be studied for its own sake: the familiar must be defamiliarized through critical analysis before we can claim to understand it.

Nonetheless, let us consider these initial criticisms of the genre. The audience for discussion programmes may be small in comparison with soap operas or situation comedies, but still it must be counted in its millions, especially if we consider the reach of programmes over one month instead of audience size on one day. Also, as economic pressures for popular and cheap television grow, audience discussion programmes may be expected to occupy an expanding slice of the schedules. Further, surprising to some, around 40 per cent of the British population is available to watch television first thing in the morning, when some of the main discussion programmes are shown, including one-fifth of full-time workers as well as the retired, the unemployed, shift-workers, students, part-time workers and housewives (Chapter 3).

The cheap-and-trashy argument has been critically reappraised in relation to the soap opera (Livingstone, 1990), where the intentions of producers have been separated from the experience of and effects on viewers. The ridiculing of soap operas by academic critics has been reappraised as often elitist and sexist. For those who watch or take part in audience discussion programmes, they may offer a constructive experience which demands analysis rather than dismissal. Finally, whatever the intentions of broadcasters in making these programmes, these do not determine the nature of the product. This must be revealed through textual analysis, and the programmes have many unintended consequences which only audience research can discover.

The original empirical research reported in this book is based on a multi-method project on the structure and reception of television audience discussion programmes conducted between 1989 and 1992. The research consisted of 12 focus group discussions following viewing of an episode of an audience discussion programme, 16 individual in-depth interviews with viewers and programme participants, textual analysis of a wide range of discussion programmes, and a survey questionnaire from some 500 respondents from a diary panel (BBC/BRB for BARB; see Chapter 3). All interviews and discussions were conducted by the authors and were taped and transcribed for analysis. Each focus group discussion was content analysed. Throughout this book, extracts from individual and group discussions are labelled to indicate the category of interview (expert or lay) or, for quotations from focus-group discussions, the group and statement code (see Appendices for further details). Extracts from programmes are transcribed verbatim.

The ideas expressed in this book have evolved gradually through many reformulations and qualifications as we watched numerous audience discussion programmes. We allowed our themes to emerge from viewing while also listening to many hours of participant and viewer interviews. The analysis is also informed by an interdisciplinary research literature which links diverse theoretical debates. The research is restricted to television programmes, but as the meaning of texts depends significantly on how viewers make sense of them, the research includes texts, viewers and participants. Few have considered this genre of television programmes and to our knowledge no research has yet interviewed either the viewers of these programmes or, more generally, those who appear on television.

The book is divided into six substantive chapters, each of which combines analysis of viewers' and participants' talk about the genre with analysis of the programmes themselves, in the context of broader theoretical debates. Chapter 2 considers recent debates over the role of the mass media in the public sphere, raising issues of the relations between participation and democracy, discourse and action, media and everyday life, citizenship and public opinion. In Chapter 3 we focus specifically on the genre of audience discussion programmes, revealing that their conventions are drawn from different discursive domains such as the debate, the romance and therapy. Through the idea of participation framework, we analyse what it means to participate either in the studio or at home, and ask about the meanings generated through such participation.

In Chapter 4 we consider debates in audience research about the critical viewer, asking how viewers respond to television programmes, what critical resources they bring to bear when making sense of programmes, and in what ways critical reception is social rather than cognitive. The relationship between expertise and common sense, as represented in discussions between experts and the public in discussion programmes, is addressed in Chapter 5. Interviews with experts and ordinary people are contrasted and the assumptions about knowledge and knowing which guide the media's management of this relationship is examined. Next we analyse the arguments that make up the discussions in relation to research on argumentation and rhetoric: what forms of argument are used and how successful are they? Finally, we return to the question of the public sphere, asking about the kind of social space in which these arguments and discussions take place. Does 'real conversation' take place in these discussions and does this produce a community of citizens talking among themselves about issues of public concern?

The studio is the institutional discursive space of radio and television. It is a public space in which and from which institutional authority is maintained and displayed [and in which] it can define the terms of social interaction in its own domain by pre-allocating social roles and statuses, and by controlling the content, style and duration of its events.

(Scannell, 1991: 2)

Throughout the book we are concerned with the ways in which certain forms – of organizing political debate, of genre, of knowledge, of argument and of social arrangement – continually escape classification. Empirical analysis of audience discussion programmes reveals a plurality of classifications or ways of understanding which coexist in a local and provisional manner. Rather than adding up, jigsaw fashion, to a complete picture of a television genre and its organization of discursive relations among participants, our analysis reveals the tensions and flux, the conflicts and mutual dependencies, of these different forms. We trace this through the issues of political debate, genre, knowledge, argument and social space, as they are illustrated by the interaction of voices participating and talking about audience discussion programmes.

THEORETICAL APPROACH

How shall we understand social communication and political action in a symbolic, media-dominated society? If talk is action, is the talk show also action–forming public opinion, making visible society's plural or marginal voices? An understanding of the media as separate from, indeed as reporting or reflecting on, political life is increasingly untenable. Whether we see the media in optimistic or pessimistic terms, we must recognize that they play a growing role in public discourse, including political participation and election campaigns. Political life is constituted through its immersion in a media-dominated world. It becomes critical to ask who has, and should have, access to and control over mediated public debate. Is open-access programming a democratic opening up of elite broadcasting practices, facilitating the contribution of special interest groups among the public to general debate? Is the viewer a member of the public (a citizen), or part of a mass audience (a consumer)?

Over 20 years ago, Blumler (1970) discussed four potential roles for television current affairs programmes: acting as spokesmen for the government; conveying information to the public; providing independent comment and criticism; editorializing on behalf of preferred policies or parties. Blumler argued that political television in Britain was moving from an emphasis on the second, informational function of disseminating expertise and representing issues of public concerns to the viewing audience, towards the third, critical function, thereby raising controversies over the media's interpretation of critical judgement, civic participation and dispassionate debate. Moreover, television has taken on an additional, populist role concerned with accountability as 'it sets out to hold politicians to account for their policies and decisions on behalf of the public by proxy' (Blumler, 1970: 97).

These controversies over critical judgement, civic participation, populism and accountability are still current. Furthermore, we suggest that, with the growth of access and discussion programmes, the mass media are now attempting three additional roles. They can act as spokesmen for the people to both government and experts, conveying opinions, experiences, information and criticism 'upwards' to the elite. They can allow the public to hold politicians and experts to account directly, rather than by proxy (raising questions not of whether the media represent public concerns without bias but of whether studio audiences are representative of the public). And they can provide a social space for communication among the lay public itself, both in the form of the studio audience and in the relation between studio and home audiences, and thus give everyday experiences and opinions a new and powerful legitimation. Thus 'in the British case, there has been a significant shift in the communicative ethos of broadcasting from an earlier authoritarian model to a more populist and democratic manner and style' (Scannell, 1991: 10) and, as Scannell also notes, from a monologic to a dialogic mode of talk. It is probably true that American broadcasting has always been more populist and conversational, having fewer elitist, Reithian restrictions on who is allowed to speak and who, supposedly, is worth hearing.

Mass media public discussions construct a role for the ordinary person who participates in them, a role which affects our understanding of the public–as citizen, consumer, client, social problem, individual or mass. They affect our expectations of social debate, our understandings of its rules and goals, and our skills in taking part. As we become increasingly familiar with the ever-broadening range of media technology and open access forms, the media become more deeply integrated into everyday life. Both cultural optimists and pessimists have discussed the role of the media in these symbolic processes in our culture. As television gives ever more space to public discussion, television itself enters into these debates, framing the discussions, offering its own perspectives and opinions, moulding the discussion to meet its own demands and purposes. Public debate, previously managed elsewhere, increasingly occurs within a media context. This context is itself discursive and is both tailored to, and simultaneously, transforms the conventions of public discourse. Through the construction of social identities and the circulation of arguments and rhetoric, mediation also transforms ordinary, private discourse.

How people talk about television affects much in our daily lives. It may direct viewing behaviour – we watch what our friends watch. It may direct our habits – we plan our meals and phone calls as well as viewing around the television schedule. It may frame programme interpretations – we negotiate which pop stars we admire, which comedies we find funny, which news we most trust. It may set conversation topics: Hobson (1982) reports discussions about last night's soap operas among women at work; Goodman (1983) discusses how families interact around the set. Anecdotally, we understand 'did you see?' as a conversational opening which may be about, or merely triggered by, a recent television programme.

Thus in many ways, talk about television may frame social relations – we negotiate our identities through talking about programme content and may reject people who make different interpretations. The effects of television depend on television talk, for example, on how parents discuss programmes with their children after viewing (Huesmann et al. 1983). No-one knows how much conversation is implicitly or explicitly triggered by television viewing, for naturally occurring conversation is notoriously hard to record (Heritage, 1991). But we know that television sets the agenda for people's concerns, that it is the major source of information for facts which are new or unavailable from the immediate environment, and that television dominates most people's leisure hours.

Relating talk on and talk about television, Scannell (1991) argues that there are considerable similarities between broadcast and face-to-face talk: both are communicative interactions intended to be heard by their audiences which are either live or simulate liveness and which may or may not permit responses (direct or simulated) from their audiences. Through everyday talk, 'individuals hold each other accountable and responsible for the maintenance of the self- evident nature of the world' (ibid: 4); through broadcast talk, the self-evident nature of the world is produced and reproduced.

The communicative interaction between programme and audience depends crucially upon the ways in which audience interests and understandings are anticipated in the construction of the programmes (through the 'model reader': Eco, 1979). It also depends on their reception by audiences. Audience reception occurs under diverse and unpredictable social conditions and these contexts of viewing, as well as the structures of the text, influences the meanings which circulate. The relationship between audience and programme or genre may be seen as contractual in that the construction of meaning is not only negotiated on-line during viewing, but is also determined in advance by a set of conventions, frameworks and expectations which each party holds of the other, formulated on the basis of past experience. While aberrant or diverse forms (of either text or reception) may occur, in general, audience and programmes operate within a fairly predictable framework of mutual expectations, for example, a framework of known genre conventions.

The evolution of a new genre, such as that of the audience discussion programme, results in unstable and diverse expectations from viewers: as we show, viewers understand this genre in different ways, resulting in different relationships between text and viewer. The programmes frequently move between diverse generic forms (see especially Chapters 3 and 6). This is not simply because the genre is at a formative stage of development but because it is inherently unstable, drawing on a variety of generic conventions in a provisional manner in order to achieve a diversity of sometimes contradictory aims: we can 'identify a self-reflexive playfulness–with language, with identity– as central characteristics of contemporary television and radio' (Scannell, 1991: 9).

Forester (1985) suggests that Habermas's theory of communicative action can be used to explore contemporary social issues, for it concerns five themes which may guide critical research:

(1) the phenomenologically meaningful experience of social action; (2) the structural staging of that action; (3) the institutional contingencies of practical actions; (4) relations of control, authority and power; and (5) the requirements and possibilities of resistance, of social action cast not simply as instrumental politics but as emancipatory political praxis.

(Forester, 1985: x)

These themes capture the approach we take to audience discussion programmes. We regard such programmes as meaningful experiences for participants and viewers, as staged by mass media institutions, as actions which have an institutional 'place' in contemporary society, as situations which involve relations of control, authority and power, and as possible sites of resistance. While Habermas's theory (1987b, 1989) proves central to our analysis of these programmes, we would also hope that our analysis may inform critical exploration of these five themes more generally.

Recent social theory has been concerned with the relations between action and social structure, discourse and power: 'how does the play of power depend on and work through the fragmentation of meaning and sense, the confusion of issues, the silencing of voice?' (Forester, 1985: x). We assume that television debates and audience discussion programmes cannot be understood as social practices without considering the sense-making activities of participants and the institutional context in which they are produced. An understanding of their social and political significance must encompass an account of the programmes as meaningful social practice.

The underlying political issue is the 'social construction and management of political consent' (Forester, 1985: xi) through participatory mass media practices in contemporary liberal democracies. The fear is that of the 'colonization of the life-world'–the propensity for capital and its admin-istrative functions to take over culture, threatening the autonomy of everyday life through the encroachment of organized instrumental power relations. Habermas's contribution, which for Forester sets the critical research agenda, is to locate social practice within social structure through the instrumental control processes which are required to embody action and through the moral issues of legitimacy by which normative social relations are constructed. Both colonization and resistance to the colonization of the life-world (the symbolic environment within which everyday lives are conducted) can take place in diverse and multiple sites. We have chosen the empirical study of audience discussion programmes as a site where life-world processes of opinion formation, group discussion and public debate are potentially colonized and undermined by media institutions and by the experts and politicians who represent established power.

In this book we examine 'the way discourses are constructed in order to achieve certain effects' (Eagleton, 1983: 205): particularly, we examine the ways the media are taking over this discursive process. In studio debates, the media present social life as conversation, bringing together its disparate elements and managing their interaction. The studio debates offer a model of a citizen's participation in the ongoing debates in society. It is our duty as responsible citizens to be informed and to have opinions about current affairs. We the audience feel obliged to make our contributions to public debate, our role beckons, the pressure is on, but the opportunity to influence the powerful and public debate is the potential prize. We all have the competence to act under these constraints because the role of the public on television is expressed through conversation. Thus we are all constructed as experts on everyday life: supposedly we all have something authentic and unique to say and no-one else knows more or better than us (Lentricchia, 1983). What opportunities and dangers lie within this model?

Graham argues that citizens can 'learn to become effective political agents on the basis of experience in more limited contexts' (Graham, 1986: 151). Regarding public debate, we ask how audiences respond to the media's implicit claims that through the studio audience debate, the dignity and worth of the individual is recognized and celebrated and that a contribution is made towards public-spirited sociopolitical decisions; both claims which Graham (1986) argues are requisite for a participatory democracy. Regarding knowledge and the public interest, we ask whether the trustworthiness and credibility of expertise is sustained through more participatory programming, so that television may still hope to inform and educate? Alternatively, are experts becoming subordinated to the 'authenticity' of lay experiences, as retold through anecdote and case history, and thus also becoming increasingly accountable to the lay agenda? Are lay and expert communicators rendered equal in the melting pot of the media forum, sharing a converging language? As the mass media are part of more general cultural changes, our analysis of audience discussion programmes is intended to illuminate broader questions concerning the nature of mass communication in contemporary society in relation to issues of the public, democracy, critical rationality and expertise.

Chapter 2

The mass media, democracy and the public sphere

INTRODUCTION

In this chapter we explore the role played by the mass media in political participation, in particular in the relationship between the laity and established power. There is a long-running debate in media theory over the ways in which the media not only disseminate elite, critical opinion but also influence the formation, expression and consumption of public opinion (Halloran, 1970; Lang and Lang, 1968). How far do the mass media provide a public sphere in which citizens may debate issues in a democratic forum and in which those in power may be held accountable to the public? In this chapter we examine the way television is responding to economic and regulatory pressures to move from a public service model towards a market model (Blumler, 1992; Collins et al. 1986; Garnham, 1990; Qualter, 1991); the media are changing their relation to political processes.

These changes affect the relationship between ordinary people and elite representatives of established power. There is a concern in liberal democracies about having an involved public. Here we are interested not so much in the degree of involvement but in different types of involvement. There is a difference between an elite democracy where communication between established power and the laity takes the form of dissemination from the powerful and the representation of ordinary beliefs as mass opinion, and a participatory democracy where established power is engaged in some kind of dialogue with the public. Recently this debate has centred on how to conceive of the role of the citizen in modern western democracies.

Both the left and right of the political spectrum are concerned with the individual as citizen, and with undermining the authority of the expert or elite (Andrews, 1991; Barbalet, 1988). The right attacks experts for their abstract, biased or ungrounded authority over the laity. They argue for reductions in restrictions on broadcasting to encourage competition according to market forces and audience demand, thereby putting pressure on the existing broadcast channels to become more accessible and populist. The left has also been concerned with the rights of individuals and the validity of everyday experience. While for the political right, citizenship signifies community, self-help and 'Victorian' morality, for the left, citizenship emphasizes human rights and civil liberties: 'citizenship, therefore, combines in rather unusual ways the *public* and *social* with the *individual* aspects of political life' (Held, 1991: 21).

Access programmes, talk shows and audience discussion programmes all capture elements of these concerns, providing a diverse appeal for both the audience and the experts, who, whether on the left or the right, have reasons and justifications for participating. It may be reason enough that the media are a powerful force in contemporary society, being increasingly implicated in the construction of political events and the management of political decisions (see, for example, Garton et al. 1991; Keane, 1991; Raboy and Dagenais, 1992).

Thus the debate over political involvement and communication has recently focused on the notion of 'citizenship', and one aspect of this concern is with the notion of the 'public sphere'. If the citizenry is to play a role in a democracy then it needs access to an institutionally guaranteed forum in which to express their opinions and to question established power. We will argue that the media now constitute the major forum for political communication. Thus the debate about public involvement of citizens in political communication leads to questions about the media as a public sphere where the relations between established power and the citizenry take place.

The starting point we have chosen for our discussion of the media as a public sphere of political communication is the work of Habermas (1984; 1989) on the bourgeois public sphere. Influenced by critical theory, Habermas sees the media as creating a society of private and fragmented individuals for whom it is difficult to form the public rational-critical opinion which could oppose established power. He attacks the media for providing a pseudo-public sphere which distracts the laity from political action, being a sphere of public relations and passive spectatorship rather than genuine public debate. However, Habermas's position (1987b) contains within it an ideal of public communication: if unfettered by institutional control, this ideal public communication might generate the critical consensus which he considers necessary for public participation in democratic political processes. Can the media potentially provide sites for public participation, expert accountability, integration of expert and lay knowledge and the provision of ideal com-municative situations?

Habermas's position reflects the ambivalence felt by many towards the mass media – that here is a great power, but can it be harnessed for the public good? We suggest that pessimistic answers tend to underestimate the complex and contradictory or fragmented nature of the contemporary mass media which opens the way for some escape from institutional control, while more optimistic positions often set too high ideals for the public sphere. Those alternative formulations of the public sphere which recognise and build on the complex and fragmentary nature of the media suggest more positively that the media could facilitate and legitimize the public negotiation – through compromise rather than consensus – of meanings among oppositional and marginalized groups.

ELITE AND PARTICIPATORY CONCEPTIONS OF DEMOCRACY

'Democracy' is generally used to refer to the rights and responsibilities of citizens in capitalist economies. The will of the people, as expressed through representation, consent and participation, plays a central role in legitimating a democracy:

> Any claim that a certain state or government, regime or society is 'really' or 'in the last analysis' democratic, however implausible it may seem, must involve the implication that in some way or other the government, regime or state in question serves or represents the people.
>
> (Arblaster, 1987: 8–9)

> The starting point for modern theories of democracy is consent, for it is the idea that government is an artifice, legitimated only by the agreement of subjects who are 'naturally' free, that revived the democratic tradition.
>
> (Phillips, 1991: 23)

The mass media play a crucial role in the modern political process, for even in elite forms of democracy, the polity requires some mediated communication with the populace to gain consent. Freedom of expression has long been seen as essential to protecting the rights of the individual from political tyranny: a government legitimated through consent depends on a free press (Keane, 1991; Koss, 1984). However, this mediation is not neutral but affects how political processes are communicated. Talking of general elections, it is clear that 'talk is endlessly circulated around all these sites [media, politics, public relations, press conferences] in practices of commentary, quotation and polemical reformulation. Statements are thus re-presented in different discursive domains, and in this re-presentation they are transformed' (Garton et al. 1991: 100).

As the implied audience for the liberal press was the bourgeois individual, the individual was affirmed as the basic social, moral and political unit. Within the democratic tradition one can envisage a dimension of public involvement in political processes. At one end the populace has little direct role in politics but policies should be enacted in the public interest with the consent of the people. At the other extreme, ordinary people participate in the political process through voting, lobbying, inquiry, membership of political parties and trade unions, and so forth. The poles of this opposition can be used to understand a transformation from an elite to a participatory democracy. One can account for recent changes in contemporary democracies in terms of this transition.

Two problems beset this progressive conception of democracy; one is bureaucratization and the other is inequalities in political influence. The mass media contribute to both these problems, for they are social organizations which institutionalize particular forms and rights of access, modes of participation and types of influence. The political role of the media is not, therefore, simply dependent on the nature of the political process; because it mediates political communications, the workings of the mass media are also constitutive of that process. Mediated political control of the masses is easier in an elite democracy, where the media are under pressure to propound critically the ideas of the political elite to the populace. Under a more participatory democracy, control over and access to media production processes by the public becomes a vital dimension of political participation.

However, there is no necessary connection between the development of mediated systems of communication and the development of participatory democracy. For example, while there is a vast difference between the practice of democratic government in ancient Greece and the modern democratic tradition, significant features of participatory democracy also existed in those earlier times (Held, 1987). Although some were excluded from the status of citizen, the argument for individual rights has gradually led to their inclusion (see, for example, the extension of the franchise to women; Phillips, 1991). The idea of citizens' political participation suggests a democracy where individuals have a responsibility to act in the political process beyond their personal interest. This contrasts with a democracy whose concern is the provision of protective environments within which individuals can conduct their own business. For Locke, this latter was to be achieved by restricting the rights of rulers and the legitimate sphere of political decision making, resulting in a political culture based on respect for leaders and on very limited involvement in the political process for the ruled. As one of our respondents commented:

> That is certainly one of my worries, that people don't think about what is happening, and it's not really their fault, it's just the way society is going now. You work, you get a pay cheque, and you want to spend the rest of the time having fun and you don't want to think about that sort of thing [i.e. politics]. (P2.157)

While one might have expected that the gradual move towards participatory democracy would have produced a greater sense of public involvement in politics, there is some evidence of growing public apathy and a less stable electoral profile, with swings and unpredictable election results resulting from more uncommitted voters (Heath and Topf, 1987; Parry et al. 1992). There are two arguments to be made here. Firstly, the shift to participatory democracy coincides with the expansion of the mass media, and many, including Habermas (see below) attribute public apathy to the effects of the media in undermining traditional class affiliations and transforming political debate into a managed show. Secondly, Heath and Topf (1987) suggest that we are seeing a change in modes of participation as social changes since the war have produced a greater section of the population who are politically confident and competent. Ideally, they suggest a widening of the definition of civic culture beyond that of deference and involvement to include attitudes to the economic and social order: economic equity, civil liberty, and law and order are all issues which constitute the political consciousness of the modern electorate:

> What we have found, then, is evidence of widespread but long-standing distrust of politicians, coupled with a widespread and growing self-confidence on the part of the electorate to try to bring influence to bear on parliament. There is no evidence, however, that either phenomenon implies any loss of respect for democratic procedures.
>
> (Heath and Topf, 1987: 58)

Let us not take too simplistic a view of political involvement and power. If we conceptualize the political subject only as a voter then the intersection between political and social life is restricted to struggles over the franchise. However, as forms of political involvement diversify to include broader aspects of social relations, then the political subject incorporates the multiple subject positions that characterize these social relations. If the person becomes political then what constitutes a political person becomes more complicated:

> I affirm . . . the existence in each individual of multiple subject positions corresponding both to the different social relations in which the individual is inserted and to the discourses which constitute these relations.
>
> (Mouffe, 1988: 90)

However, Mouffe (1988) argues that the politicizing of social relations is a function of the post-war expansion of market capitalism and need not imply greater political power for those involved. Indeed, the contrary may be true, and she points to 'new social movements' such as feminism which offer resistances to new types of oppression which are emerging in advanced capitalist societies. The questions which she asks of these social movements might also be asked of other parties drawn into this wider conception of political participation, including the mass media:

> (1) What kind of antagonism do the new social movements express? (2) What is their link with the development of capitalism? (3) How should they be positioned in a socialist strategy? (4) What are the implications of these struggles for our conception of democracy?
>
> (Mouffe, 1988: 89)

PARTICIPATORY DEMOCRACY AND PARTICIPATORY MASS MEDIA

Carpignano et al. (1990) argue that in audience discussion programmes:

> The crisis of the bourgeois public sphere is fully visible and displayed in front of our eyes. The crisis of representational democracy is the crisis of the traditional institutions of the public sphere, the party, the union etc., and

most importantly, the present mass refusal of politics. If we think about the reconstitution of a public sphere in terms of the revitalization of old political organizations . . . then the embryonic discursive practices of a talk show might appear interesting, but ultimately insignificant . . . but if we conceive of politics today as . . . consolidated in the circulation of discursive practices rather than formal organizations, then a common place that formulates and propagates common senses and metaphors that govern our lives might be at the crossroad of a reconceptualization of collective practices.

(Carpignano et al. 1990: 54)

This view captures the ambivalence of many towards the potential of the mass media. Optimists and pessimists base their cases on different and opposed constructions of modernity (Seidman, 1990): one can analyse the media as part of the secular, millennial myth of progress or as part of the apocalyptic myth of darkness and decline. For the pessimistic approach of the critical theorists of the Frankfurt School, rationality is lost as mass culture increasingly dominates popular consciousness, offering only a consumerist culture to satisfy false, commodified desires. Some would argue that a culture of critical discourse still exists, both in academia and also as a strand surviving in public organizations and the mass media (Gouldner, 1976).

The position of the Frankfurt School has been attacked most recently by postmodern theorists for whom society is too fragmented and heterogeneous for any unitary description. Instead they advocate 'an ideal of a more open, decentralised society that values differences and permits fluidity in desires, identity, and institutional order' (Seidman, 1990: 234). Either position suggests a potentially radical role for the media through, for example, the audience discussion programmes. The programmes may offer either a forum for the critical discussion of contemporary political and social issues or alternatively they may provide opportunities for the expression of diverse social identities.

The move from elite to participatory social and political arrangements is resulting in changes within the mass media from the paternalistic 'auntie' of elite programming to a potentially more responsive and open medium. Our focus is on the growth of broadcast genres involving open access or audience participation. These can be seen to challenge traditional oppositions between producer and audience, text and reader, expert and laity, and the response of the audience has been shown by recent media research on the active, interpretive, sometimes resistant, and even subversive audience of popular culture (Curran, 1991; Livingstone, 1990; Morley, 1980). Consequently, some are enthusiastic about such forms of programming (Scannell, 1990), anticipating greater participation and involvement for the viewers, a transfer of power from a paternalistic media to an 'active viewer' (Livingstone, 1990) or 'citizen viewer' (Corner, 1991).

Nonetheless, a critical perspective on the mass media in general and on audience access and participation programmes in particular has long existed, suggesting that such programmes are a trick to capture a passive, mass audience through the illusion of influence and involvement. Lazarsfeld and Merton (1948) argued that the media have a narcotizing function on their audience, undermining the practice of democracy: 'modern media may encourage citizens to know more, even to be more opinionated, but to do less about public affairs' (Tuchman, 1988: 604). Similarly, commenting on media debates, Habermas claims that 'critical debate arranged in this manner certainly fulfils important social-psychological functions, especially that of a tranquillizing substitute for action' (Habermas, 1989: 164). Lang and Lang (1983: 21) claim that 'the mass public is still condemned to a bystander role . . . privy to, but not part of, the give-and-take through which parties with conflicting interests hammer out an acceptable policy'. The ever-increasing importance of opinion polls in elections suggests to some one way in which 'the media discourage political participation and meaningful social change' (Tuchman, 1988: 604), providing a 'managed show' (Thompson, 1990) of public participation without any accompanying influence, role or power. Elliot (1986) argues that we face 'a continuation of the shift away from involving people in society as political citizens of nation states towards involving them as consumption units in a corporate world' (Elliot, 1986: 106).

THE PUBLIC SPHERE

By 'the public sphere' we mean first of all a realm of our social life in which something approaching public opinion can be formed. Access is guaranteed to all citizens. A portion of the public sphere comes into being in every conversation in which private individuals assemble to form a public body.

(Habermas, 1984: 49)

Habermas (1987a, 1987b; see also Fraser, 1989) argues for four domains of modern social life, divided according to two dimensions: public versus private and system-integrated (roughly, based on strategic calculations and mechanistic functions concerned with money and power) versus socially-integrated (roughly, based on consensual references to moral norms and values). Material reproduction is the function of the official capitalist economy and the modern administrative state; both of these are system-integrated, but the economy is part of the private domain while the state is public. Symbolic reproduction (involving socialization, solidarity formation and cultural transmission) is the function of the two socially-integrated institutions of the modern 'life-world' – the private family and the public sphere.

The two private domains have historically been linked by the roles of worker and consumer, while the public domains have been linked by the roles of citizen and client. Habermas makes the further, historical argument that influence, having once flowed from socially-integrated to system-integrated domains, is now flowing the other way around, colonizing the life-world and undermining the public sphere. Fraser (1989) notes that these roles are gendered (consumer and client are feminine, worker and citizen are masculine) and adds in a fifth role, that of childrearer. She argues that influence also flows from the family to the economy and the state. However, she would agree with Habermas that the relations between system and life-world and the 'health' of the contemporary life-world are major concerns.

The mass media, primarily concerned with symbolic reproduction, address both family and public sphere and have complex relations with both economy and state. Does the impact of the media inevitably result in the fragmentation of public opinion or can a more positive role for the media in the formation of a discursive public sphere be worked out? For Habermas (1989), the public sphere (*Öffentlichkeit*) is a space where private individuals discuss public matters, a space which mediates between society and the state. The public sphere has a potential influence over power by forming a critical consensus which produces a coherent public opinion and by making the state accountable to its citizens: 'the public sphere is . . . what one might call the factory of politics – its site of production . . . the space in which politics is first made possible at all and communicable' (Kluge, 1981–2: 213). Central to the public sphere is 'the necessity of discursive justification of democratic politics' (Benhabib, 1992: 119).

As widespread concern grows over the way in which the public service ethos is being destroyed and replaced by a market model (Qualter, 1991) while communication and information technologies expand and diversify, Habermas's discussion of the public sphere offers much to a critical analysis of the relationship between media, power and the public. The argument is a historical one: Habermas argues that during the seventeenth and eighteenth centuries there emerged a 'bourgeois public sphere [which] created a forum in which the authority of the state could be criticized and called upon to justify itself before an informed and reasoning public' (Thompson, 1990: 109). This forum was founded on the principle of 'publicness', 'that the personal opinions of private individuals could evolve into a public opinion through the rational-critical debate of a public of citizens which was open to all and free from domination' (Thompson, 1990: 112).

Habermas's account has attracted criticism as a historical account of the rise and fall of the public sphere, for the scrutiny of revisionist historiography suggests it to be more of an idealization than a historical reality (Curran, 1991; Eley, 1992). However, it may and does still serve as 'a usefully mobilising fiction' (Robbins, 1990a: 3), particularly in amending the failure of Marxist critical social theory to distinguish sufficiently between the state and societal forums for public discussion (Fraser, 1990). This has led to an emphasis on the coercive, hegemonic role of the state in regulating broadcasting and on the cynical aims of the commercial broadcasting model:

> Mass culture has earned its rather dubious name precisely by achieving increased sales by adapting to the need for relaxation and entertainment on the part of consumer strata with relatively little education, rather than through the guidance of an enlarged public toward the appreciation of a culture undamaged in its substance.
>
> (Habermas, 1989: 165)

Television viewers might agree here:

> People are generally having less and less time to take anything seriously, and I feel that commercial pressures will feed into that because they are totally dependent on the sponsors, so you don't want all this heavy stuff, you just want a bit of light stuff, trivialization like the *Sun* newspaper. (D3.151)

> The BBC seem to be saying that they have a free voice, and yet they have always been terribly establishment, haven't they? Are they changing? (D4.184)

The market may be transforming the media into an unrepresentative, nonparticipatory system, a system made up of major, centralized monopolies, which together offer a narrower and more uniform ideological and cultural range of meanings (Curran, 1991). However, there has been insufficient theorizing of any positive vision of a public service ethic–of how broadcasting 'should' be (although see Blumler, 1992). As market models of broadcasting are partly legitimated through a critique of the elitist and patronizing aspects of the public service ethic, an emancipatory rather than an oppressive conception of the public service ethic is needed to counter the arguments for a market-led broadcasting system (Garnham, 1990; Keane, 1991; Tebbutt, 1989). After all, 'the television network, airways, belong to all of us' (P4.150) and we all know that:

> There are countries surely where they're not allowed to talk like we are, wasn't it Russia or was it in Germany, something like this? I mean, we can raise our opinions and we can discuss. (SC.320)

Arguing more positively now, Habermas claims that:

> The *bourgeois public sphere* could be understood as the sphere of private individuals assembled into a public body, which almost immediately laid claim to the officially regulated 'intellectual newspapers' for use against the public authority itself . . . To the principle of the existing power, the bourgeois public opposed the principle of supervision – that very principle which demands that proceedings be made public.
>
> (Habermas, 1984: 52)

THE MASS, THE PUBLIC, THE AUDIENCE

The concept of 'the public' has become caught up in debates over the mass media, mass consumption, feminism and democracy (Fraser, 1989). People have become suspicious of those who speak in the name, or interest, of the public (Robbins, 1990a) – as indeed, they may have of all metanarratives (Lyotard, 1984). Robbins (1990b) analyses the various rhetorical and justificatory appeals made through the use of the term 'public', where sometimes public is opposed to the market and aligned with the intellectuals, and sometimes it is opposed to the elite and aligned with consumerism:

> The current crisis of representation that subjects all 'representatives' as such to the immediate charge of abusing/inventing the 'public' from which they claim to derive legitimacy might be seen as a phenomenon produced *by* the market, and as serving the capitalist status quo rather better than it serves the public interest.
>
> (Robbins, 1990b: 105)

Traditionally, social theory distinguishes between the public and the mass (Robbins, 1990b). In contrast with the mass, Mills (1959) characterized the public as egalitarian, for as many people express opinions as receive them, as operating a form of communication which permits immediate and effective feedback, as affording the translation of public opinion into effective action even against the *status quo* or authority; and as constructing an autonomous public opinion. Institutional control over mass communication means that fewer express than receive opinions, and feedback is made near impossible for an individual. Moreover, the authorities control whether or not the outcome of expressed opinion leads to action.

In some ways, the public versus mass debate parallels that over the active versus passive audience which has recently occupied media theory (see Chapter 4). The concept of the active viewer counters images of the viewer as duped, mindless, brainwashed or manipulated. It has been supported by both the failures of effects research (Roberts and Bachen, 1981) and the successes of audience comprehension and reception research (Ang, 1985; Corner, 1991; Liebes and Katz, 1990; Livingstone, 1991) which demonstrate that viewers play an active role in the construction of programme meanings, as influenced by the viewer's sociocultural and family context (Liebes and Katz, 1990; Morley, 1986), their uses and gratifications in viewing (Blumler, Gurevitch and Katz, 1985) and their sociocognitive processes of reception and interpretation (Livingstone, 1990).

How we think about the active or passive viewer depends on our theoretical framework. The economic and production framework of early media research led to a concern with the viewer as alienated worker (seen as passive, male, a viewer of news and action-adventure) – a problem for the private domain (Adorno and Horkheimer, 1977; Halloran, 1970). The viewer as conceived by British Cultural Studies is the consumer-viewer, seen as resistant, subversive, female – a consumer of soap opera, magazines and romances, again understood as being within the private domain (Curti, 1988; Hall, 1980; Hobson, 1982). Now we have the citizen-viewer, seen as participating, potentially at least, in democratic processes of the public sphere (Corner, 1991; Curran, 1991), processes which may be more accessible to many women than the public sphere has been hitherto, being also part of domestic, daytime television. As more ordinary people participate in making television programmes as well as receiving them, this gives new force to the concept of the active viewer. In this chapter we examine the argument that participation in the mass media, as audience or as programme contributor, may count as acting as a public rather than as a mass and hence as political participation.

THE REFEUDALIZATION OF THE PUBLIC SPHERE

Habermas (1989) argues that the public sphere exists now only as a promise. Party politics and the manipulation of the mass media have resulted in 'a "refeudalization" of the public sphere, where representation and appearances outweigh rational debate' (Holub, 1991: 6) and where the rational–critical public is transformed into a mass, manipulated by persuasive authority. The public sphere has been undermined by, among other factors, class biases in criteria of admission, the expansion of an interventionist state, new techniques of opinion management and a loss of institutional meeting places. 'This *refeudalization of the public sphere* turns the latter into a theatre and turns politics into a managed show in which leaders and parties routinely seek the acclamatory assent of a depoliticized population' (Thompson, 1990: 113). Thus:

> Large organizations strive for political compromises with the state and with each other, excluding the public sphere whenever possible. But at the same time the large organizations must assure themselves of at least plebiscitary support from the mass of the population through an apparent display of openness.
>
> (Habermas, 1984: 54)

The mass media are a medium of talk, of communicative action, of potential consensus: 'today newspapers and magazines, radio and television are the media of the public sphere' (Habermas, 1984: 49). To the extent that refeudalization has occurred, Habermas is highly critical of the role of the media in the public – or pseudo-public – sphere. He argues that we have moved from a culture-debating to a culture-consuming public:

> The deprivatized province of interiority was hollowed out by the mass media; a pseudo-public sphere of a no longer literary public was patched together to create a sort of superfamilial zone of familiarity.
>
> (Habermas, 1989: 162)

Marx 'denounced public opinion as false consciousness: it hid before itself its own true character as a mask of bourgeois class interests' (Habermas, 1989: 124). Following Marx, it has been argued that, as the public is divided against itself into property owners and the workers, there can be no unified public voice (or 'general public'), no-one can abstract from their particular class position to speak for everyone, and 'citizens' now expect services to be provided for them without having to participate politically. Political communication, particularly during election campaigns, may be seen to be managed or 'designed' increasingly by the mass media (Lang and Lang, 1983; Negrine, 1989; Nimmo and Combs, 1990). Private voting patterns do not add up to Habermas's conception of public opinion: they are not formed rationally, nor in discussion with others, and so do not constitute critical, rational participation. Parliament can be seen as evolving away from a debating body, so that the real decisions are made more through political lobbying, committees and prearranged deals (Grant, 1989), and the debating chamber becomes a display of party unity rather than of genuine debate (Thompson, 1990). The televising of parliament made this change public, and maybe exacerbated it:

> Since we have seen parliament and question time, we've all changed our views on parliament. In parliament you don't deviate from your strongly held view, you just get up and contradict. (SC.523)

As traditional social class ties weaken, a political culture of persuasion has grown up, where ideas are paraded as goods for the electorate to consume rather than as representing underlying class interest or other political ideology. In the mass media also, the elite try to persuade and the mass consume according to personal taste. As media effects and attitude persuasion research has shown (Bryant and Zillman, 1986; Petty and Cacioppo, 1981), even those who are informed and do argue in public spaces often tend only to mutually confirm their previous ideas: 'most people have got a very definite view on politics and they are not going to change their minds' (F1.149). Thus argument does not necessarily result in public opinion change but rather becomes an opportunity to express diverse persuasive appeals:

> Publicity loses its critical function in favour of a staged display; even arguments are transmuted into symbols to which again one can not respond by arguing but only by identifying with them.
>
> (Habermas, 1989: 206)

POSSIBILITIES FOR CRITICAL–RATIONAL PUBLIC DEBATE

Habermas (1987b) later holds open the possibility of rational debate, thus suggesting the incompleteness of the process of refeudalisation in the public sphere. Based on a universal pragmatics whose principles specify the conditions which make utterances possible, he outlines a model of undistorted rational communication which is essential for the potentially emancipatory role he assigns to public discourse in a democratic society. So, while the bourgeois public sphere failed because it could never satisfy the institutional conditions for open dialogue, the possibility remains that language itself may escape institutional control. That the refeudalisation of the public sphere is as yet incomplete is supported by the active audience debate. Because of the complexities and technological developments of modern media:

> The individuals who receive mediated messages have acquired new forms of power and a new awareness of rights . . . it has also given [political] leaders a new visibility and vulnerability before audiences which are more extensive and endowed with more information and more power . . . than ever before.
>
> (Thompson, 1990: 115)

Thus the individual may not simply be the passive consumer which the media – and critics of the culture industry – often assume. One may argue that in contemporary society it is not possible for the media to fashion the world so completely and consistently, that no attempt to influence can be so successful, so lacking in interstices, so without contradictions. Thus it remains possible that public interests can be served by mass communication. For Habermas, the laity can only retain influence over established power through the development of 'self-organised public spheres'. The inherent problem with any attempt to organize and galvanize public opinion in the mass media age is that 'autonomous public spheres can draw their strength only from the resources of largely rationalized life-worlds' (Habermas, 1987a: 361), thereby risking social control at the moment when the formation and the expression of public opinion takes place.

Consequently, public opinion may function as a critical influence in democratic debate and decisions, or as an object to be moulded, the result of public communication or opinion management. The process of making opinion public may correspondingly be understood as critical or manipulative but however it is understood, the mass media play a central role. In contrast to Habermas's conception of the mass media as fully institutionalized and all-powerful, there have been some recent attempts to theorize the media as being one of many sources of influence on public opinion. Garnham (1990) attempts to revalue the public service ethic, Ang (1985) analyses the diverse ways in which the media may be seen as either oppressive or emancipatory, and Curran (1991) proposes that the mass media has a radical-democratic potential. These arguments suggest that there are a number of contradictions in the contemporary political functions of television. The media contains both manipulative and emancipatory elements.

Some of the contradictions inherent in the media are illustrated by Scannell's analysis of how, since the 1930s, the British Broadcasting Corporation has aspired to a representative mediatory role between government and people. For example, it has attempted to provide the public with both an awareness of the consequences of unemployment and a role in terms of individual action to mitigate those consequences (Scannell, 1986). On the other hand, direct public access to the mass media, which raises problematic issues of political participation, citizenship, public opinion and the active viewer, has traditionally been heavily limited, especially compared to the access given to representatives of elite groups (Scannell and Cardiff, 1991; Tebbutt, 1989). Audience participation has been generally restricted to audience measurement and viewers' letters. While the industry may state that 'we owe it to our audience as well as to ourselves to establish some systematic method of inviting the public to participate in shaping what we do' (Frank Stanton of CBS, 1960, quoted in Bower, 1973), this has probably been valued more by the industry than by the audience itself and has certainly been regarded cynically by social commentators.

The attempt to treat public service listeners as citizens rather than consumers and the subsequent undermining of this attempt by the market model reflects the fundamental contradiction between conceptions of the individual in the political and economic realms (for Habermas, the public and the private realms):

> Within the political realm the individual is defined as a citizen exercising public rights of debate, voting, etc., within a communally agreed structure of rules and towards communally defined ends. The value system is essentially social and the legitimate end of social action is the public good. Within the economic realm on the other hand the individual is defined as producer and consumer exercising private rights through purchasing power on the market in the pursuit of private interests, his or her actions being coordinated by the invisible hand of the market.
>
> (Garnham, 1990: 110)

While the mass media operate across both realms, 'political communication is forced to channel itself via commercial media' (Garnham, 1990: 111), thus prioritizing the individual as private consumer over the individual as public citizen. Social commentators, viewers and viewer organizations believe in widespread and diverse participation in rational public debate. A contemporary problem is that the opposition between public broadcasting and commercial broadcasting has been linked to elite and participatory forms of democracy. Thus one line of justification for commercial conditions in broadcasting is that public broadcasting is elitist. The problem is that commercial interest uses an emancipatory rhetoric offering the illusion of involvement relative to public broadcasting. Neither model allows for the emergence of a critical public sphere. The elite model reduces public to mass opinion and communication to dissemination; the market model uses involvement to position the viewer as consumer rather than citizen. Participatory television such as the audience discussion programmes exist in the interstices of these two models. Public broadcast opens up to the public, commercial television gains a conscience. The move to participation provides the unintended consequences of involvement.

SPECIAL INTEREST GROUPS AND PUBLICITY

You need to have responsible people, authoritative people, civil servants, where the particular area being discussed is an area where civil servants are involved directly in making decisions. You want the decision makers in there, the people who actually have to deal with the problem, if it's the police, you want to have policemen in there, you know. And if it's the army you need to have some soldiers in there, and I'm sure Kilroy wouldn't hesitate in any of those cases to try and get people to express those points of view. I would be disappointed if any of the organizations concerned were reluctant to allow representatives to go along and express their own personal views.

(George, viewer)

Political parties, special-interest groups, pressure groups, charities and so forth, which operate according to their own internal public spheres, may generate a kind of quasi-public opinion. Their representatives then enter the general public sphere to express opinions which, insofar as they also represent broader public opinion, may contribute to a rational–critical public debate, influence political processes and hold the system accountable. How 'public' the opinion expressed is depends on how the organization's membership is constituted and how it relates to the state, to other social organizations, and to the mass media.

However, special interest groups arise from the private sphere and, together with political parties which arise from the public sphere, they may use the mass media to attempt to squeeze out the public, often obtaining their consent through manipulated acquiescence rather than critical discussion. Associations become concerned with the representative showing of their members in the public sphere – 'the aura of personally represented authority' (Habermas, 1989: 200) as a part of public relations and the refeudalized public sphere: 'the public sphere becomes the court *before* which public prestige can be displayed – rather than *in* which public critical debate is carried on' (Habermas, 1989: 201). If the public sphere is not genuine, accountability cannot be authentic, but is rather a matter of public relations.

Nonetheless, public debate among special interest groups may generate contestation and negotiation, if not critical discussion, as well as the dissemination of interested views. Further, special interest representatives may represent the views of particular, often disempowered publics (such as the disabled or the elderly) who are frequently excluded from the general public sphere of public meetings, public consultations and media debates. Public debate between special interest group representatives thus brings specific or local issues to a wider public and makes conflicts visible.

At least these processes bring significant, previously hidden aspects of political processes into the public domain. The opportunity of influencing the public is so great that special interest groups, established power and members of the public are compelled to run the risk of public exposure. In Habermas's theory, one gets the impression of politics as a complex, emergent process where discussions, debates and negotiations take place in private (in families, committee rooms and the meetings of special interest groups) only coming to the light of critical exposure when they have been formulated clearly and in controlled forms of debate. Participatory programming brings public exposure earlier in this process. Ideas and opinions don't have to be 'well formed' before they can be expressed. Committees don't have to make hard-and-fast decisions to respond on a given issue and special interest groups don't need to have a worked-out position from which to speak. The media thus enter the political process at a more open, less formalized stage, when there are not necessarily any clear opinions, policies or positions which the media can manipulate and control. The interaction between parties to the discussion is discursive rather than a formal exchange of views. Getting involved in discursive exchange transforms all parties, which is not true of the dissemination of information. However, whether this transformation is one of changing the mode of public relations or whether it changes the processes of politics and everyday life is a question which goes beyond the scope of this book.

THE OPPOSITIONAL PUBLIC SPHERE

The view that the mediated public sphere is an illusion which masks the hegemonic domination of the masses by the bourgeoisie is receiving considerable criticism (Curran, 1991; Garnham, 1990). Lyotard (1984) claims that power cannot be and is not centralized in any one social stratum, but rather that it is dispersed across diverse institutions and discourses, including the mass media. The very idea of 'the public', as unitary, homogenous and able to speak disinterestedly, must be problematized, for it is 'fragmented into a mass of competing interest groups' (Fraser, 1990: 59) who may or may not represent fairly all sections of the general public. At times, Habermas does speak of plural public spheres (Benhabib, 1992), although for him, it is vital that they come together, however problematically, with some kind of underlying harmony prior to, and in order for there to be, a confrontation between the public and established power.

For Habermas, the potential for a public sphere exists in the commonalities and consensus which arise through the disinterested exchange of views, weakening traditional boundaries between groups. However, more open, mediated communication between groups in society may not achieve consensus but rather have other consequences, suggesting a reformulation of the character of the contemporary public sphere. Let us consider alternative models of the public sphere based on oppositional, conflictual or radical democratic situations in which diverse social groups discuss, negotiate and dispute.

The tendency of the bourgeois public sphere which concerns Habermas is to become increasingly institutionalized and specialized, and so to increasingly exclude dissenting or critical voices. However, although apparently excluded, dissenting voices tend to form alternative forums for discussion which, for Negt and Kluge, generate an oppositional public sphere: 'a type of public sphere which is changing and expanding, increasing the possibilities for a public articulation of experience' (Kluge, 1981-2: 211), for 'in terms of community . . . what I have in common with other people . . . is the basis for processes of social change' (ibid: 213). In contrast to the bourgeois public sphere, conflicts of interest are recognized and expected in this proletarian public sphere (Negt and Kluge, 1990). The sociological conditions of this public sphere are not those of access and disinterested contribution but forms of mass communication:

> A public sphere can be produced professionally only when you accept the degree of abstraction which is involved in carrying one piece of information to another place in society, when you establish lines of communication. That's the only way we can create an oppositional public sphere and thus expand the existing public sphere. This is an occupation which is just as important as direct action, the immediate on-the-spot struggle.
>
> (Kluge, 1981-2: 212)

Others identify possibilities for the public sphere in local contexts where negotiation and debate are institutionally accepted. For example, Mann (1990: 81) distinguishes 'between the relatively universal and apolitical public sphere of mass media entertainment, and the vast numbers of de-centered yet highly politicized public spheres currently existing within specific institutional contexts'. Through analysing a specific period of conflict at The City College of New York, Mann describes the emergence of a political public sphere which aims to 'formulate unifying discourses capable of providing the basis for consciously chosen communities, in the face of myriad and conflicting interests' (ibid: 81). This model of the public sphere does not depend on the unifying reason and consensus of Habermas's public sphere nor on the inevitable conflicts between opposed counterpublics in the oppositional public sphere. Rather, it emphasizes the possibility for the negotiation of provisional unifying discourses in local spaces where a shared conception of community and joint action may have broken down.

In practice, the bourgeois public sphere excluded major sections of society (women, the working class, children). This specialization restricted the diversity of meanings which contribute to opinion formation. Ironically, it also resulted in a host of marginal and conflicting voices, supporting the development of special interest groups to represent these repressed voices in a public sphere based on opposition or negotiation:

> Arrangements that accommodate contestation among a plurality of competing publics better promote the ideal of participatory parity than does a single, comprehensive, overarching public.
>
> (Fraser, 1990: 66)

We have seen that there is a debate occurring over the constitution of an ideal public sphere which differs in terms of the implications of organizing the public sphere prior to publication and debate. The two positions we have outlined suggest that either the public sphere should only include positions organized at the level of having gained social consensus, or that the process of public debate should be opened up at the point of contest and opinion formation. The Habermasian bourgeois public sphere also differs from the oppositional (or negotiation-based) public sphere in terms of the proposed character of rational–critical public debate. In the former, rational–critical debate involves reasoned consideration of other positions to generate a genuine amendment of original positions in the light of new arguments. The latter does not generate such a consensus, but rather aims for a negotiated compromise: each side brings pre-prepared arguments which carry rhetorical rather than rational weight so as to achieve the best compromise as judged by the more persuasive side. Neither side need concede the other's arguments but merely agrees a midway position.

Both forms of debate are reasoned, democratic procedures and both may be included by the mass media although the management of these different debate forms would differ. The bourgeois public sphere requires power inequalities to be transcended in the search for a consensus in favour of the public good. The oppositional public sphere attempts explicitly to balance differences, facilitating the representation of the less powerful and regulating the discourse of the more powerful in order to arrive at a fair and workable compromise.

In all these conceptions of the public sphere a heavy burden is placed on dialogue, particularly when 'people participate in more than one public' (Fraser, 1990: 70) and when these publics may overlap. Surely the mass media have a potentially significant role to play in bringing diverse cultures or groups together in discussion? Abrams argues that 'the universality of broadcasting puts the media in a false relation to society. They are impelled to treat as homogenous what is in fact a tangle of more or less dissimilar groups' (Abrams, 1964: 53). However, in the oppositional public sphere, the media may play a potentially emancipatory role, albeit unintended, if we see appearing on television as cutting across the exclusions of traditional forms of representation. Television potentially disrupts the attempt to control involvement in and access to public debates, not simply by influencing such events but by transforming them into 'media events' in which a more diverse public may play a role. This forces the political into the personal arena and makes possible a form of life politics (Giddens, 1991). In contrast, Habermas is mainly concerned with the ways that the media as industrial institutions may disrupt the expression and construction of consensus in the life-world. While Habermas focuses on the disruption of the life-world and Fraser focuses on the transformation of political processes, both these are concerned with the potentially disruptive and transformative effects of the mass media.

Drawing on both liberal and critical traditions, Curran (1991) offers a radical democratic theory of the mass media. A democratic mass media should represent all significant interest groups, thereby 'assisting the equitable negotiation or arbitration of competing interests through democratic processes' (Curran, 1991: 30). While this requirement is operationalized differently in different countries, it has always been present over the history of the mass media, at least through the radical and alternative press. Curran argues for wider public access to the mainstream media so that special interest groups, pressure groups and so forth, may counter the privileged access and impact of elite groups. On this view, 'the media are assumed to be caught in an ideological crossfire rather than acting as a fully conscripted servant of the social order' (Curran, 1991: 37).

For Habermas, public criticism has been appropriated by the culture industry, transforming the public into a mindless mass. As the system increasingly penetrates the life-world, any institutional space from which the public might oppose established power, such as that once provided by the bourgeois public sphere, is undermined and a crisis of legitimation results. Proponents of the oppositional public sphere regard the legitimation crisis as resulting from established power imposing elite views on the public, (mis)conceived as a homogeneous mass, such that the actual diversity of voices is excluded from the public sphere. For while the mindless mass undermines the critical rationality demanded by Habermas, the homogeneous mass undermines the diversity perceived by, for example, Fraser. Habermas wants the public to create a position from which it can debate with established power. He also implies that critical rationality is now lost to the life-world as the public sphere has been refeudalized. Fraser thinks, in contrast, that the life-world is rich in critical voices which go unheard by established power.

Underlying these debates is a question as to whether the public has become fragmented, making collective action impossible or diversified, where diversity has the potential to subvert those ideological processes which construct the public as a mass to be governed. Different answers suggest different solutions to the legitimation crisis. One can focus on instituting a public sphere to produce a consensus which can engage with established power through critical discussion. Here a liberal conception of the self-conscious individual as the locus of reason is presumed – the bourgeois gentleman (Dews, 1987). Or one can aim to give voice to the diversity of subject positions in society so as to subvert the hegemony of the elite and challenge established power into taking account of the various oppositional interests in the public sphere. Or at least, on this latter view, the public might escape or resist state control by deflecting or reappropriating meanings, exploiting the fact that control can only be applied locally and provisionally and refusing the subject position of the mass by responding in unpredictable ways to the dictates of the state; we borrow here from Foucault's (1970) analysis of power in modern society as distributed, negotiable and ever-shifting.

For Foucault, the possibilities for change are rooted in the fragile, dispersed and contestable nature of power in modern society, not in the construction of an ideal individual or public who will debate 'head to head' with established power. Thus we should not then inquire about the possibilities for an emancipatory media in the sense of either constructing a consensual public opinion to challenge an idealized, centralized established power or giving the oppressed an opportunity to resist. Rather they may provide a site where the distributed processes of power can be enacted and resisted in diverse ways.

To the majority of the public who support the *status quo*, these expectations of conflict and diversity may appear unreasonable:

> You have to have a minority to make sure that the other side has its say, whether the minority is the people who complain about their GPs or the gay community or drug pushers. And on the box it looks like it is an equal say. Sometimes you don't always appreciate that the minority is a very small minority. (D4.202)

> Sometimes it is an equal voice which they don't deserve. The chap who keeps the rottweilers must be allowed to have his say – the rottweiler is a very nice dog. (D4.204)

POLITICAL ACTION

How do discussions in a public sphere, however conceived, translate into action consequences? For Habermas, there are no longer any such consequences, for in a democracy:

> The citizens themselves participate in the formation of collective consciousness, but they cannot act collectively . . . today politics has become an affair of a functionally specialized subsystem.
>
> (Habermas, 1987a: 360)

Political action is commonly understood in terms of voting: 'according to the theory of democratic government, an informed populace is the bulwark of freedom . . . it is the citizen's duty to form an opinion about public affairs and to express it at the ballot-box' (Oskamp, 1977: 97). However, other forms of expression of public opinion may also be significant, broadening the notion of political action to include the discursive (see Curran, 1991; Gastil, 1992). Indeed, the common-sense opposition between talk and action, with its implicit devaluation of talk, has itself been challenged: talk is action, action is communicative (Austin, 1962; Quinn and Holland, 1987). Mann (1990) provides a case study of how a public sphere, in this case, a local community-based public sphere, can promote actual political action, although she sees the media as relatively disengaged from lived social practices and hence concerned with escape from rather than connection with everyday experiences. Nonetheless:

> Public spheres of discursive interaction, such as television, play a large role in bridging or mediating the gap between our unrealized political ideals and our lived social relationships. The interesting questions involve the *quality* of that mediation.
>
> (Mann, 1990: 87)

Fraser links the public sphere to a Goffmanian dramaturgical model: 'a theatre in modern societies in which political participation is enacted through the medium of talk' (Fraser, 1990: 57; Goffman, 1981). Thus an analysis of the public sphere is indispensable to critical social theory because, broadly speaking, political theory has hitherto neglected the role of public communication in the democratic process, even though 'changes in media structure and media policy . . . are properly political questions of as much importance as the question of whether or not to introduce proportional representation, of relations between local and national government, of subsidies to political parties' (Garnham, 1990: 104). One wonders why talking face-to-face with one's member of parliament in the MP's surgery or at a public meeting is regarded as political participation, but not talking to one's MP on television, or watching someone else talk to one's MP.

If not political participation, public forums such as access and participation programmes, can be thought of as social events and so involve informal, social participation. This raises questions about the rights and responsibilities of the ordinary person when he or she is transformed into a public social actor and hence about his or her relations to those in power. In a participatory democracy, consent and public participation are mediated in a discursive context which affords opportunities for involvement and dangers of persuasion for the various interested groups in society (Gastil, 1992). Surely the public sphere must affect voting, trade union and pressure group activities and so forth, by affecting the climate of public opinion, by setting the agenda for discussion, and by framing the meaning of key terms in political debate? Interestingly, political participation as narrowly defined is a minority activity – few among the general public participate in pressure groups, trade unions or public meetings, and even voting is dropping off in advanced capitalist countries. A more discursive notion of participation may be as significant for involving the majority of the public in the fairly undemanding activity of talk and opinion formation. Even some of the medium's critics argue that in some programmes:

Not only is information of some public importance effectively communicated, but a contribution is made to the discussion of public issues and
a public hitherto excluded from such discussions at any influential level is
given access – if only as spectators – to the arenas in which public issues are
decided. Television functions, as the Press once functioned, to create and
maintain an informed and politically relevant public opinion.

(Abrams, 1964: 69)

This positioning of the media as marginal to political processes is being
challenged by proponents of oppositional, local and negotiated public
spheres. These latter would distinguish between the events which are
peripheral and those which have the appearance of the marginal but which
significantly affect the negotiation and circulation of meanings in contemporary society (Giddens, 1992; Shields, 1991). Conceived as such a space,
the media and popular culture in general are part of discursive democracy
rather than a sphere of social activity separated from the political.

THE MASS MEDIA AS CULTURAL FORUM

The development of broadcasting in its institutional forms has had major
consequences for modern democratic politics . . . It became a forum for
debate and discussion on current matters of general concern, and thus a
new site for the formation of public opinion.

(Collins et al. 1986: 212)

Isn't that the climate of today, that people will not be muffled. So you can
demand something from television and radio, it is more independent than it
used to be. (D4.187)

It's part of the democratic process. It is a good thing to air issues, in general.
(D4.91)

Informal, mass mediated participation results in what Newcomb and Hirsch
(1984) have termed a cultural forum for topical public discussion and debate,
as distinct from, although potentially overlapping with, the public sphere. The
cultural forum may not generate a clear and consensual position but rather
offers a range of diverse positions, providing an active role for the viewer in
debate. In this respect, it is more akin to the oppositional than the bourgeois
public sphere. For Newcomb and Hirsch (1984), even if conservative
viewpoints are advocated, this is less significant than the airing of the debate: it
is the '*range* of response, the directly contradictory readings of the medium,
that cue us to its multiple meanings' (Newcomb and Hirsch, 1981: 68). While
this media discussion occurs in public it is echoed and continued privately in
the living room, connecting public forms of argument on television and the
formation of private opinion.

What is the product of a public debate? The traditional forum, based on the public sphere, implies not only a multiplicity of voices in debate and disagreement but also rules of debate by which conflicts are addressed, not evaded, and arguments are analysed rather than simply aired. These may be too stringent requirements for the present-day mass media cultural forum, which may more simply place arguments side by side without analysis or integration: the discussion may hold together because it functions as a recognized, and thus 'coherent', social occasion (Livingstone et al. 1992). To debate without conclusion is to celebrate the wisdom of the populace but to fight shy of promoting the insight of popular decisions beyond the bounds of the programme.

Beyond providing people with a 'place' in which to meet (see Chapter 7) and permitting the expression of diverse voices, media debates also provide a source of social representations: 'the equivalent, in our society, of the myths and belief systems in traditional societies; they might even be said to be the contemporary version of common sense' (Moscovici, 1981: 181). Indeed, television is increasingly a major medium for the generation of social representations or myths, and discussions and debates play their part here, particularly in popularizing expert knowledge for mass consumption (Livingstone, 1987; Moscovici, 1984).

Moscovici (1984) outlines four conditions for the emergence of social representations, each of which fits the audience discussion programmes (see Chapter 3): the representation of an issue must emerge through the conversation of ordinary people (the studio audience); a vital contribution is provided by 'amateur scholars' who mediate between scientific knowledge and the laity (the experts); the debate is typically held at a time of social concern or crisis (the topical issues); finally, the social representation may emerge through a variety of debate forms, resulting in a vocabulary, lay theories, causal explanations, cognitive frames and prototypical examples (see Livingstone et al. 1992 for this process in discussion programmes).

If participation includes talk as action, then a further consequence of audience participation is the construction and maintenance of social identities and of power relations. However, social and psychological implications of participating in public spheres, pseudo or genuine are unclear – these form a significant concern of this book. Audience discussion programmes are a forum in which people can speak in their own voice, which, as Gilligan (1982) emphasizes, is vital for the construction of a gendered or cultural identity.

PUBLIC CONTESTATION AND PLURAL VOICES IN THE AUDIENCE DISCUSSION PROGRAMME

For some commentators, the audience discussion programme is an example of the pseudo-public sphere, with little to recommend it:

The very call for a space of open public discussion is closed by the structural demands of that media form in which most discussion today takes place. Reason reveals itself to be what it really is: a show, a spectacle in which truth is not a content but, à la Russian Formalism, a *device*, an alibi, to get excitement going, to make a scene. One watches really more for the excitement, the good fight, than for the enunciating of reasoned positions within the society.

(Polan, 1990: 260)

The audience discussion programme may not conform to the bourgeois debate and yet may still be compatible with oppositional conceptions of public spheres as sites of discursive contestation. Apparent lack of structure and control of argumentation may signify communicative conflict rather than emotional noise. For in addition to the specific and diverse public spheres, there must also be:

The possibility of an additional, more comprehensive arena in which members of different, more limited publics talk across lines of cultural diversity . . . our hypothetical egalitarian, multi-cultural society would surely have to entertain debates over policies and issues affecting everyone. The question is: would participants in such debates share enough in the way of values, expressive norms, and, therefore, protocols of persuasion to lend their talk the quality of deliberations aimed at reaching agreement through giving reasons? In my view, this is better treated as an empirical question than as a conceptual question.

(Fraser, 1990: 69)

One approach to this empirical question forms a central focus of this book: are audience discussion programmes a possible space for such communication? How could we determine the success of this communication and what character would the space have? These programmes may be partly about working out ways in which such communication can take place – negotiating a process of communication – rather than actually exhibiting a successful product: less a site where successful communication across diverse publics occurs than one where the exploration of such possibilities is undertaken. Television has a role to play in constructing a space rather than providing one, in negotiating an interactional style, and in bringing together diverse publics rather than displaying a common, unified public.

There are other criteria we can suggest to evaluate audience discussion programmes as public spheres. Following Mills's distinction between public and mass, the participants must be constructed as a public rather than a mass – with equal rights to speak, with feedback, with action consequences and without media manipulation. Also in this oppositional and plural public space, all topics must be permissible (as hosts of audience discussion programmes will agree) – no-one can speak for humanity in general by pre-specifying topics of concern to diverse groups. The public agenda must emerge: it is typically thrown up by events of the day–the contests 'out there'. Similarly, the definition of a successful conclusion cannot be specified in advance, for different participating publics may draw different conclusions from a debate: emergent conclusions may be plural and not necessarily consensual.

Audience debates also raise issues of the relation between the expert or elite and the public, focusing on questions of knowledge, access and accountability. Lang and Lang (1983: 297) concluded from the reporting of Watergate that 'the ubiquitous presence of television most directly affects the political actors themselves. It forces them to be responsive to norms binding on other members of society'. They argue further that public debate complicates the resolution of political controversies because the media 'modify the rules of the game, forcing politicians to justify themselves to an ever larger public' (ibid: 305). Moreover, 'to have influence, opinion has to be visible' (ibid: 19). By providing a space for expressing public opinion, access programming implicitly allows public opinion to have influence – a populist move by which broadcasting organizations may claim accountability in terms of an 'extra-political power base' (Heller, 1978), apparently 'seeking direct guidance from the people on the details of policy' (Lang and Lang, 1983: 15).

The cultural significance of putting ordinary people on television, then, is that the viewer is constructed as citizen, with the right to decide policy and the information – the data of everyday experience – on which decisions are based. Audience discussion programmes provide a space in which ordinary experiences are collected together as grounding for a decision, with the help or hindrance of experts:

> He managed to fill the studio with people all of whom had something different to contribute, people who were victims, there was a magistrate, there was an MP. You know, he had really done a good job of getting a group of people together who could all add something, and I've found this is rather characteristic of Kilroy's programmes . . . I found it quite interesting that he had managed to obtain two people to sit in his audience and say that they would not condemn terrorism.
>
> (George, viewer)

However, the participants in Habermas's public sphere are private citizens, not state officials or official representatives of public bodies. In contrast, audience discussion programmes include members of various 'official' bodies (for example, parliament, the health service, charities, the police). These representatives of official state bodies are present in an official 'public relations' capacity, and so their presence has no necessary decision-making consequences. They are not acting as private citizens for they are there to be publicly accountable, as part of their official role. For Habermas, it is important that these discussions do not result in decisions, or else the critical potential would be lost– the public would become the state.

However, some public debates do also have decision-making consequences – Fraser discusses the case of parliament; we could add the self-regulating activities of many local publics, as in Mann's City College of New York example, or residential communities, trade unions, etc. As Fraser (1990) notes, as soon as such internal forums or 'strong publics' translate opinion into action, questions arise about their relation to the general public ('weak publics') whom they supposedly represent, and issues of representativeness and accountability come to the fore. There is a trade-off implicit in the construction of public spheres: they may provide open access or establish representatives; they may form opinion only or they may translate this into actions with questionable accountability.

Having argued for plural public spheres rather than a unified consensus, we must ask about the (plural and diverse) relations between public spheres. Particularly, what forms of communication are possible, and how are these managed in relation to state intervention and power inequalities between participants? Fraser argues for a 'post-bourgeois' conception of the public sphere which raises crucial questions for a democratic society. She outlines four criteria for a post-bourgeois public sphere, which resemble Mills's four criteria for a public as opposed to a mass, and which we can here ask directly of audience discussion programmes. Are social inequalities rendered visible? (Who goes on these programmes, how are they selected, what are their motivations for appearing?) How are different publics differentially empowered? (Who speaks, who is silent, who determines what can be said, how is the debate managed, whose voice concludes?) Which topics are labelled public or private? (How are topics selected, what is omitted, how are topics covered or selectively ignored?) How is public opinion translated into political or social action? (What social value or impact do these programmes have?)

Extending the political franchise bestows political rights, which promote political interest beyond voting, and leads to a broader struggle to gain more political power and to the 'widening of social conflict as the extension of the democratic revolution into more and more spheres of social life, into more social relations' (Mouffe, 1988: 95; see also Giddens, 1992). In this context, the audience discussion programme, as a forum for the expression of diversity, the contestation of multiple positions, and the interfacing of many discourses, becomes a part of contemporary political processes.

CONCLUSIONS

We have proposed that there are, broadly speaking, two approaches to analysing and assessing the role of the mass media in public life. One account, drawn principally from the work of Habermas, suggests that there is an ideal form of public debate which, if it can find an institutional context, potentially allows equality of access and equal rights to all citizens. This supports the development of public opinion which in turn limits the incursion of bureaucratic and political control into everyday life. On this view, we can ask whether the broadcast media, through access and participation programmes, are offering an institutional forum which orchestrates critical opinion, promoting or undermining the development of consensus between disinterested parties.

Alternatively, critics such as Fraser and Mouffe suggest that the media can facilitate the expression of diverse political and social interests in order to form a working compromise between negotiated positions. Access and voice remain priorities but the underlying model of argumentation (negotiation versus critical discussion) and the underlying functions of the dialogue (compromise versus consensus) are changed, and the significance of social identities and social relations is no longer marginalized. Access and participation programmes should, according to this view, be evaluated in terms of how well they express a diversity of public voices and challenge established power to recognise the complexities of everyday life.

The debate in social theory about the character of the public sphere relates to different political possibilities for the broadcast media:

> Among the key advantages of the revised public service model sketched here is its theoretical and practical recognition of complexity. Moving out from under the shadow of Lord Reith, it recognises that 'freedom of communication' comprises a bundle of (potentially) conflicting component freedoms. It acknowledges that in a complex society the original public service assumption that all the citizens of a nation-state can talk to each other like a family sitting down and chatting around the domestic hearth is unworkable; that it is impossible for all citizens simultaneously to be full-time senders and receivers of information; that at any point in time and space some citizens will normally choose to remain silent and only certain other individuals and groups will choose to communicate with others.
>
> (Keane, 1991: 164–5)

Chapter 3

Studio debates and audience discussions

A television genre

THE AUDIENCE DISCUSSION PROGRAMME

> Maybe speaking as an American and growing up with these shows, it becomes an acceptable forum for these issues. We don't really read about the issues in such a controversial way and I think people would turn on *Oprah* and just look and it would become a forum for everyone in the room to just have a little chat about it.
>
> (Marie, viewer)

In audience discussion programmes such as *Kilroy, The Time, The Place, Donahue* and *The Oprah Winfrey Show* the audience is placed directly in the television studio as joint author of the text in order to debate social, moral and political topics as part of a mixed studio audience of experts and the lay public. This genre may be seen as challenging traditional oppositions of programme and audience, producer and subject, expert and laity. It contributes to the reformulation of the rules of public debate by offering new opportunities for ordinary people and representatives of established power to argue and debate topical issues in public.

Through diverse programme forms, including audience discussion programmes, the mass media offer an informal, unofficial, but nonetheless large-scale, institutionally managed forum for public debate. The nature of this forum varies with the broadcasting regulations in different countries and, where these have been influenced by the public service ethic, the forum may be an official part of the broadcasters' brief (Curran, 1991). In the British and American context, broadcasters point to access and participation programmes, as well as to the dissemination of information, as a means of fulfilling their public service obligations. The popular American host, Phil Donahue, claims that 'we discuss more issues, more often, more thoroughly than any other show in the business. We also involve the audience in our act more than any other show on the air, period' (Carbaugh, 1988: 3). British broadcasters also claim an important role for the studio audience:

> The BBC is very proud of *Question Time* . . . It is the only place where senior politicians and public figures are questioned by ordinary members of

the public. It must be at the heart of the debate occupying public attention that night.

(James Hogan, editor of *Question Time*, letter to *The Independent* 10 October 1990

This implies that public access genres are an integral part of processes of discussion, debate and diffusion in modern societies. Such programmes have been around for several decades, but their place in the galaxy of television programmes is far from simple. In this chapter, we discuss the generic form of audience discussion programmes, for the genre affects the relationship between the viewer and the medium. Do these programmes open up new forms of relationship between television and its audience?

GENRE BOUNDARIES AND THE TALK SHOW

Television is a recent cultural form which is still changing rapidly. Literary concepts such as that of genre, themselves much debated (Dubrow, 1982), can be difficult to apply to popular culture. Indeed, audience discussion programmes challenge existing conceptions of genre, particularly the distinctions between entertainment and current affairs, ideas and emotions, argument and narrative: as a source of 'infotainment', talk shows are popular, cheap, and have become a commonplace part of most television and radio channels (Robinson, 1982). Nonetheless, some classification of programme conventions and commonalities provides a useful starting point for analysing the relationships between programmes and the mass media generally, and between a programme and its audience.

Because television is constantly looking for new programmes, genre boundaries are fuzzy and evolving, resulting in diverse genre overlaps and subtypes. The talk show is especially intertextual in its dependence on other forms of media. Just as 'common sense betrays its own inadequacy by its incoherences, its contradictions and its silences' (Belsey, 1980: 3), so do the contradictions within broadcasting challenge its own assumptions about providing a public – or indeed, a commercial – service. Broadcasting is supposedly both a public service to be regulated for the public good, and a medium of entertainment, a commercial enterprise which exists outside sociopolitical processes. We suggest that the audience discussion programme, which is growing in popularity and variety and yet resists categorization in established genres, raises questions about information, entertainment and public service.

Carpignano et al. (1990) discuss how 'the general public' appears on television, ranging from passive presence as a mass audience to contributing to public discourse and common sense through active participation. First, they may appear as the 'audible public'. By providing the applause and laughter which accompanies game shows, sitcoms, quiz shows and talk shows, they create the sense of a live event. Second, 'the visible but inarticulate public' is presented as a vast mass, cast in the role of spectator as at a sporting event where the crowds are seen, waving banners, singing songs, quiet at tense moments. Third, the public, presented as 'real people', is made into an object of ridicule, as in *Candid Camera*. Fourth, the 'edited public' presents public opinion through 'on-the-spot' or 'vox pop' interviews in news and documentaries so as to provide visual interest for a journalist's report. Fifth, there is the public as 'protagonist' in the talk show – active, participating, conversing, debating as part of 'a public rite of hospitality', where guests and hosts converse in a 'living room' – 'a type of television uniquely suited to the demands of television' (Rose, 1985: 329).

The talk show spawned a new form when Phil Donahue, Sally Jessy Raphael, Oprah Winfrey and others in America and elsewhere created what we have termed the audience discussion programme or studio debate in the late 1960s:

> 'The Phil Donahue Show' became a forum for exploring every issue in society . . . in an open manner not previously attempted by any daytime talk show. As a host, Donahue was a probing interviewer who placed great emphasis on letting his studio audience . . . ask the questions as well.
>
> (Rose, 1985: 338)

No accepted term for this now-familiar 'genre' has emerged. Carbaugh (1988) distinguishes between personality-type talk shows, based on dyadic conversation, and issue-type talk shows, based on group discussion. However, in the latter the personality of the host is still important. One must also distinguish group discussions which include ordinary people compared with those where experts alone discuss an issue. There is a wide range of access and participation programmes which involve experts and ordinary people. Some programmes are based on the voices of ordinary experience or involve the public in order to help experts. In others, the public directly challenges experts or the media challenge experts on our behalf. In others still, experts debate among themselves for the benefit of the public or provide information and advice in response to audience questions. In audience discussion programmes, the public is actively engaged in dialogue with experts, able both to participate and challenge. They vary in approach and seriousness, depending on the topic, the skills and interests of the host and the target audience and they are growing in popularity and numbers of programmes (Robinson, 1982; Rose, 1985). While they are generally known by the personality of their host, some current affairs programmes and documentaries occasionally, and it seems, increasingly, include a studio debate.

The audience discussion or participation programme is not quite current affairs or consumer affairs though it deals with current issues as they affect ordinary lives. It uses experts but is not documentary. It shows the impact of current issues on ordinary people's everyday lives through story-telling but is not soap opera. Like the soap opera, it constructs the viewer as community member and repository of common sense (Livingstone, 1990), but it takes issues beyond the private domain of the domestic and local, for the viewer is also constructed as citizen, with a duty to be informed about and act upon the wider world.

Let us characterize the main features of the television audience discussion programme, although different programmes vary somewhat. First, the guests or experts and lay studio audience sit together (typical of British programmes such as *Kilroy, The Time, The Place*) and experts are singled out only insofar as they are seated in the front row and are identified by a visual label. Alternatively, the experts and guests are placed on a stage and faced with a studio audience (as in the American programmes *The Oprah Winfrey Show* and *Donahue*). In this case, most speakers, lay and expert, are labelled.

Second, the host, typically a television 'personality', roams among the studio audience with the microphone, selecting who may speak and re- sponding to self-selected contributions. Third, each episode focuses on a particular topic of social, political or personal concern, often stimulated by events in the news. Fourth, the programme consists of lively, controversial conversation and argument on the chosen topic, expressing oppositional and diverse views. Fifth, while the conversation is managed by the host and production team, the selection and ordering of participants also depends on the flow of the argument and the contributions of the studio audience. Sixth, contributions appear as emotionally significant to the participants, being grounded in their personal experience rather than hearsay or scientific facts. Seventh, the programmes are generally cheap to produce, low in production values, broadcast in the daytime or late at night and so not part of prime-time broadcasting. Eighth, the programmes are either 'live' or recorded in 'real time' soon before broadcasting, with little or no editing.

Audience discussion programmes offer a sense of a community where everyone belongs, there is consensus about the social, political and psycho- logical agenda, and common sense is the key to addressing everyday problems. The resulting debate may be considered an open text (Eco, 1979) or dialogic text (Bakhtin, 1981), where multiple meanings flourish and diverse perspectives are interrelated. Participants and the home audience are relatively free to make diverse interpretations, depending on their own circumstances. Carpignano et al. (1990) propose the audience discussion programme as candidate for the (oppositional) public sphere:

> What is conceived as a confrontational device [the exaggerations, the personal revelations, the management of conversation] becomes an opening for the empowerment of an alternative discursive practice. These discourses don't have to conform to civility nor to the dictates of the general interest. They can be expressed for what they are: particular, regional, one sided, and for that reason politically alive. Few other shows on TV today can make that claim.
>
> (Carpignano et al. 1990: 52)

INSTITUTIONAL CLAIMS: A GENRE OF THE PUBLIC SPHERE

The programme descriptions in the *Radio Times* and *TV Times* clearly indicate the official view of a participatory audience active in the public sphere. Excerpts from descriptions in the *Radio Times* for one week of access and participation programmes are listed in Table 3.1. When asked about the relationship between hosting an audience discussion programme and being a politician, Robert Kilroy-Silk, who has done both, comments:

> There are a lot of similarities. It's just a different platform. I'm a communicator: whether it's teaching, politics or the media, it's all part of the same pattern. The BBC wanted someone who could take on a cabinet minister, but who could also understand the problems of an unemployed person in Liverpool. An MP straddles all those areas. I make no concessions to the time of day the programme's shown. The fact that it's on at five past nine in the morning is neither here nor there. The show would be no different if it went out at five past nine at night. We're doing serious television. I didn't come from the House of Commons to do kids' programmes. There's no way I'm going to tone it down in case there are five-year-olds watching. It's an adult programme, talking about adult issues, in an adult way . . . I'm very lucky: through *Kilroy* I can be far more effective than when I was an MP. Instead of making a speech about something in the House of Commons I can do a show about it, and have an audience of millions, instead of five-year-olds.
>
> (*New Woman*, November 1991, interview by William Cook)

The claims of broadcasters may be ignored as naive, motivated or ideological. However, let us remain open about the potential of these programmes for the public sphere. The production team probably puts more effort into staging the conversation than biasing its content, for when frequent and regular episodes are required, any controversial argument is welcomed, any boring or consensual argument is not. Moreover, while the shows are managed, so too are other social situations in which debates and conversations occur: all are structured according to power inequalities, tacit rules and implied audiences. 'The real confrontation in the show is between those who espouse an ideology of therapeutic solutions and those who keep open the continuity of a discursive practice' (Carpignano et al. 1990: 51).

THE TALK SHOW AND THE CONSTRUCTION OF IDENTITY

Discussion programmes such as Donahue are a rare location in which 'millions have gathered daily, to talk' (Carbaugh, 1988: 2). These programmes offer a 'cultural performance of individuality' (ibid: xiii) which produces and reproduces the American understanding of the self as individual through conventions of talk. For example, Carbaugh analyses the construction of two genres of communication–genres of speaking ('being honest', 'sharing

Table 3.1: Official claims for access and discussion programmes

Right to Reply, C4: 'Viewers tackle the programme makers.'

The Last Word, C4: 'Censors and the censored discuss issues arising from Channel 4's *Banned* season.'

Gloria Live, BBC1: 'Gloria Hunniford discusses topical issues with her guests. Audience: if you would like to take part in a future programme call . . .'

The Time, The Place, ITV: 'Discussion programme with Mike Scott.'

Family Matters, BBC1: 'More parents nowadays are delaying starting a family until well into their 30s . . . But what about the children of older parents?...Paul Heiney has been talking to parents and their children.'

Panorama, BBC1: 'Beyond the Poll Tax: in the week when millions vote in local elections and the government unveils its replacement for the poll tax, the spotlight is on local government. What should it do and how should we pay for it? From Nottingham, David Dimbleby leads a debate with politicians, councillors, experts and ordinary citizens.'

Open Space, BBC2: 'The series where the public can make programmes under their own editorial control.'

Drink Talking, BBC2: '[Names] were all alcoholics. None of them is drinking now, and here they reflect on their continuing recovery. Also contributing to the programme is [name], a pioneer of the treatment of alcoholism.'

The Cook Report, ITV: 'More hard-hitting investigations on matters of public concern by Roger Cook.'

Comment, C4: 'Another personal view on a particular issue.'

The Lowdown, BBC1: 'Real life stories about children, told by the children themselves.'

How was it for you?, ITV: 'Discussion programme . . . [names] talk to host Henry Kelly about adolescence.'

Donahue, ITV: 'Phil Donahue hosts a late-night discussion about good parents whose children turn out bad.'

Famous for Four Minutes, C4: 'Ordinary Britons talk about their lives, hopes, values and fears.'

Points of View, BBC1: 'Anne Robinson with your comments on television . . . '

People Today, BBC1: 'Including a medical phone-in on . . .'

The Oprah Winfrey Show, C4: 'Convicted drunken drivers and their surviving victims come face to face.'

Question Time, BBC1: 'Peter Sissons presents live debate and discussion . . . Audience: if you would like to be in the Question Time audience send a large sae to . . .'

A Problem Aired, ITV: 'A series in which people with emotional problems talk them through with a therapist.'

Ask Oddie, (ITV): 'Children in the audience join in a debate about blood sports with [name] from the League Against Cruel Sports and [name] of the British Field Sports Society.'

The Day, (ITV): 'A crucial day in someone's life.'

The James Whale Radio Show, (ITV): 'Tonight's subject is rape. Viewers can express their views by phone . . .'

Source: As listed in Radio Times, 27/4/91 to 3/5/91.

feelings') and symbols of personhood ('the individual', 'self', 'social roles', 'rights', 'choice').

Further, any interaction involves the construction of mutual identities. When a studio audience member asks the expert, 'How do you know what it's like to be poor?', they simultaneously reaffirm the expert status (the person is worthy of challenge) and question it (implicitly constructing the lay-expert, 'I', who knows about poverty from experience). The central function of discourse is not to refer to a pre-existing world but to create and sustain the social order: 'what we talk of *as* our experience of our reality is constituted for us very largely by the *already established* ways in which we *must* talk in our attempts to *account* for ourselves' (Shotter, 1989: 141). As social orders are inevitably structured by power relations, 'it is not so much how "I" can use language in itself that matters, as the way in which I *must* take "you" into account in my use of it' (ibid: 141).

Talk on television is not simply conveniently available conversation through which we may analyse the construction of identity, for the media plays an active role in managing and transforming that talk. Some are concerned that the media are invading the previously autonomous, private self – assuming such an authentic self ever existed:

> In an operation that might be called 'post-modern', the individual hailed or fixed by the television talk show format is disseminated, collated, fragmented, even simulated and represented as it recognizes itself in the mass/public act of telling its own story.
>
> (Masciarotte, 1991: 82)

For Masciarotte, cultural criticism tends to emphasize the negative consequences of television talk because of a prejudice against the supposed superficiality and falsity of women's talk. However, if politics includes issues of identity and the right to speak in one's own voice, then television talk may be revalued, for after all, the personal is political:

> Oprah Winfrey is not a simulated self, and so a fetish for the endless lack of consumer desire, but a tool or a device of identity that organizes new antagonisms in the contemporary formations of democratic struggle.
>
> (Masciarotte, 1991: 84)

The topics of talk shows are often 'women's issues'; they are frequently scheduled for housewives in the daytime; they are concerned with gossip and story-telling. They can be understood to draw on the way in which feminism has 'redefined the relationship between the public and the private', transforming the political towards a reliance on 'the circulation of discursive practices [rather] than on formal political agendas. In this sense, the talk show can be seen as a terrain of struggle of discursive practices' (Carpignano et al. 1990: 51–2). Thus, the talk show, and the critical commentary which surrounds it, is gendered: 'talk shows afford women the political gesture of overcoming their alienation through talking about their particular experience as women in society' (Masciarotte, 1991: 90). As Oprah Winfrey says, 'we do programme these shows to empower women' (quoted in Squire, 1991).

Audience discussion programmes vary. Masciarotte (1991) argues that Donahue tries to construct a generic citizen, demonstrating 'union within diversity' and so undermining the potentially radical consequences of creating a space for contestation among truly diverse voices. In contrast, Oprah opts for opposition rather than pluralism, self-disclosure rather than discretion. While Kilroy offers some self-disclosures to show he is one of us, Oprah's disclosures are far more personal and are offered as a challenge: I've told you all about me, now you reveal your secrets and emotions. Although different, both strategies encourage the private person to talk in public: the one reassures through heroic identification, the other invites through therapeutic challenge.

Kilroy resembles Oprah in his antipathy for experts and his tolerance of a lack of conclusion, although he is also one of the white male professional broadcasters, like Phil Donahue and Mike Scott or John Stapleton (presenters of *The Time, The Place*), for whom conclusions are desirable and the private life of the host remains private. While audiences may identify less with these hosts than with Oprah, it is not identification but parasocial interaction (Horton and Wohl, 1956) which is the key to the television talk show. The audience – in the studio and at home – is encouraged to tell its own stories, to agree or disagree, confirm or contradict, confront or support the speaker, generating a polyphony or 'cacophony of narratives' on and beyond the small screen (Masciarotte, 1991: 86).

PARTICIPATING IN THE TALK SHOW

> To read America, then, we need first to learn how to read talk shows, which are the controlling contemporary form of public discourse ... for American television, the talk show is not trivial but definitive.
>
> (Fogel, 1986: 150)

Although 'the television talk show seems almost extravagantly participatory' (Masciarotte, 1991: 81), little research has examined the experiences of participants and home audience. We know more about the now commonplace radio phone-in to which, research suggests, some 70 to 80 per cent of radio listeners tune in every day (Avery and Ellis, 1979). Avery and Ellis (1979) claim that, through the radio phone-in, 'social reality is defined and becomes significant for the communicators. Interaction within the context of talk radio, then, is an important event for those people who participate' (ibid: 112). Talk radio serves as a companion for lonely people, countering the growing isolation of many in modern society, for 'talk radio is one of the few public media which allows for spontaneous interaction between two or more people' (Avery, Ellis and Glover, 1978: 5).

Those who call radio shows tend to be single, to live alone, to be alone when they call, and they are less likely to be members of organizations, compared with the average population (Bierig and Dimmick, 1979). Callers admit to seeking interpersonal contact through the radio: 'while substantial numbers of people called to use the talk radio format as company and as a forum, the gratification prompting the greatest frequency of calling was companionship seeking' (Tramer and Jeffres, 1983: 300). Armstrong and Rubin (1989) identified seven motives for listening to talk radio: relaxation; excitement/ entertainment, convenience, voyeurism/escapism; information utility; passtime/habit; and companionship. Compared with listeners, callers experienced these motivations more strongly, listened to talk radio for longer each day, and felt it as more important in their lives. Callers also found face-to-face communication less rewarding and were less mobile in their everyday lives.

THE HOME AUDIENCE FOR AUDIENCE DISCUSSION PROGRAMMES

We now consider in more detail who is available to watch audience discussion programmes, who actually does watch them, and how much people enjoy them (Tables 3.2–3.6).

Based on a diary sample, the BBC daily activities survey shows what people are doing at around 9–10 on the average weekday morning when the British audience discussion programmes are shown (see Tables 3.2 and 3.3). Of the whole population, some 40 per cent can be classed as available to watch broadcast television although only 7 per cent of the population are watching television at this time.

> They say that they have got the kids off to school and they have sat down to have their breakfast, so on goes *Kilroy*. (F2. 194)

> I work fairly close to my house, and there are occasions when I work very late so I don't start very early in the morning, and it's nice to sit down with a cup of tea and watch something. And this is just the time of day when I tend to be doing that and so I do watch it from time to time.
> (George, viewer)

Women are more often available to watch television than men at this time (one half compared to one third), although similar percentages of the available women and men actually watch. Until the mid-fifties in age, one-third of the population are available to watch television and this figure rises steeply thereafter, although again there is no clear association between availability and actual viewing. Nor is there a clear association between availability and social class.

Part-time workers are twice as likely as full-time workers to be available to watch television at this time, although a similar proportion of each is actually

Table 3.2: Daily activities (%) at 9.15 to 9.30 a.m., by demographic group,[1] showing
availability for and watching of broadcast TV

Demographic Group	Available to watch TV[2]	Watching TV[3]	Watching TV as sole activity
All	40	7	3
Men 16+	31	6	3
Women 16+	50	7	2
Age 25–34	37	9	3
Age 35–44	36	7	4
Age 45–54	37	4	1
Age 55–64	48	6	3
Age 65+	65	7	4
Class AB	37	3	1
Class C1	36	6	3
Class C2	41	10	4
Class D	32	6	3
Class E	58	10	3

Notes: Based on figures for winter 1989 (averaged over Monday to Thursday, 11/2/89 to 24/3/89).
[1] Figures for 10.00 to 10.30 a.m. are similar.
[2] Availability is defined as being awake, in the same room as a TV set (either at home or
   elsewhere). Availability at home is slightly lower.
[3] Total percentage of the population watching TV, where percentage watching at home is
   slightly lower.
Source: Daily Life in the Late 1980s, BBC. Printed with permission.

watching. The unemployed, however, while only slightly more available than part-time workers, are twice as likely to be watching, and nearly two-thirds of housewives and retired people are available to watch morning television. Housewives are especially likely to be doing something else at the same time. Shiftworkers add to the profile of morning viewers, for one-third of these are available and 7 per cent are watching. Finally, those who live alone are slightly more likely to be available to watch and to be watching than those who live with others.

Tables 3.4 and 3.5 show that each episode of *Kilroy* is viewed by one million people on average (2 per cent of the population) and receives a 29 per cent share of the viewing audience available after breakfast television in the morning. There are almost twice as many female as male viewers. This is because more women are watching television at this time: of the men and women watching, a similar proportion choose to watch this programme compared to other programmes. The lower one's social class and the older one is, the more likely one is to watch, although higher-class viewers watching television at this time are more likely to be watching *Kilroy*. While these figures refer to the number of people watching an average episode, the reach of the programme (the number of people reached in any one week or month) would be far higher, as many people watch a few rather than all of the available episodes.

Table 3.3: Daily activities (%) at 9.15-9.30 a.m., by occupational group,[1] showing availability for and watching of broadcast TV

Demographic Group	Available to watch TV[2]	Watch TV[3]	Watching TV as sole activity
All	40	7	3
Full-time[4]	22	5	2
Part-time[5]	45	7	1
Unemployed[6]	50	14	4
Retired[7]	65	6	4
Housewife[8]	61	9	2
Shiftworker[9]	32	7	3
Live alone	59	9	3
Live with others	37	7	2

Notes: Based on figures for winter 1989 (averaged over Monday to Thursday, 11/2/89 to 24/3/89).
[1] Figures for 10.00 to 10.30 a.m. are similar.
[2] Availability is defined as being awake, in the same room as a TV set (either at home or elsewhere). Availability at home is slightly lower.
[3] Total percentage of the population watching TV, where percentage watching at home is slightly lower.
[4] Work 30+ hours/week.
[5] Work 8-29 hours/week.
[6] Age 16+, work 0-8 hours/week, looking for work.
[7] Work 0-8 hours/week, regard self as retired.
[8] Work 0-8 hours/week, regard self as housewife.
[9] Work 8+ hours/week, work between 7 p.m. and 5 a.m. on 6+ days/month.
Source: Daily life in the late 1980s, BBC. Printed with permission.

Each episode of *The Time, The Place* is viewed by some two million people on average, representing 4 per cent of the population and a 65 per cent share of available viewers, although again, the reach of the programme over a period of one week or month would be higher. There are between two and three times as many female as male viewers, although the percentage of women and men viewing this programme compared to other programmes is similar. Regarding class and age trends, the percentage of viewers in each subgroup ranges from 2 per cent of class AB to 6 per cent of class DE viewers, and from 3 per cent of young adults to 6 per cent of retired people.

The Oprah Winfrey Show is watched by over one and a half million viewers on average, some 3 per cent of the general population and 9 per cent of those watching television at this time (mid to late afternoon). There are almost twice as many female as male viewers, although again, the percentage share of this programme is similar for women and men. The age and class trends are as for other discussion programmes. In America, *Donahue* is watched by some five million people daily (Robinson, 1982).

Finally, *Question Time* is watched on average by over four million viewers (8 per cent of the population; a 36 per cent share of available viewers). The number of female viewers is similar to that of male ones and the programme attracts a similar percentage share of the viewing audience among women and

Table 3.4: Audience composition for audience discussion programmes, averaged for period 1 Oct–17 Dec 1991, showing thousands of viewers, percentage of potential audience who viewed, and percentage share of viewers, by sex and social class

Viewers	Programme			
	Kilroy[1]	*The Time, The Place*[2]	*The Oprah Winfrey Show*[3]	*Question Time*[4]
Total	1035	2025	1635	4275
	2	4	3	8
	29	65	9	36
Male	344	541	573	1984
	2	3	3	10
	34	65	11	38
Female	644	1336	956	2169
	3	6	4	9
	30	73	12	36
Class AB	143	179	228	861
	1	2	2	8
	39	56	10	42
Class C1	220	413	336	995
	2	3	3	8
	32	66	10	36
Class C2	277	524	387	1063
	2	4	3	7
	28	59	8	33
Class DE	395	909	684	1356
	3	6	4	9
	26	72	11	35

Notes: Each cell contains three figures: (a) the number of people who viewed an average minute of the programme, in thousands; (b) the television rating – the actual viewers expressed as a percentage of the potential viewers (number of people in a specified category); (c) the percentage share – the percentage of the specified category watching the programme compared to those watching other television programmes at the same time.
[1] Shown at 9.00 to 9.50 a.m. on BBC1 on each weekday.
[2] Shown at 10.00 to 10.40 a.m. on ITV on each weekday.
[3] Shown at 5.00 to 5.50 p.m. on Channel 4 on Wednesdays and Thursdays.
[4] Shown at 10.30 to 11.30 p.m. on BBC1 on Thursdays.
Source: BBC/BRD for BARB.

men. There is no consistent trend by social class in terms of audience size, although the percentage share is greatest for AB viewers. There is a clear trend by age: only 3 per cent of young adults but 18 per cent of retired people watch this programme.

Audience appreciation indices indicate enjoyment and/or interest in programmes (Goodhardt et al. 1975). Table 3.6 shows that of the audience discussion programmes, *Kilroy* appears to be marginally the most liked, although all score reasonably well. They are generally liked by viewers as

Table 3.5: Audience composition for audience discussion programmes, averaged for period 1 Oct–17 Dec 1991, showing thousands of viewers, percentage of potential audience who viewed, and percentage share of viewers, by age of viewers

		Programme		
Viewers	Kilroy	The Time, The Place	The Oprah Winfrey Show	Question Time
Total	1035 2 29	2025 4 65	1635 3 9	4275 8 36
Age 4–15	45 – 11	138 1 33	106 1 3	122 1 23
Age 16–24	59 1 23	207 3 68	135 2 8	226 3 20
Age 25–34	141 2 25	353 4 59	201 2 10	407 5 24
Age 35–44	126 2 28	271 4 67	146 2 8	573 7 30
Age 45–54	156 2 36	263 4 75	221 3 14	575 9 34
Age 55–64	175 3 37	287 5 75	248 4 12	733 13 41
Age 65+	335 4 34	607 6 77	578 6 14	1637 18 54

Note: Each cell contains three figures: (a) the number of people who viewed an average minute of the programme, in thousands; (b) the television rating – the actual viewers expressed as a percentage of the potential viewers (number of people in a specified category); (c) the percentage share – the percentage of the specified category watching the programme compared to those watching other television programmes at the same time.
Source: BBC/BRD for BARB.

much as most other programmes, for example, documentary and consumer affairs programmes, and as much as other debating programmes, such as *Question Time*, and access programmes, such as *Video Diaries*. Direct feedback programmes, like *Right to Reply* and *Comment* receive slightly lower appreciation indices. For any programme genre, the AI scores vary by gender, age and class, for different programmes are geared to different audiences. In general, women and men give similar appreciation scores for the programmes listed in Table 3.6, although women tend to be slightly more appreciative of

Table 3.6: Audience appreciation indices (AI) for audience discussion programmes, by demographic group

Programme	AI[1]	M	F	12–34	35–54	55+	ABC1	C2	DE
The Time, The Place[2]	75	70	77	67	75	80	73	75	76
Kilroy[3]	77	69	80	70	73	82	70	76	81
Gloria Live[4]	73	67	75	70	65	75	75	73	70
The Oprah Winfrey Show[5]	75	73	76	75	76	74	73	76	75
Donahue[6]	70	72	68	66	66	79	–	64	79
Family Matters[7]	72	68	75	70	71	74	71	72	74
Question Time[8]	76	73	79	70	73	79	74	74	80

Notes: Figures are based on aggregated data for weeks 14-26, 1991, unless otherwise
   indicated.
[1] Weighted summary index of enjoyable and/or interesting ratings (scale from 0–100).
[2] AI averaged over five weekday shows.
[3] AI averaged over Monday and Tuesday shows, based on aggregated data for weeks 14–25,
   1990.
[4] AI averaged over five weekday shows.
[5] AI averaged over two weekly shows (Wednesday, Thursday).
[6] AI averaged over two weekly shows (data for ABC1 too few for reliable reporting).
[7] AI based on aggregated data for weeks 14–25, 1990.
Source: National Audience Appreciation Summary, BBC/BRD for BARB.

television overall. However, for the British audience discussion programmes,
women are considerably more favourable than men, and older people also
tend to like these programmes more.

VIEWERS' PERCEPTIONS OF THE GENRE

In collaboration with Mallory Wober at the Independent Television
Commission, the AGB/BARB panel of viewers was asked to complete a
questionnaire about audience discussion programmes as part of their regular
weekly diary task in March 1992. The 17 per cent of the sample of 3,000 people
who had watched at least two episodes of *Kilroy* or *The Time, The Place* in the
previous fortnight were asked a series of questions about the genre (see
Livingstone, Wober and Lunt, in prep. , for details of the questionnaire and
statistical analysis).

   We found that to a moderate extent, viewers considered the genre to offer a
public sphere in which they can participate, with little difference between
viewers of different age, sex or class. All viewers fairly strongly believed that
the genre provides a fair and valuable debate. Generally, viewers were neutral
about whether to judge the debate as chaotic and biased, with older viewers
being more critical. Some viewers, especially older ones, were concerned that
the genre invades individuals' privacy. Most considered the hosts to be
relatively unbiased, although the middle-age group tended to be most critical.
Viewers preferred the contributions of laity over experts, or at least considered

them equally worthy, with older and more working-class viewers emphasizing this less strongly. Men, younger viewers and viewers of higher social class were more likely to think that the debates were pointless insofar as they reached no clear conclusion and had little influence. Finally, viewers showed a slight tendency to prefer American and/or personal shows to British and/or political shows. This was more true for women and for the youngest age group.

Further analysis of these responses was used to answer a series of questions about viewers' involvement in audience discussion programmes. We first asked why some watch more episodes of audience discussion programmes than others. The results suggested that people watch more discussion programmes if they want to know what others are thinking, if they become emotionally involved, if they do not consider the hosts rude, and if they watch more television in general. Generally, it is difficult to predict the frequency of viewing from judgements about the character of the programmes – it probably depends on whether people are free early in the morning for television viewing.

We also asked why some find audience discussion programmes more entertaining to watch than others. This, it seems, depends on how much viewers: value 'ordinary people' (members of the general public) having a say, value discovering what ordinary people are thinking, discuss or think about issues discussed on the programmes after viewing, consider that the hosts do a good job, would like to go on themselves, value ordinary people having a chance to argue with experts, consider that the experts come over well, prefer personal issues to political ones, consider that the programme issues are important in their own lives, consider that the experts are unbiased, and consider that the programmes include a good mixture of people. To watch the programme with pleasure is to treat it as a public forum for rational debate, and pleasure in the programmes is fairly well predicted by viewers' judgements of the genre's character.

Why do some value hearing ordinary people's views more than others? People are more likely to value a programme for giving a say to ordinary people if they want to hear what people are thinking, if they think the programmes give people a fair hearing, if the debate makes them think, if they value the chance for ordinary people to argue with experts, if they would like to go on such a programme, if they think the programmes have a social influence, if they feel views similar to their own are expressed, if they think a good mixture of people are invited on, if they become emotionally involved, and if they feel the experts are unbiased. Hearing ordinary people's opinions is valued by those who believe that these programmes provide a fair forum for such a hearing and that such a debate has real-world consequences and further, if the issues debated are personally and emotionally relevant to their own lives.

Why do some value the opinions of experts more than others? People value the experts' views over those of ordinary people the more they think there is little point in hearing ordinary people's opinions, the programmes are out of control, the experts should not be on an equal footing with the laity, the hosts are rude, the invasion of privacy should not be encouraged, the host should support the ordinary person (clearly interpreted patronizingly). These beliefs are stronger for those from higher social classes and for male viewers.

Why are some more likely to discuss or think about what they have seen than others? People are more likely to discuss or think about things they have seen dealt with on these programmes if they consider that the programmes make them think, if they become emotionally involved, if views similar to their own are included, if they want to know what others are thinking, if they think ordinary people's opinions are worth hearing, if they are older, if they find personal problems more interesting than political ones, if the programmes deal with issues important in their own lives, if they consider the American shows to be more honest, if they prefer the host not to support the ordinary person, if they value people getting the chance to argue with experts and if they do not like to see the experts on an equal footing with the laity.

Clearly involvement in the issue and relevance to one's own life are vital to thinking about the issue afterwards. So too is a belief in the programme as providing a valuable public sphere. They see the experts as superior, but the laity as of value, and they see the interaction between lay and expert as important (see Chapter 5).

DISCUSSING THE NATURE OF AUDIENCE DISCUSSION PROGRAMMES

> No subject is taboo on *Kilroy*, which takes its cue from the controversial Oprah Winfrey show in Chicago and has developed its own distinctively intimate style . . . [and] keeps things up-to-the-minute.
>
> (*Radio Times*, 19 March 1988: 19–25)

The media present this genre as open to all topics, as current and relevant. How does the audience see it? Respondents in the focus group discussions spontaneously made a large number of comments concerning the nature of audience discussion programmes as a genre. Many referred to an implicit trade-off between relevance and chaos, involvement and control. Central to the genre is its relevance to viewers as topical, involving and contentious:

> It is a kind of programme that produces people not normally seen on television, a lot of experts and politicians and so on . . . and it is quite interesting to see what people think. (P1. 132)

> I mean, he [Donahue] gets in there, because it's an open discussion and he's much more involved. (D3. 43)

However, these features run the risk of taking the programme out of control: if topics are involving, some people will talk too much, if lots of people must speak, no-one has time to say much, if discussion is open, conclusions cannot be guaranteed.

> It must be extremely difficult when you are trying to control a programme like that on such a subject, and some people have very positive definite views one way or another and it's very difficult to try and control them or shut them up. (P4. 95)

> Everybody can't speak together, you can only go around with the mike to one person, and in three-quarters of an hour how many people had a good five minutes? Nobody. (D3. 72)

> One of the problems with that type of programme is that there is no end conclusion to it, you just get a discussion and there is no idea of what is going to go beyond that point. (P1. 19)

The structural tension between openness and closure, which also underlies other television genres (Fiske, 1987), is a major dynamic for the public sphere. As there are benefits and costs to forums which strike different balances between these two concerns, one might advocate a diversity of genres within which to locate the public sphere, as well as a plurality of publics and topics. Different programmes manage this tension in different ways. Some may prioritize the critical–rational discourse of the experts, some prioritize the variety of personal experiences among the studio audience, some prioritize the direct contests between participants, and some prioritize the diversity of the issues. Viewers have different preferences and so evaluate certain features differently:

> I would rather listen to experts, I would rather have a programme organised and under control. (D2. 98)

> Even these politicians on Robin Day's programme [Question Time] are very long-winded and go all round the houses and they don't actually tell you anything. (F1. 114)

> *After Dark* is far better because it allows people to go over all sorts of stages in a discussion and they are not shut off. Well I suppose they are on for three or four hours, but I think that is a really good idea, that you can really work everything out for yourself. (D2. 85)

When asked to compare the genre with documentaries as a forum for putting over a social or political issue respondents again disagreed over the trade-offs. Should one prefer depth (the documentary) or breadth (the audience discussion programme)? Should one prefer the conclusiveness of the former or the openness of the latter?

> You don't hear enough from each individual, whereas the documentary is normally concentrated on one or two circumstances. This doesn't give enough detail for anyone to get a real idea of what their life is like. (P1. 60)

A documentary concentrates on one person, and I like the way this [audience discussion] tends to try and balance the arguments, and I can think of both sides and decide for myself. (P1. 184)

Each genre offers a kind of direct evidence – we can see people's lives *in situ*, as put into broader context by experts or presenters, or we can hear from them in their own voice in the context of a studio discussion:

A documentary can actually show where they live, how they live. (P1. 61)

You get the immediate personal impact [in audience discussions], you wouldn't from a documentary. (D4. 64)

But the documentary . . . it tends to be the presenter who is the one who puts the point across, whereas here it is the actual people, whether they are correct or not is another matter, but they do have something to say about various circumstances and I think that you can only find out what is going on by listening to people's own experiences. (P1. 188)

One can regard the control of a documentary as facilitating a more orderly argument or as preventing the spontaneity of ordinary speech:

On a documentary people have more of a chance to think before they speak, also it is rehearsed to some extent. (D1.110)

You're getting somebody's opinion in a documentary, but in a studio audience you're getting a cross-section. (SC. 272)

Similarly, people differ on the issues of bias and balance:

A documentary is very easily swayed. Whereas at least in this [audience discussion] you have got at least more possibilities for making your own mind up, in an unbiased sort of sense. (P3. 98)

If you had a documentary you would have a much more balanced point of view. (D2. 37)

In all, half the comparisons favoured the documentary over the audience discussion programme, one-quarter favoured the latter and one-quarter expressed no preference. Most comparisons favouring the documentary used dimensions relating to the bourgeois public sphere – order, conclusiveness, expertise, argument, seriousness, while those which favoured audience discussions related to problematic areas for the public sphere – access and openness, involvement and spontaneity, ordinary experience and confrontation.

PARTICIPATION FRAMEWORKS FOR PUBLIC COMMUNICATION

How shall we understand public, mediated communication? Who is speaking to whom? Who is the hearer? The sender–message–receiver model of communication, which focuses on the transmission of information, is too simple for communications which involve the construction of understandings and social identities among many interconnected participants. Goffman (1981) argues that everyday communication is too complex, dynamic and ambiguous to fit neatly into the categories of speaker and hearer – the two fully involved individuals taking orderly turns presumed by the traditional dyadic model. He reconceptualizes the hearer in terms of a 'participation framework': in a discussion, a hearer has a communicative role – hearing what the speaker says, and a social role – official status as ratified participant. As 'a ratified participant may not be listening, and someone listening may not be a ratified participant' (ibid: 132), these two aspects of the hearer must be distinguished, for their communicative roles and responsibilities differ. Going beyond the dyad, as both interpersonal and mass communication generally do, complicates things further. A subordinate communication may be interleaved with the dominant communication, and nonaddressed or nonratified participants may engage in various forms of byplay, crossplay or sideplay. While some subordinate communications are relatively public, they may also be concealed, as in collusion or innuendo.

The concept of the speaker is also too global a folk category. Goffman identifies three aspects of the speaker which frequently and mistakenly become rolled into one: the animator, who produces the speech; the author, who has selected the words and sentiments; and the principal, a social role established through the speech and which gives the words their authority. When a speaker 'changes hats' during a meeting, the social role changes, but animator and author remain constant. To quote another person is to separate animator and author (or to imply multiple authors). To argue on behalf of another person is to separate animator and author from principal: 'the notions of animator, author, and principal, taken together, can be said to tell us about the 'production format' of an utterance' (Goffman, 1981: 145).

The role of the reader or viewer (Eco, 1979; Livingstone, 1990) is to construct a communicative framework which specifies the perceived participants as the reader sees them. Interpretation depends on various factors: the reader's understanding of the genre; on their critical judgements; on their view of expertise and the validity of ordinary experience; and on their selection of real and imaginary participants (for example, personal acquaintance with a member of the group being discussed, comparison with other hosts, perception of the government as represented by an expert). The framework constructed by the reader specifies the perceived rights of the variously arranged participants to affect the course of the communication, their responsibilities to act in certain ways and according to certain evaluative and epistemological criteria, the overall gratifications which are to be achieved, and the nature of the social process of which this event is one part. As this framework specifies the social arrangements among participants (speakers and hearers) to the communication, we will generalize Goffman's terminology to refer to the whole as a participation or communication framework.

Returning to television discussions, we will use Goffman's analysis to explore how the conventions which frame television talk construct the viewer as citizen or consumer, how they construct participants as expert or lay, and how talk about or reception of television may renegotiate these constructed identities. Who is talking to whom in a television debate? Who is 'I' or 'You', hearer or overhearer? Who addresses whom, constructing identities of both self and other? How are the multiple participants interconnected? The reception of audience discussion programmes involves the construction of a particular relationship between viewer and programme which has implications more generally for the construction of selfhood, the validation of personal experience, and the formation of public opinion.

> I was very conscious of making a fool of myself really. And also I was very aware that my mum knew I was going to be on it, so I knew certain people knew I was going to be on the show, it was just the embarrassment of it really.
>
> (Ruth, studio audience)

> I also underestimated the significance of the meeting in the sense of how it might impinge on my life because on the way back from the programme, two people stopped me in the street and said that they'd seen me and one of my mother's friends phoned her to tell her I was on which mortified me absolutely.
>
> (Martin, studio audience)

Throughout the discussion, studio audience, experts and host all have the home audience in mind. The studio audience, apparently the hearer, is invited also to create the message as speaker, personifying the tacit invitation offered to the home audience. Some speakers also may not be listeners, merely waiting for the opportunity to tell their story but hearing little of the discussion in their nervousness. Not only are a number of participants physically present, acknowledged or not, at the interaction within the studio and its extension in the home, there are also imaginary participants who play a vital role in this communicative process. These latter may not be common across participants, but they form part of the participation framework.

For example, the host has one eye on the media world, his peers and superiors (as Kilroy says on the doctor–patient communication programme, 'I'd better watch this, my doctor's watching, my doctor – you're wonderful'). Similarly, experts may be conscious of their scientific colleagues, knowing that they are continually overstepping their expertise under the pressure of answering lay questions in an unfamiliar forum; the studio audience are concerned to communicate to, and on behalf of, an idealized representation of the 'public' and also of specific target groups under discussion, such as victims of drunk drivers, the poor or divorcing couples – these target groups are also in some sense part of the framework, with their own rights, responsibilities, and acknowledged or unheard voices. Imagining one's friends listening at home may constrain the contributions of the studio audience, thinking of the unemployed affects the vehemence with which a politician argues her case.

The nature of the participation framework offered by these programmes depends on the genre conventions which are themselves peculiarly open and ambiguous. This generic ambiguity is clearly seen in the role of the host: is he or she the chair of a debate, the adored hero of a talk show, a referee, a conciliator, a judge, the compere of a game show, a therapist, the host of a dinner-party conversation, a manager or a spokesperson? At times, the host plays any one of these roles, thus altering the roles of other participants and listeners. We consider below three influences on the programmes – the debate, the romantic narrative and the therapy session. Each of these results in the construction of a different participation framework and a different perception of participants' rights and responsibilities, and each contributes to the 'intergenre' character of audience discussion programmes.

THE DEBATE GENRE

> The media play a constitutive role in British political life, especially during general elections.
>
> (Garton et al. 1991: 100)

The main 'relevant' topic of the public sphere must surely be political campaigns and elections. During at least one American presidential campaign, Donahue hosted a debate among Democratic candidates (Carbaugh, 1988) and more recently, presidential candidates have appeared on talk shows. The 1992 British election campaign also saw a wide range of programmes adopting the studio debate format (as do election campaigns around the world) including *The Channel 4 Debate*, *First Tuesday*, *Special Inquiry* and *Midnight Special*. Other radio and television programmes also gave extensive airtime to ordinary people's opinions, doubts and questions. For the three weeks preceding the election, *Kilroy* was replaced by *Election Call*, a live phone-in, simultaneously broadcast on Radio 4 and BBC1 television, in which the public asked questions of ministers of all parties. Just before the election itself the leaders of the three main parties sat in the hotseat and answered voters' questions. As *The Sunday Times* commented, this was 'remarkable':

> Politicians are totally exposed: they have no idea what questions they are going to be asked. For once, it's the voters who set the agenda, not the campaign managers. In addition, callers can and do talk with real passion on topics of which they have personal experience, a course not open to professional interviewers.
>
> (*The Sunday Times*, Paul Donovan, 5 December 1992: 6)

Ordinary people can go beyond the rules of professional interviewing: as the programme editor commented in the same article, 'it's the one programme politicians tend to be worried about, it's totally unpredictable . . . professional interviewers can *report* a problem, but they don't *have* the problem, that's the difference'. As a consequence, politicians have been pushed by the public into answers, admissions and reactions, which they would rather not have given. John Naughton in *The Observer* made a similar argument: 'the daily *Election Call* (BBC1) was often the programme most worth watching, because it alone broke through the protective shield and allowed the voter direct access to senior politicians' (TV Review, 12 April 1992). Of course, the media manage interaction: of an estimated 8,000 calls to the party leaders, only some 15 to 20 were broadcast, so the media have considerable gatekeeping powers and may thereby set the agenda (Verwey, 1990).

When audience discussion programmes provide a forum for election issues, they are acting to channel public opinion up to the decision-makers and to circulate it among the public. When they provide a forum for government information campaigns, with the Christmas drunk driving campaigns, they channel information and advice from experts to the public. In each case, they provide not only information but also a social space for the public – experts, politicians, interested parties, ordinary people – to debate issues of general concern.

For many viewers, audience discussion programmes are essentially debates, and most important, they are debates among ordinary people, held in a public place, unlike the traditional media form where experts debate issues in the presence of an audience:

> What I like about Kilroy's approach is that you get more flow and interaction. I think interaction is what makes it work more. The Peter Sissons [*Question Time*] style of things is traditional – it's a good formula and it provides good television and good debate, but the debate is debated between the politicians about issues suggested by the audience.
>
> (George, viewer)

So, these programmes certainly seem at first like a classic debate, and this fits with the public sphere claims made for them by the media itself. They focus on a social problem, posed in terms of two sides (Should fox hunting be banned or is it just good fun? Should we legalize euthanasia or not?), and they invite experts and representatives of the public, including all relevant and valid contributors, to offer their opposed arguments, supporting one side or the other in an orderly, rational and informed discussion. There is a chair, the host, who ensures that both sides get a fair hearing, and one hopes for the best conclusion at the end. The host attempts to turn the discussion away from consensus, seeking out disagreement. For example, Kilroy says about one speaker to another, 'she's doubting you'; checks with the studio audience, 'what do you mean, there's nobody that says "no" '; interrupts an anecdote to provoke a confrontation, 'let me just stop you there, how do you respond to our friend?' In sum, it is a public space for the public to talk:

> Why should only professionals have their chance to air their views on television. It's our television, it's our country, why shouldn't we, as ordinary people, have a chance to air our views? (P4. 148)

> I like the way this tends to try and balance the arguments, and I can think of both sides and decide for myself. (P1. 184)

Studies of the radio phone-in suggest that they do meet some criteria of the public debate. Callers recognize the programmes' lack of legitimate authority or ability to take action, but believe that they 'stimulate political communication, educate the public, formulate issues, recruit civic activists, [and] promote free political expression' (Crittenden, 1971: 201). Many messages are strongly political, even when dealing with private matters, and are often critical of the status quo, containing 'realistic comment on practical problems of local political life' (Crittenden, 1971: 207). Thus while generally presented in a supportive style of agreement and information exchange (Avery et al. 1978), the content of contributions is often oppositional. Turow (1974) found that callers wanted to add new elements to the discussion, set the facts straight, have their opinions heard, give information and be part of something. In Crittenden's study, some 15 per cent of the home audience talked to others about issues discussed on the programmes, 11 per cent reported becoming interested in local community issues as a result of the programme, and 17 per cent of 'community leaders' thought their decisions were affected by the programmes. Verwey's (1990) analysis of Canadian and British radio call-ins identified 'their capacity to get regional public works done and public complaints attended to' (ibid: 233) and argues that even for commercial stations, the call-in has become a political arena which makes political candidates available to the public.

The participation framework of the debate genre places the host at the centre as the chair. It then lines up those for and against the motion in order of prominence – experts higher than lay people – and all contributors are divided into two camps linked by the host. As in a debate, the studio audience are both speakers, often in the fairly minimal sense of being able to ask questions and vote at the conclusion, and, more prominently, hearers. The whole is mounted for the benefit of the home audience, the general public, who must be paying full attention as ratified listeners. While the dyad is lost, the participation framework is simplified by the division of all participants into two sides, with an all-powerful host keeping order and regulating contributions.

THE ROMANCE GENRE

> I think he is very much aware that he is the star. (D2. 45)

He enjoys the limelight, that's very obvious. (D3. 218)

I think he thinks of himself as a sex symbol. (SC. 591)

While many debates are introduced as having two sides, others are not. The poverty programme began with Kilroy saying:

Can you be poor if you've got a colour television? And a washing machine? Can anybody really be called poor in Britain today? Who's poor?

Discussing older people getting married on *The Time, The Place*, only one person spoke against it; discussing boxing on *Kilroy*, little space was given to those who considered it harmful or aggressive. Often hosts make a moral judgement rather than remaining neutral. Oprah asked one self-confessed drunk driver, 'don't you think it [the memory of the victim] should stay with you?' Conclusions are generally lacking, despite the implicit promise of one, and may not be expected by viewers:

I think it is better if they don't [draw conclusions] because I think people are smart enough, anyone is smart enough to come to their own conclusion and think things through for themselves and I don't think we should all think what Oprah or Donahue say.

(Marie, viewer)

I think it would be very dangerous to give a conclusion from a programme like that anyway. They have been criticized for being a debate but not actually having a vote at the end, but if you have a vote at the end of what has been decided by the programme, that could prove quite dangerous.

(Jack, viewer)

Viewers know that 'the talk show format privileges the process over the product of consciousness raising, the narrative over the self' (Masciarotte, 1991: 91). So what are viewers expecting? In significant ways, the genre resembles a romance, with the romantic hero, constructing identities as real, authentic and hence relevant:

One of the things about this is that it's real, and it is real people and is different to the normal reality of television. (P2. 177)

With normal people, they are bad actors, they can only act for a few minutes and then they revert to themselves. Eventually it all comes out and you can see their true selves. (D1. 155)

The argument that the genre adopts features of the mythic, romantic narrative (Dubrow, 1982) parallels Silverstone's (1984) analysis of scientific documentaries as heroic romances. In the audience discussion programme, as in the romance, we start with a social problem which directly affects the studio audience, who represent the inhabitants of the 'kingdom'. At the centre of a romance is the hero:

He is naturally pretty and the programme revolves around him rather than the others. (D2. 197)

It just seemed as if he was more keen on him holding his own role rather than on what people had to say. (F2. 158)

People like to be on his [Kilroy's] programme because girls think he is handsome. (P2. 133)

Instead of being a neutral outsider, overseeing the action, the host plays a central role as the hero who undertakes to solve the problem affecting the kingdom (the public) and restore social order (through advice, understanding or validation of experiences). Consequently, he or she strides through the mythical kingdom (studio), setting out on a journey of discovery, brandishing his or her sword (microphone). On the way, the hero encounters those who can offer information and advice, and those who hinder by posing problems and undermining information (and who are chastised: 'this is getting us nowhere'). Having attained the goal – an understanding, a decision, a body of evidence– the hero returns triumphant to the community in need, for whom social order is restored and celebrated.

On the poverty programme, Kilroy moves away from the position of neutral chair, saying, 'I'm on Joe's side, no problem about that'. He claims ordinariness in response to a lay speaker who attempts to determine the purpose of the programme, saying 'this programme is about what anyone talks about, and I'm one of them too'. The host is on the side of the people, although at other times, the host may reassert his or her power: 'I don't want us to go on about the arcades any longer, I want to try to . . .'

In distinguishing between myths and fairy tales, Bettelheim (1976) offers an additional hero role. While the heroes in myths have superhuman capacities, exerting great powers to reaffirm the *status quo* and offering an image to be emulated, in the fairy tale it is one of us, an ordinary person with whom we may readily identify and whose achievements we may delight in. In the myth, the hero is a member of valued categories – adult, male, white, a prince, while in the fairy tale, the hero is often a child, the village idiot, female. The typically white, male, middle-class host of discussion programmes is the mythic hero: the object of romantic articles in popular magazines, the figure with the superhuman powers of the media, symbolized by the microphone, the hero we admire but cannot truly emulate.

However, as Chesebro (1982) notes, over the past decades television programmes have shifted from mythic 'superman' tales towards the mimetic realism of ordinary lives, reducing adulation and increasing identification. The audience discussion host falls more clearly into the fairy tale category. Oprah Winfrey has no problem claiming ordinariness – a large, black, working-class woman who offers her own abused, victimized, suffering past to empathize with her audience:

There are a lot of black issues and a lot of incest things. I think she was an incest survivor, and she tends to do topics like that and she does them very sentimentally, very much presenting it as the most important aspect of it is the person who was violated. She definitely has her opinions and they're known.

(Marie, viewer)

Even though Kilroy is a media host, an educated politician, an academic, and a white male, he claims to be an ordinary member of the working class: 'Britain's a class society. You've got to be one or t'other. It's us and them, (Robert Kilroy-Silk, interviewed by William Cook, *New Woman* magazine, November 1991).

More fundamentally, the audience becomes hero: in these programmes, we are all the small child lost in the wood who by dint of only ordinary cleverness and great good luck manages to find her way home again. We all tell our own stories and everybody claps. The romantic reading endorses an individualistic ethos which celebrates the ordinary person and the authenticity of direct personal experience and which legitimates the expression of emotion. This contrasts with the debate genre where the abstract principles of truth, rationality and justice are celebrated (see Lyotard, 1984, on the conflict between narrative and scientific modes of knowledge). The frequent absence of a conclusion is problematic for the debate but not for the romance, for the programmes celebrate the brave act of searching for the goal. Appearing on the programme to tell one's story may itself be a celebration of resolutions to personal narratives: 'this is now, and this is my story' and 'I've done it, I've been off the street for six years (applause)'. All kinds of 'achievements' are celebrated in these programmes. One woman, discussing the effects of children on a relationship, notes in passing that she has six children, and is interrupted by the applause. When discussing sibling rivalry, one speaker was introduced as someone who 'got married on Saturday' and a round of applause followed before he could make his point.

Personal stories provide a platform from which one can offer advice to others: 'this happened to me and my advice is . . .' and 'this happened to me and I finally learned . . .'. Here the genre resembles a self-help group where people confess their failings and share their hard-won advice (Squire, 1991). However, as Squire further notes, in constructing the individual as hero through confession and celebration ('you did it!'), the medium hides its own claim to heroism ('television did it!'). Boorstin (1982) takes a more cynical position still, suggesting that the host, who is being represented as if he or she were a hero (whose achievements were created by him or herself), is maybe only a celebrity (an image created by the media).

There is a generic struggle here between debate and romance conventions. While debate conventions are undermined by the host's biases or stardom or the absence of two sides, the romance conventions may be undermined also. Some resist opportunities to tell their story, making instead an abstract point.

Asked to tell her 'poverty' story on *Kilroy*, one woman subverts this invitation and makes a clearly pre-planned political point:

> I think every one of us has got a story to tell about poverty, but the most important thing I think is when I read about babies being born with rickets that went out the window 80 years ago, TB being on the rampage, polio, pawn shops springing up all over the place, second hand furniture shops and second hand clothing shops. That is a sign of the times.

The host's role also represents a struggle between conventions, for the charming and moral hero may undermine the impartial chair:

> His role, you know, ought to be quite neutral, so that he is supposed to be there organising things, but he does try to be because he is dreadfully good looking, dreadfully charming, I think that sometimes rather than making their point, people will allow themselves to be distracted by him. (P2. 134)

> I was surprised that he said that because he is supposed to be neutral, and at that stage his guard really fell. (P3. 167)

The participation framework established under the romantic reading of the genre locates the lay participants in centre stage. Rather than mediating between producers and audiences, the programmes mediate between audience members themselves. The ordinary person, whether at home or in the studio, is the main actor, appearing both directly and personified in the sympathetic figure of the host-hero who advocates their position, although 'the star male moderator automatically and persistently competes with his guest and the callers for centre stage. He treats both his guests and his callers either as competitors or as exploitable stage props' (Verwey, 1990: 239). The expert is a major protagonist, cast at times in the role of villain, to be redeemed only by listening and being converted. Arguably, the debate format marginalizes the public for it is too restrictive and intimidating for ordinary people to express their opinions, while when the anonymous caller is the star, as in the Canadian call-in, 'both the anonymous callers and the silent listeners feel that commercial call-ins have become their very own medium, and thus a real public service' (Verwey, 1990: 239).

THE THERAPY GENRE

> The mass media recommend themselves as addressees of personal needs and difficulties, as authorities for advice on the problems of life. They offer abundant opportunity for identification – for a kind of regeneration of the private realm out of the readily available pool of public support and counselling services.
>
> (Habermas, 1989: 172)

The purpose of the talk show is not cognitive but therapeutic . . . not a
balance of viewpoints but a serial association of testimonials . . . not an
argumentative line . . . [but] the aura of a ritual.

(Carpignano et al. 1990: 51)

For Bettelheim (1976), fairy tales are therapeutic because, through symbolic
disguise, they address basic fears and threats of existence – death of parents
and children, divorce and separation, loss and disfigurement. Maybe for
adults the symbolic disguise can sometimes be dispensed with and
ceremonially, we can confess our fears and doubts directly. We also celebrate
the bravery of those who expose themselves, and gain a sense of community
through sharing our problems. The host on *The Time, The Place* tells a
contributor, 'I think you're extremely courageous to come on this programme
and talk about it and approach it in that way with a smile'.

I felt really good because I'd spoken because in the past I've actually spoken
to friends about it and they hadn't been in difficult situations and so they
couldn't quite relate and strangely enough the audience was really really
sympathetic and I felt more empathy with them than I had with friends who
hadn't been through it. It felt really like the audience was on your side so it
was actually a really nice feeling, you felt like you were being supported.

(Margaret, studio audience)

A lady on a show about meningitis that I found very moving and that
almost brought me to tears . . . came up to me after the show and she said,
'I've wanted to stand up on a rooftop and scream for six years, and on your
programme, I've just done it. Thank you very much indeed'.
(John Stapleton, host of *The Time, The Place*, speaking on *TV Weekly*,
ITV, 19 November 1992).

It makes good therapy. Some people may think there are people worse off or
there are people saying they are in isolation. You don't know what it will
trigger off. (P2. 169)

We would not argue that these programmes offer 'good' therapy, but rather
that any occasion on which painful emotional issues are discussed in a
personal manner must at times resemble a therapeutic situation, recasting host
(or sometimes, expert) and lay speaker as therapist and patient. Labov and
Fanschel (1977) argue that therapeutic discourse is rendered coherent as
conversation through the interlinking of the surface level of what is said with
the deeper level of what is felt and done: the two levels are linked through
challenges, requests, assertions and denials. At the same time, the participants
must maintain 'save face' and manage their social identities through
euphemisms, vagueness, omissions, etc. Despite the public nature of the
occasion, the sense of private interaction persists. The programme generates a
supportive intimacy which is offered, however briefly, to each story-teller in
turn and therapeutic insights may be gained. Labov and Fanschel outline

various sources of insight which, we suggest, may plausibly occur even within the unusual framework of a television programme: concatenation of topics, provoking the patient to realize parallels and contrasts; interpretation, sometimes offered by the therapist through an analogy; direct suggestion to put the patient in touch with her emotions.

Consider how Kilroy plays the therapist role in a programme on the effect of children on a relationship. He sympathetically puts his arm around people, speaking in a lowered voice and maintaining steady eye contact. He uses a range of therapeutic interventions: asking questions, 'what were the problems that children caused?'; challenging emotions, 'what's all this about, Jackie, what are you reacting like that for?'; putting interpretations to people, 'what, you felt that he was competing with the kids?'; restating a story in analytic terms, 'so, you found that he was invading your space?' and 'you felt jealous'; provoking people into helping themselves, 'but you can change that'.

While generally the host asks questions rather than makes statements, embedded in these questions are a range of interpretative assumptions which, tacitly, the host puts to the speaker and which the speaker may accept or reject: for example, 'are there other men that have this kind of mother-complex, as it were?' The host's 'therapeutic analysis' may be resisted: when Kilroy says, 'is it the husband that's jealous . . . because there's a special bond between a mother and a child, isn't there, and then –' he is cut off by a cry of disagreement and laughter from the studio audience. Similarly, the experts may resist the therapeutic conventions: in a programme on sleep problems, one woman asked the psychologist about her problem to which the latter replies: 'sometimes very individualistic problems require very individualistic analyses and I don't think we would have time to go into it now'.

The Time, The Place asked 'Britain's best-known agony aunt', Clare Rayner to discuss sibling conflict. When asked to make an analysis she first offers a personal account: 'there's a whole lot of stuff here. By the way, I'm the eldest in my family, I had two sisters, hated them, they hated me . . . Mothers have no right to turn children into looker-after-ers'. She then launches into her analysis, having established her 'lay' credentials, saying 'parents are totally unreasonable, they think it's a terrible thing for an older child to be jealous of a younger child' and thus she legitimates the denied jealousies and hostilities which many have expressed in the studio and which presumably viewers feel at home, following this up with an abundance of advice. New understandings may result. Discussing the pressures women feel from their husbands, one husband says: 'I'm asking the women really, you feel a sort of pressure to– from your husband coming home? See, I never realised that'. He offers his realization as both an excuse and a sign of progress that women and men are beginning to talk to each other. When one woman responds, Kilroy encourages this process, saying 'talk to Mike, he asked the question'.

Oprah uses confrontation as a therapeutic technique: supposedly, as at Alcoholics' Anonymous, everyone confesses and then feels better. Secrets must come out, hypocrisy must be revealed, putting a brave face on things is emotionally destructive, the pain of family life must be recognized (Masciarotte, 1991). The multitude of positions expressed resists organization and so marginalized voices, repressed experiences and taboo thoughts are given a legitimate place:

> The bitterness was hurting me, the anger was eating at me like a cancer.
>
> (Mother of drunk driving victim on *The Oprah Winfrey Show*)

> I feel he should have been put in prison, he should have paid a stiffer penalty for what he done . . . this man killed my son and yet he was allowed to walk free. Since the accident we're just a broken family. My husband left me because we couldn't cope with each other's emotions and feelings. Now that man's left me a legacy of pain, anger, bitterness, remorse.
>
> (Mother of drunk driving victim on *Open Space*)

The therapeutic aspect of the genre holds dangers for participants, and may be exploited, for where does sympathy end and sensationalism begin? Does it depend on the judgement of the confessee, the host, or the observer?

> I also felt very pissed off with him because he was picking on a woman and her boyfriend in the audience and really put them on the spot and said 'do you use it?' and she was put in a position where she had to say 'yes' because of the comment she'd made but she actually didn't want to and I thought that was very sensationalized, and she said afterwards that she'd felt very forced into it, very uncomfortable about it, and that made me very angry.
>
> (Martin, studio audience)

> He got really upset and he actually started crying and Kilroy was really nice. And I thought that Kilroy would say OK, we'll move on, that kind of thing, and he didn't, he kept with the guy – one was in tears and the other angry – I was quite surprised that he actually stayed with the guy and waited for him to compose himself and then he carried on with it.
>
> (Margaret, studio audience)

For the therapist, the distinction lies in how the person's emotional needs are handled. One therapist contrasts the audience discussion programme with a programme specifically concerned with portraying the therapeutic process on television:

> In *A Problem Aired*, where things are carefully monitored, people have counselling afterwards . . . we really make sure beforehand that it's not going to damage them, and that they're not too vulnerable to do this, because one of the signs of somebody being healthy is that actually they don't want to do too much disclosing . . . they made an enormous effort to protect people.
>
> (Expert 3, psychologist)

In her follow-up survey of participants, she concluded that this programme did indeed help people:

> I just measured the changes people had made in their lives after *A Problem Aired*, and there were really very dramatic changes. Big life changes, and there were so many of them that it wasn't just coincidence . . . I did one thing with a woman who'd had panic attacks for years and years and years, and they had 230 calls afterwards, and there must have been thousands of others who'd watched and realized there was a very simple explanation for panic and a relatively simple cure. I think that has to be terribly helpful.
>
> (Expert 3, psychologist)

In contrast, she felt that Kilroy:

> Is there for his own glorification, and that really comes across, and if you're dealing with . . . audiences of damaged people then I think that's a pretty terrible experience for them . . . I think that the way he flicks his microphone around and just cuts people off – and it's actually quite a demoralizing experience to be cut off in that way.
>
> (Expert 3, psychologist)

One host feels that these programmes do act responsibly towards the needs of their studio audiences:

> I think a lot of them, the vast majority of them, get a very great deal out of it and they find it very therapeutic and very helpful. But we have responsibilities, broadcasters, without wishing to sound too pompous, to make sure that we don't let them overstep the mark and do themselves damage.
>
> (John Stapleton, host of *The Time, The Place*, speaking on TV Weekly, ITV, 19 November 1992)

Viewers disagree among themselves:

> He is bad in that way because he seemed to wind people up to see what they could do, and then he left them in a state of distress. I didn't think that the programme solved people's problems. (D2. 06)

> There was one where there were emotional people in the audience, because of hurt or upset of some description, and he was very caring, I must say, he spent time with the people who were crying, or what have you, and trying to assist them in how they were trying to get through what they wanted to say. He was caring. (D3.210)

In many ways, the audience discussion programme uses relatively uncontrolled self-disclosure with few boundaries to create a safe space, little significant analysis can occur, and the pressures of 'good television' rather than good therapy dictate the encouragement and attention given to participants. Nonetheless, as we have noted before, in an uncontrolled environment, the therapeutic as well as the sensationalizing may occur. The genre holds opportunities as well as dangers for its participants, both lay and expert.

Experts talk of being pressured into personal disclosures rather than professional advice. They are concerned about the absence of therapeutic follow-up for those lay people who express distress on the programme. The absence of preparation for the programme on the part of all participants leaves them vulnerable to its surprises. The time–space compression of any therapeutic content – therapy in two minutes, here and now – severely limits that content. Nonetheless, it can be argued that the visibility accorded to people's problems could itself be therapeutic, encouraging people to recognize their problems and to desire a solution: certain experiences are recognized, legitimated and shared, the expression of emotions may be cathartic, and ordinary people can prove to themselves and to the public, 'this happened to me and I survived'. Producers report significant numbers of letters following programmes, thanking them for highlighting an issue or for the advice offered, and phone-lines or information packs made available after selected programmes receive a considerable take-up.

Are we really talking about therapy? We suggest that there is no other way of understanding the creation of intimacy and the emotional self-disclosure which forms part of the genre. The initial catharsis – getting emotions off one's chest, feeling one is not alone – can indeed be seen to occur, but there is relatively little therapeutic follow-up. Generally, the effects on participants and audiences are largely unknown: maybe for those who have already begun working on their problems, the programme may offer encouragement or development rather than initiation of a therapeutic process. Concerns about both therapeutic or cathartic uses and voyeurism, exploitation and sensationalism raise questions for audience research.

Some research shows that people listen to call-in psychology shows to learn about their own lives and about psychology and to hear about others' problems as well as for entertainment (Bouhoutsos et al. 1986). In this study, listeners were not demographically different from nonlisteners although those who called in to the programmes were more likely to be unmarried and female. Callers were also more likely to be alone, unemployed and less well educated – characteristics associated with poorer psychological health. Klonoff (1983) discusses some of the positive consequences of giving psychological advice through the mass media. For example, teaching breast self-examinations has increased the number of women seeking early treatment. One may reach those who would not otherwise seek help and so prevent future problems. Balter (1983) discusses his role as a radio psychologist in terms of providing information, referrals, reassurance that one is not alone, and pragmatic suggestions, rather than therapeutic encounters.

Indeed, there is a question about whether media therapy is ethical (Klonoff, 1983), and Robinson (1982) expresses concern that talk show experts tend not to make their frequent value judgements explicit. Balter (1983) defends radio psychology: for example, concerning the expectation of follow-up consultations, he notes that this often does not occur in clinical practice, despite one's best aims, while the continuity of a radio psychology programme does indirectly allow regular communication with the psychologist. When a sizeable group of psychologists were asked to assess tapes of caller–host discussions, they found that generally callers were offered a moderately valuable source of social support and that, at their worst, they were useless rather than harmful (D. Levy, 1989). Raviv et al. (1989: 71) note that callers 'seemed to know the limits of the medium and emphasised primarily the expectation to receive information and increase their self-awareness', which indeed, they generally felt was what resulted from their calls.

The 'therapeutic' participation framework of the audience discussion programme is composed of numerous patient–therapist dyads. Each dyadic interaction, while public, is constructed as if it were private, so that all listeners are overhearers who are ambivalently ratified, provided they vicariously play the role of patient or are emotionally supportive as in a group therapy session. The host-as-therapist uses many of the non-verbal cues of a private dialogue to create a mood of intimacy and security in which confessions may be heard and advice given. The discussion moves from one such dyad to another, particularly at the start of a programme, when a series of personal narratives are heard, inviting the overhearers to share one intimate moment after another. While the public nature of the moment is thus mystified, therapeutic discourse is nonetheless being transformed into public discourse. Through these private-yet-public encounters, the programmes suggest, the truth may be told: 'the real expert on the issue at hand, the 'true' voice, is the storied voice of the audience and the caller' (Masciarotte, 1991: 86).

THE INTERPRETIVE CONTRACT

The genre ambivalences, moving in and out of the conventions of debate, romance and therapy, rearrange the relations between participants as the conventions change and so allow considerable flexibility for both programme and viewer. Various participation frameworks are legitimate and a process of negotiation is opened up between text and reader. The programme offers various cues, through its themes, degree of openness or closure, criteria for evaluation and so forth. The reader too has various concerns – different levels of experience with the topic, different kinds of knowledge, desire for certain kinds of involvement. In effect, a contract that specifies the roles and responsibilities of each party must be worked out. Maybe part of the attraction of these programmes lies in the fact that the nature of the genre, and hence of the viewing experience, is underdetermined. Gratifications gained (e.g. admiration of the hero) can be re-presented – and justified – in other ways (e.g. concern for the topic under debate). Viewers may respond in various ways to the mix of modes used in the discussion programme: they may see the discussion as a debate and applaud its presentation of basic declarative knowledge – at last we hear someone expressing certain views or get to the truth of the matter; they may identify with one of the imperative positions expressed by a heroic figure and feel themselves or others to be persuaded by them; or they may respond to the interrogative whole, which 'disrupts the unity of the reader by discouraging identification with a unified subject of the enunciation' (Belsey, 1980: 91; see also Benveniste, 1971). In this genre, the subject positions constructed are inherently unstable, resisting any permanent or hierarchical 'I' and 'You'.

Chapter 4

The critical viewer

THE SIGNIFICANCE OF CRITICAL RECEPTION

If the mass media are to provide some kind of public sphere, the audience must be capable of critical response. Not only are certain institutional arrangements required for democratic participation, but citizens must possess and exercise certain skills. For many, including Habermas, the mass media is often seen as undermining critical response and, hence, as undermining the public sphere. However, a growing body of research would seem to counter these arguments and those of the Frankfurt School more generally, suggesting that audiences are diverse and informed, able to respond critically to the mass media as well as to other sources of talk in their everyday lives. Moreover, the members of the audience are ever more experienced, critical and sophisticated in their reception of the media as they become increasingly familiar with its forms and production processes.

The Marxist conception of critical or rational argumentation is essentially emancipatory, revealing the connectedness of facts and norms, science and ethics (Holub, 1991). On one level, we suggest that audience discussion programmes themselves represent critical knowledge: the lay people and the experts personify the construction of facts and norms or science and common sense; and through these programmes, the media attempts to position itself as the forum that brings together these otherwise segregated spheres of science and common sense so as to challenge traditional assumptions and construct critical knowledge.

In the present chapter, we are concerned with the different but related issue of whether the home audience is critical or passive, analytic or superficial, informed or ignorant of the textual forms and production conventions through which these programmes are constructed. The emancipatory pay-off of critical response is frequently hinted at throughout audience research: if audiences are critical then presumably they will not be taken in: they will have more control over the possible effects of viewing, they may opt for resistant or subversive interpretative stances rather than accepting and normative ones, and they may both reflect upon and participate in the construction of any consensual world view which results from such programmes. Fraser quotes

Marx's definition of critical theory as 'the self-clarification of the struggles and wishes of the age' (Fraser, 1989: 113). Through their responses to the mass media, we suggest that viewers may take some part in this struggle.

When analysing audience reception in terms of critical response, we note that the term 'critical' designates a distanced, informed, or analytic approach to programmes, rather than simply a negative or rejecting one (Cantril, 1940; Liebes and Katz, 1986). Critical–cognitive versus impressionistic – accepting responses result in different responses to persuasive messages and so people's relationship to the text mediates its effects (Petty et al. 1981). Moreover, the more people depend on the media for information, having no other social knowledge about an issue, the more it affects them (Ball-Rokeach, 1985). Viewers' critical responses reveal the status and hence the power given to the media by viewers, they reveal the interpretive resources used by viewers, and they reveal the relations which hold for viewers between media meanings and social knowledge.

THE CRITICAL VIEWER

A common assumption is that people are not critical of television programmes in any informed or informative sense. They may be either accepting or rejecting, but not critical. Thus the audience is frequently described as mindless, undiscriminating, duped, vulnerable, and so forth. However, listening to ordinary people's responses to television programmes shows that they routinely make a wide range of critical comments about what they see, leading Himmelweit et al. (1980) to liken viewers to literary critics debating the merits of works of high culture. People spontaneously comment upon, say, the coherence of arguments, on the adequacy of the data presented in support of claims, on the motivations behind media appearances, on what could have been said but was omitted. Listening to the audience also reveals that people are aware that programmes are constructed: they comment on biases introduced by production processes, on the constraints of programme form or scheduling, and on the uses and effects of programmes.

Viewers are able both to introduce criteria by which to evaluate the arguments presented in programmes, thereby referring to alternative interpretative frameworks, and to acknowledge the constructed nature of the programme as a product, not simply seeing the programme as a 'window on the world'. In this chapter we focus on the ways in which critical viewing can and does occur. In the research literature, the recent concern with the critical is part of a broader process of upgrading the often demeaned status of the viewer. Conceptually, the critical viewer or reader derives from parallel developments in literary theory (moving from an emphasis on fixed texts to recognizing actual readers who negotiate meanings), in Marxist cultural analysis (moving from an emphasis on domination and hegemony to recognizing the occurrence of resistance, opposition and subversion), and in media theory (moving from an emphasis on passive, accepting, and mindless viewers to one of active, selective and informed viewers). As McRobbie (1986) and others have noted, audience research is only recently being upgraded from 'market research': while textual and production analyses have long been valued, there has been an undertheorizing of the ways in which the media are embedded in the accomplishment of everyday life. Incidentally, a parallel argument can be made regarding the neglect of everyday discourse in the literatures on political discourse, argumentation and expertise.

The term 'critical viewer' is often used in different ways which tend to be confused under the currently fashionable label, 'the active viewer' (Livingstone, 1990). For example, for Himmelweit et al. (1980), a critical viewer bears a different relation to programme appreciation and programme effects, particularly in terms of emotional and evaluative orientation, than does an uncritical viewer. After all, 'an audience has views about programmes, can express them, and much can be learned from such descriptions' (ibid: 69). For Liebes and Katz (1990), a critical viewer draws upon different interpretative frameworks to make different readings of programmes compared with an uncritical viewer, resulting in the experience of different modes of involvement and gratification. For cultural studies, a critical viewer is politically resistant to hegemonic meanings, being motivated for sociopolitical reasons to make oppositional or subversive readings 'against the grain' (Morley, 1980; Fiske, 1987; Radway, 1984). For example, a group of trade unionists make oppositional readings when 'they not simply *reject* the content or 'bias' of the particular items – they *redefine* the programme's problematic and implied evaluations into quite other terms' (Morley, 1980: 116).

Both the evaluative and interpretative notions of the critical can subserve the political notion of the critical: it is by making different evaluations and interpretations that political resistance or acceptance is achieved. In any case, as Eagleton (1983) notes, all criticism is inevitably political. We offer here a grounded account of the variety of viewers' critical responses examined in relation to various theories of the television audience. Our approach will be to look for evaluative, critical and political contributions in focus group discussions, and then draw these together to reconsider the idea of the critical.

While evaluative criticism seems fairly straightforward, at least as discussed by Himmelweit et al. (1980), interpretative criticism as discussed particularly by Liebes and Katz (1990) requires some explanation. Responding to concerns that the world-wide export of American television constitutes a form of ideological imperialism (see Silj et al. 1988), Liebes and Katz attempted to see whether viewers have the critical faculties and interpretative resources necessary to resist this persuasion. They argued that resistance depends upon the cultural factors which support or undermine active viewing. Particularly, resistance to persuasion is facilitated by an awareness of programme production processes (so viewers see programmes as a construction), by an ability to abstract underlying messages, themes and issues, and by being self-aware in making critical interpretations. It is interesting to note here that the locus of resistance is social-psychological. The processes of resistance to persuasion through awareness of the attempt to persuade, generating arguments against the message and self-persuasion are well documented in social-psychological studies (see Petty and Cacioppo, 1981, for a review). Central to their argument is the assumption that such critical practices spontaneously occur in conversations between families and friends while viewing programmes (Jensen, 1986; Iyengar and Kinder, 1987).

In their study of cross-cultural interpretations of the prime-time soap opera, *Dallas*, Liebes and Katz (1990) suggest that viewers respond according to either of two basic modes of interpretation, referential and critical. When making referential readings, 'viewers relate to characters as real people and in turn relate these real people to their own real worlds. The critical (Jakobson's metalinguistic) frames discussions of the programme as a fictional construction with aesthetic rules' (ibid: 100) such that 'the critical involves awareness either of the semantic or syntactic elements of the text or of the roles of the reader as processor of the text' (ibid: 117).

By semantic criticism, Liebes and Katz mean that viewers might make an inference about the theme of the programme or about the producer's didactic aims, they might suspect the producer of trickery, identify underlying archetypes or reflect on how the programme presents reality. By syntactic criticism, Liebes and Katz mean that viewers might be aware of genre conventions (e.g. as a soap opera), of the dramatic function of characters/ events, of the commercial/business constraints on production, of their own involvement/reactions to the programme, or of the programme as having been constructed. In contrast, in referential readings, the programme is regarded more as a window on the world, and as an extension of the viewers' own world, so that connections may be made between the world as perceived and as known. Here, viewers regard the programmes as 'real' rather than constructed, and so are more inclined to accept and take for granted the naturalized meanings in the text that a critical reading would have made explicit.

Liebes and Katz (1990) illustrate the difference between referential and critical (or metalinguistic) readings through the responses that their focus groups' participants made to the question, 'why all the fuss about babies [in Dallas]?' For example, a referential answer concerns the importance of babies for the characters:

> The emphasis on the issue of babies in the family shows the importance of babies in a monarchy. They cannot risk [the possibility] that the empire they have built would vanish with their death; continuity is important.
>
> (Russian group: 115)

In contrast, a metalinguistic/critical answer concerns the importance of babies for the producers and writers:

Table 4.1: Varieties of critical response, as indexed by coding schedule categories

Category	Frequency	
Respondents (see present chapter)	417	(20%)
Respondents: viewing of discussion programmes	58	
Respondents: viewing of television	29	
Respondents: effects on selves	75	
Respondents: own reception of programme	90	
Respondents: particular others in their lives	51	
Respondents: own world experiences	103	
Respondents: other	11	
Studio audience (see Chapter 5)	350	(17%)
Studio audience: selection and motivation	95	
Studio audience: evaluation	24	
Studio audience: particular others in their lives	18	
Studio audience: effects	28	
Studio audience: interaction style	111	
Studio audience: other	74	
Host (see present chapter)	263	(13%)
Host: motivation	51	
Host: evaluation	58	
Host: interaction style	107	
Host: particular others in his/her life	3	
Host: other	44	
Home audience (see present chapter)	52	(3%)
Home audience: selection and motivation	30	
Home audience: effects	19	
Home audience: other	3	
Experts (see Chapter 5)	112	(5%)
Experts: selection and motivation	32	
Experts: evaluation	29	
Experts: interaction style	28	
Experts: particular others in their lives	0	
Experts: other	23	
Topic (see present chapter)	49	(2%)
Topic: selection	12	
Topic: interest	29	
Topic: other	8	
Argument (see Chapter 6)	281	(14%)
Argument: coverage	97	
Argument: premises/definitions	22	
Argument: closure	28	
Argument: debate	61	
Argument: in/coherence	10	
Argument: validity	18	
Argument: worth	29	
Argument: agreement or disagreement	13	
Argument: other	3	
Production (see present chapter)	174	(8%)
Production: purpose	53	

Production: making of programme	82	
Production: programme as construct	14	
Production: other	25	
Genre (see Chapter 3)	167	(8%)
Genre: other discussion programmes	37	
Genre: documentary	66	
Genre: radio phone-in	4	
Genre: Question Time	13	
Genre: discussion programmes generally	29	
Genre: other	18	
Public sphere (see Chapters 5 and 7)	213	(10%)
Public sphere: nature of ordinary knowledge	76	
Public sphere: nature of expertise	35	
Public sphere: social value of genre	102	
Total	2057	(100%)

Note: Table shows frequencies of response in each category over twelve focus group discussions. These critical responses are discussed in different chapters in this book as indicated in the Table. The coding procedure is described in Appendix 3.

There are a lot of problems around babies in such a family – the real identity of the baby, sickness, kidnapping – which provide a lot of possibilities for the writer of the series in constructing the plotline.

(Kibbutz group: 116)

On analysing the frequency of these different types of statement in their focus group discussions of Dallas, Liebes and Katz found differences across cultures, even controlling for educational differences: the western groups (Russians, Americans, Kibbutzniks) made some 30 per cent critical framing statements, while the Arab and Moroccan groups made some 10 per cent critical framing statements and, consequently, far more referential statements.

Whether viewers make referential or critical readings is presumed to have implications for the meanings constructed on viewing, the experience of distance from or involvement with the programme, and the likely effects of viewing in terms of social learning, opinion formation, reality orientation, or normative expectations. Nonetheless, this approach to critical response is not without its problems, not the least of which is that the implicit link to effects has not yet been demonstrated (this is also true of cultural studies research on critical or oppositional audiences). Also unexplained is the link between modes of response and particular cultural formations. In practice, the distinction between referential and critical can itself be difficult to apply, and often descends into the simpler distinction of agreeing or disagreeing with programme content. This latter distinction forms the basis of much social-psychological research on persuasion, where response to persuasion often depends on whether the message is pro- or counter-attitudinal (Petty and Cacioppo, 1981). How this distinction relates to the viewer's mode of involvement, whether critical or referential, remains unclear.

Let us now turn to the varieties of critical response offered by respondents in our focus groups after viewing an episode of an audience discussion programme. As shown in Table 4.1, these responses were classified in terms of comments about the participants to the communication framework – the respondents themselves, the lay studio audience, the host, the home audience, and the expert participants. These comments also concerned the nature of the discussion – the choice of topic and the arguments, and the nature of the programme – the production, the genre and the social value in terms of the public sphere (see Appendix 3 for details of the coding procedure).

PERCEPTIONS OF THE HOST'S ROLE

Many comments (17 per cent of all discussion comments) focused on the role of the host. Whether the host is the chair, the hero or the therapist, he or she is highly salient to the viewers and attracts many comments which reveal viewers' broader critical response to the genre. There is some interest in the host as a person – their motivation, aims, private life, but most interest centres on the host's role in facilitating and managing the discussion and on evaluating that role. The concern is with both the programme as product and how that product is constructed, a process personified in the interaction style and management activities of the host.

The host's motivations were seen as various. Clearly the job is seen as interesting and well-paid. However, for some, the host hopes to generate a public sphere in which opinions are aired and issues discussed:

All he is doing is highlighting things rather than changing things. He is just bringing them to the public. (P1.23)

Less neutrally, some saw the host as having a political purpose:

The fact that Kilroy was a socialist did come over. (P3.162)

He wants to encourage people to complain about doctors. (D4.167)

He is forcing his opinion on the programme in so far as he is choosing which ones will speak, because he has been with them for an hour or two before it goes on. (D1.136)

However, most praised him for being neutral:

On the whole, you don't know what his views are on the subject, which is good, as it should be. (D4.173)

He was unbiased and unpolitical, don't you think? (P3.143)

Many saw the job in terms of the demands of television rather than the public sphere, and so the host's primary motivation was seen as the production of entertaining television:

I think that he tried to keep it light. (P2.42)

He is an entertainer, isn't he, as well as a supposed social commentator. He has to be good to look at and listen to. (P2.137)

The largest group of comments focused on the host's construction of a heroic position. This supports the romantic reading of the genre: while the conduct of the debate and the participation of lay and expert speakers may support the reading of the genre as a public sphere debate, the position of the host is clearly seen as that of a hero:

Really I think to show Kilroy-Silk on television is the prime aim. (P2.139)

He wants to be a media superstar, doesn't he? He's had enough of being a Labour MP. (P2.140)

He is set for stardom. (P4.75)

The role of the host in managing what was generally seen as a difficult and fast-moving situation attracted much critical attention. There was disagreement between those who saw the host as out of control compared with those who thought he was in control of a deliberately lively situation:

There was a lot of heckling and talking going on, and he didn't seem to be able to control the situation and say, that is who is to speak next, and that's why we didn't get the answers. (P4.94)

This chap didn't seem to be always good in controlling the audience or the participants, so I think that half the programme was taken up with people talking across each other so you couldn't hear anything anyway and then it gets very frustrating for the people who are taking part. (D2.37)

It is just perfect television, and that is why Kilroy earns 50 grand a year, because he manipulated the audience, he manipulated the medium absolutely brilliantly, and the audience know what is expected of them. (D1.45)

He is usually in control of his audience. (F1.15)

Indeed, for one viewer, the point of the programme is precisely that, at certain points, the studio audience may subvert the control of the host to achieve their own ends:

It's an unusual style of programme in that the content can't be totally programmed by the presenter. To a degree I believe they can orchestrate it, but I don't think they can totally orchestrate it.

(George, viewer)

A further debate centred on judgements of Kilroy himself: for some, he was emotionally manipulative – malicious, uncaring, stirring things up, and upsetting people:

> Sometimes he seems to be malicious. (P2.135)

> If any argument comes up, he doesn't try to calm people down as much as I would have thought. He just seems to sort of stir the argument up quite a lot. I think he's there to get people going. (SC.030)

For others he was sympathetic, sensitive, charming, and good at putting people at their ease:

> I think that he is trying to be friendly, putting people at their ease. (P1.70)

> Some people are very distressed about what they are talking about, and he comes across as a very sympathetic person, which I like. (P4.65)

How the host affected the quality of the discussion was also debated. For many, he prevented the development of the argument by frequently cutting people off, often rudely. Others saw him as maximizing the number of speakers to gain a wide range of opinion. These points are compatible: it seems the host is willing to sacrifice argument development for argument breadth. Respondents' frustration or praise depends on which aspect of argument they value more:

> I think that it was unsatisfactory that he didn't allow people to finish their sentences, that he cut them off and was dashing off to someone else, I think rather rudely. (P1.14)

> He was stopping them at the initial question, he wouldn't let them develop it and go onto a second stage, which as far as they were concerned was probably the more important question. (P1.180)

> You have to let as many people as possible have their say, and I think that is what he tries to do, and I think that he does it. (P1.17)

> He certainly seemed to get around the audience, a good sprinkling all round of people. He didn't really let anybody dominate, or only for a short time, which I thought was quite good. (P3.53)

In general, respondents were evenly split in evaluating the host: half made positive comments – he was unbiased, professional, skilful, charming and sympathetic; and half were negative, regarding him as rude, patronizing, out of control, not listening, superficial and poor at relating to people.

PERCEPTIONS OF PROGRAMME PRODUCTION

> People outside think you do the whole thing. They think you've chosen the subject, selected every person . . . but there's an enormous amount going on behind the scenes.
> (Robert Kilroy-Silk, interviewed in the *Radio Times*, 19–25 March 1988)

While it is indeed true that viewers credit the host with considerable power in terms of programme production and that they are often ignorant of production features, they are by no means naive about the organization behind the programme. In the popular press, 'behind the scenes' views of programmes are frequently provided, supporting a critical awareness among viewers of the constructed nature of programmes and challenging the illusion of a single charismatic individual making it all happen.

> Well, of course it's produced. (SC.553)

A number of respondents were interested in why the programmes were made (8 per cent of all comments) and there was a debate about whether the programmes were intended to be entertaining or educational, superficial or serving the public sphere. People's perceptions of the social value of such programmes and of public debate determined their responses regarding programme intention. No particular political, social or institutional purposes were attributed to the producers of such programmes, beyond the general aim of filling airtime in a manner which would attract audiences.

What do respondents know of how audience discussion programmes are made? Their responses to the programmes were frequently interrupted by speculations about the production processes and their evaluations in particular were framed by their understanding of the limitations or constraints under which these programmes are produced. Much of their understanding about how the programmes are made is itself framed by their understanding of the genre: it must be entertaining, it must be a debate with two sides, it must select participants who are articulate, it must keep things moving and be lively, and so forth.

As was frequently noted, the programmes make some production knowledge visible:

> They ask after one programme, they say, we are doing a programme on . . . next, and people write in or ring and say they want to take part. (P1.13)

> So they all ring up and say, yes please, and then the researchers ask them questions and find out if they are fluent. (F1.90)

Similarly, because the cameras start recording apparently in the middle of an ongoing discussion, respondents were aware that a warm-up session had been held:

> It's not like walking in cold. They rehearse for two or three hours before that. Not to know actually what they are going to say, but to get them used to the cameras around them. (P1.83)

It is also obvious that programmes must fit a time schedule and financial budget, and a number of comments excused or blamed aspects of the programmes by reference to temporal or financial constraints. As with the soap opera and glossy films, viewers have a rough idea of which genres are cheap and which attract large budgets. They also have a rough idea of scheduling: that programmes shown in the daytime, as well as being cheaper, are geared to a different and more restricted audience (supposedly, housewives, the retired, students) than are prime-time shows:

I thought it was very superficial, with not enough time, and necessarily shallowish because of the length of time. (P2.108)

There will be more of these sorts of programmes because people enjoy watching these programmes and they are cheap. (P1.145)

There is an attitude, right or wrong, that says we don't need to put on serious things throughout the day because we have mums with kids who are going to be shouting and doing the vacuuming, or old people and I think maybe we don't have to worry about these people so much. I think that we have a very patronising thing happening here. (D2.183)

Otherwise, there are a range of production issues of which respondents are generally aware, but they lack specific information about audience discussion programmes. For example, respondents felt that their evaluation of the programmes would differ if they knew whether or not programmes were live or pre-recorded, edited or not, rehearsed or spontaneous:

I don't know if it was set up beforehand or if they just hope that they fall out. (D2.19)

Is the programme edited? I am not sure about that. (F1.96)

If the programme is live, really the programme makers couldn't have stopped it. The programme makers must realize that what they are going to get is a series of anecdotes, and that is what they got. (D2.167)

Occasionally, they or a friend had participated in an audience discussion programme, and then respondents shared their greater production knowledge with the group. Another source of production knowledge is the popular press – newspapers, magazines, TV guides – which frequently feature television 'stars' and provide information about their personal lives. While this applies especially to films and soap operas, this is less true of audience discussion programmes: while the hosts may receive their share of popular attention, the other participants do not:

Kilroy-Silk is an ex-Labour MP and he writes this column in *The Times* and I think people expect him, probably wrongly, to have something reasonably serious to say. (D3.201)

There was a suggestion by some that television constructs rather than reflects the debate. This construction is seen to occur not just in the ways in which the production team selects participants to represent opposed sides but also in the way it might actually transform their positions, creating rather than reflecting existing oppositions:

> I just felt it was a shame they became polarized – she was labelled aggressive and he, well you were sort of fighting yourself not to label him fuddy-duddy old-fashioned. Probably neither of them were true representations of their character types. I felt that television made them something that they weren't. (D2.17)

> Sometimes the person feels that they have to speak very critically into the microphone about what they are saying. (P2.46)

> I think that he was trying to lead people on, I suppose that this is his job, to make the programme interesting. (P4.04)

PERCEPTIONS OF PROGRAMME TOPICS

Relatively little interest in the choice of topics was expressed in the focus groups (2 per cent of comments). While generally, controversial topics were considered best, a few were sceptical about this apparent intention to raise public controversy:

> It has to be a controversial subject where people do have strong opinions. It is no good where people would agree. (P1.135)

> They probably pick issues that aren't extremely controversial, that won't upset a lot of people, that there are certain general agreed standards of what is right and wrong in these areas, so you tend to be discussing fringe issues rather than basic sets of values. (P2.124)

And yet, it seemed that many social taboos are discussed:

> They have programmes on everything that you can think of – child abuse, incest. (P1.142)

The programmes themselves differ considerably, of course. One programme on how to tackle drunk driving (Livingstone et al. 1992) indeed discussed mainly 'fringe issues' in so far as it was taken for granted that driving when drunk was wrong. Nonetheless, the ensuing discussion centred on a basic thematic opposition contrasting individual with societal responsibility for drunk driving, raising issues of duty, agency, policy and unintended consequences. In contrast, the programme on poverty watched by our discussants was highly controversial, opposing the view that poverty is a social problem where certain groups suffer from societal exploitation and prejudice against the view that poverty is caused by individual inadequacy and is a necessary consequence of an entrepreneurial capitalist society which rewards effort and ability; a familiar controversy no doubt, but nonetheless strongly felt and argued by the participants.

Even when programmes address controversial and taboo topics, underlying moral issues may be avoided through the concern to maximize audiences. Controversy is itself double-edged: it is a requirement of the oppositional public sphere and of a good public debate; yet it is also one means of obtaining audiences, for controversy means excitement and emotion as well as, if not instead of, good argument and genuine involvement. The public sphere need not only emerge through intentional actions: while setting out to gain audiences in many different ways and through a variety of genres, the media may, as an intended or unintended consequence, also meet some of the requirements of the public sphere.

Interesting topics are generally seen as relevant and as emotionally involving: people present themselves as having a personal agenda of 'things they care about':

Something to do with poverty I was interested in, abortions and such, real things I was upset about, I find that very interesting. (P1.127)

Something that is worth thinking about . . . religion, there was one very recently on mixed marriages and the product of them . . . most of them are very topical. (P1.130)

There was one on suicide, young people, which was very amazing. (P1.131)

Furthermore, topics are generally seen as those that affect participants and viewers directly:

Some subjects are alright, but especially the situation in China, I mean I don't think that many people's opinions in this country are worth all that much, they don't know what is going on really, they are not interested enough to turn up in a studio 100 miles away and make a contribution in front of the camera, whereas if it's a personal thing, AIDS or something, education, water, crime. (F2.204)

Nonetheless, this respondent was very interested in China: if publics are recognized as plural, they may become too small or too dispersed to meet anywhere except through the mass media. The problem experienced by health campaigners regarding those who feel that AIDS is not relevant to them, suggests there are no universal issues, and there will always be enough people who want to debate China's or Russia's problems. Audience discussion programmes are often interesting only for some of the people some of the time, but that does not preclude their candidacy for the public sphere, provided those who find the issue relevant are able to participate.

RESPONDENTS' INVOLVEMENT IN VIEWING

When people talk about a television programme, they inevitably talk about themselves as well (20 per cent of comments), revealing concerns in their everyday lives. For example, comments on programmes indicated how they fit into daily routines. Frequently, daytime television is treated more like radio than like primetime television, for people listen while engaged in a household or childcare activity. And the time and attention one gives to the programmes affects how one evaluates them.

> I watch it when I am doing the dusting. I don't watch it every day, but if I am in, I'll do the dusting or hoovering, that sort of thing, while I am watching, and just sort of half a mind, it's not meant to be taken seriously. (D2.168)

> I don't watch *Kilroy* very much because it is on at the wrong time of day. I watch a lot of *Donahue* and occasionally *Oprah Winfrey* and *The Time, The Place*. (P2.110)

> It comes on after breakfast. Sometimes when I am making the beds, I put the television on, the upstairs one. (P3.32)

What gratifications do these programmes offer? For some the programmes are enjoyable, for others they are not:

> I watch it because I enjoy it. I enjoy seeing the subjects they tackle and I enjoy seeing ordinary people's thoughts about the subjects they tackle. (P4.126)

> I found it boring. Having people around to talk about their problems doesn't interest me. (D2.08)

Similarly, some find the programmes interesting or absorbing ('I found myself stirred up': D4.78) and others are left uninvolved or unstimulated by them.

There is a consensus about the value of hearing experts. There was also general agreement that discussing current affairs is a good thing. So one dimension which determines viewing gratifications concerns the value one places on hearing ordinary people speak in public. Following this, some feel they can learn about their social world through these programmes, while others feel the discussions are too superficial compared, say, to a documentary, to learn anything useful. As with soap operas, some social stigma may be attached to watching audience discussion programmes, and so a certain amount of denial is attached to viewers' comments:

> I happened to see it this morning, not that I ever watch it, and . . . (F3.10)

Others use their involvement to present themselves positively to others. For example, this respondent constructs a 'liberal, caring, modern' self-image:

> The last one I got really mad at was the one on HIV/AIDS. Those stupid churchmen started saying it was the wrath of God and all this, that sort of dogmatic approach to it, and it really made me so cross. (SC.282)

Respondents experience a dilemma in assessing their reactions: are the programmes 'real' and genuine emotionally and are they 'real' and thought-provoking intellectually? For some respondents, the referential mode of viewing (Liebes and Katz, 1990) is unproblematically positive: the programmes arouse their sympathies and interest, so that they feel they are made to think and learn from viewing:

> I could identify with some of the problems that those people were putting forward. (D3.226)

> Personally, it's as though I am having an argument with some people, that's the effect it has. (D4.86)

> It's astonishing really. You say, good gracious, does it do that? Do they live like that? Different people's lives. (F2.240)

These people perceive the programmes as genuine, as a valid, though not necessarily agreeable, part of their own world, rather than, as the critical mode of viewing would emphasize, as a commercial production. Others find the programmes similarly unproblematic, but use the critical mode to explain their lack of involvement, feeling irritated or frustrated by production features like switching rapidly from one speaker to another:

> I don't think that he had control of it very well, and there were many times when I lost interest because everyone was talking at the same time. (D2.04)

The referential/critical dimension is, however, independent of the involved/distanced dimension. While in the above examples, referential viewers are involved and critical viewers are distanced, many other examples show how some critical viewers are critical precisely because they care about the aims of the programmes, particularly in relation to the public sphere and the value of hearing the opinions of ordinary people in public. For them, the management and production of the programmes must be critically examined for its furtherance of these aims. Similarly, some consider the programmes as part of the world–real people talking about things they have experienced–but not as an interesting part of their world and so, while regarding the programmes referentially, they do not feel at all involved.

The referential mode can be problematic. A few respondents rejected the polarization of their views which many gained from the debates, and instead were provoked into difficult self-realizations:

> I must admit that I did find it disturbing, I think because it rouses very different feelings in me. On the one side, one wants to be compassionate with these people, but on the other side, I am a reasonable practical person, I think, why the hell are you doing that? I found it very difficult to come to conclusions about that. (P3.148)

> I feel uncomfortable about that programme because the question it was asking was, are they poor? I have sympathy for people who obviously were fairly unhappy at being so poor. I felt sympathy for them because there

were the fat cats on the other side who were so complacent. I think to myself, OK, we are not poor, I am complacent. (P4.183)

Respondents frequently related experiences from their own lives to check the validity of those recounted on the programme. Part of critical ability (Cantril, 1940) includes conducting external validity checks on, for example, the claims of the poor – by recalling past student days, or by ascertaining whether jobs for the unemployed are really hard to find:

> I have had some experience in studying all the advertisements in the press for quite some time. Now I do notice that what there is no shortage of whatever is cleaning jobs. (P3.19)

Less obviously related to programme reception, respondents frequently used the programme topic as an opportunity to tell of their own problems with their doctors, their friends or their budgets. These stories may be vaguely supportive or critical of the studio audience's accounts, but essentially they represent a separate discourse in which the media provide the opportunity for viewers to manage their identities in relation to others. Thus the focus group, which simulates other, more ordinary situations – coffee-time at work, chatting to friends, meal-times with the family – allows respondents to express their own views on the issues discussed in the programme. Indeed, one can hardly listen to the debate without formulating an opinion of one's own. As respondents often refer to an acquaintance's experiences of the issue, we may say that these acquaintances join the participation framework for that respondent, adding their imaginary voice to the debate, and further locating the debate between studio and living room rather than just in the studio:

> Well, I say this because I know somebody who started off with a six or eight room bed-and-breakfast and now they have at least ten of those. (P1.45)

> Yes, that's right. Like my son. (P3.26)

What effects do respondents suppose viewing audience discussion programmes have on themselves? Mainly, people felt that the discussions provoked thoughts or analysis which they might not otherwise have had:

> It does make you think of your own view on these things. You can't listen for 40 minutes with people talking on a subject like that without thinking in your own mind how you would react or feel about it. In that sense it is educational but not to a given point of view. It makes you sort out your own thoughts a bit more. (P1.91)

Surprise at discovering how others lived or felt was a commonly expressed emotion:

> What surprised me was that some receptionists asked patients what was wrong with them. I have never had that, I think that that is appalling. (D2.117)

Others felt that they learnt little from the programme beyond a repetition of the obvious:

> What did we learn? We know that we have bad patients, we know that we have bad doctors. (D1.56)

> It's one of those kinds of programmes where you think, 'yes, that's nice' and you felt that you were in the majority view and programmes where you can identify with the majority view are always satisfying. (F2.65)

One difference between involved and uninvolved viewers is whether they see the discussion as addressing issues, for which individuals are merely the exemplars, or whether they see the discussion as presenting individuals, from which issues may or may not successfully emerge:

> I think that it is just being presented with a problem in society, or what some people find a problem, and because you are actually listening to that sort of thing, everyone is trying to deal with it. That is why I find it stimulating. It's not seeing individuals in certain circumstances, it's being aware that there are problems which perhaps I identify with myself. (P1.182)

PERCEPTIONS OF THE HOME AUDIENCE

Rather few comments concerned the home audience for audience discussion programmes (3 per cent of comments). They may suppose the home audience to be similar to or different from themselves. So, they imagine that the home audience also watches because they are at home at that time of day and want entertainment while doing the housework. They may also see the home audience as being voyeuristic or prejudiced:

> You can just see people watching who have been treated badly, but they wouldn't be listening so much to their doctors who would be defending themselves, they would be saying, 'hear, hear', you know. (D1.117)

They also wonder about the possible effects on the home audience of watching audience discussion programmes – does it make you think about issues or does it leave you unaffected?

> Well, it gives people food for thought, perhaps changing their minds about themselves. Perhaps the people that were there, or the people watching, put themselves in that position, feel something change inside them. (P3.178)

> I don't think that anybody would change their opinion having seen the programme, they know that there is poverty in society. (P1.22)

THE CRITICAL VIEWER?

From respondents' comments in this and other chapters, we have tried to ground the variety of ways in which viewers are critical of television programmes. Most simply, viewers differ in their evaluation of the genre. Whether viewers like or dislike, approve or disapprove of a programme affects their involvement or distance from the programme, their interpretations of its structures or purposes and, of course, their likelihood of watching it at home. However, this notion of critical is limited, and it would be misleading to conclude that those who dislike the genre are the more critical viewers. Rather, both positive and negative responses to the genre rest upon interpretation: viewers vary in their analysis of the social value of the genre and of its relation to the public interest and commercial entertainment.

The relation between interpretation and evaluation may be complex. Often, those who take against the programmes – maybe they dislike the host – tend to see it as commercial entertainment, trivial escapism and voyeurism. On the other hand, those who are sensitive to television's commercialism express their frustration at being addressed as consumer rather than citizen by disliking the programmes. Similarly, those who see the programmes as part of the public service may feel more positively about it while those who appreciate hearing ordinary people's stories may be more ready to attribute public service rather than commercial goals to the genre. As discussed in the previous chapter, the generic form of these programmes is unstable and so, consequently, are viewers' critical and evaluative responses.

These evaluative responses cut across the critical/referential notion of interpretation. Independently of whether they like or dislike the programmes and of whether they interpret the programmes as meeting public service or entertainment aims, respondents vary in whether they make referential or critical (metalinguistic) readings. Those comments that are revealing of the respondents themselves are referential, as are some of those made about the lay and expert participants. Here, viewers focus on people's opinions and experiences, seeing them as part of the real world, on the emotions or frustrations expressed, and on their own involvement or interest in the issues discussed. Many other comments reveal an awareness of production issues, seeing the genre as a constructed product, the participants as having specific motivations and as being selected for specific reasons, and seeing the lay and expert speakers as facing particular communicative and generic problems. Respondents were also aware of some issues of genre conventions, epistemology and argument structure (Chapters 3, 5 and 6).

Referential and critical comments are unrelated to the evaluative responses to the programmes: both positive and negative orientations could lead viewers to comment on production aims or generic conventions (whether seen as public service/debate or entertainment/romance). Similarly, both could lead viewers to see the programmes as part of the real world, whether this consists in the triviality or the significance of hearing ordinary people's opinions on television.

Many varieties of literary criticism (Belsey, 1980) may be seen to have filtered into common-sense assumptions about the critical. As in Leavis, the question of expressive realism is a problem for television viewers: is the programme authentic? What are participants trying to tell us and can they be relied upon? In what sense is this a fair picture of a contemporary issue and what can we learn about the world by watching such programmes? In a similar way to the New Critics, viewers are concerned about the form of the text: is it coherent, does it make sense in its own terms, is it a valuable contribution to the public domain? Like in Frye's structuralist approach, viewers are concerned with classifying the programmes, with identifying their underlying conventions, to make comparisons with other genres. Like for reader-response theorists, viewers may occupy or challenge the subject position inscribed for them in the text, connecting the text to their own experiences or rejecting the assumption that, for example, they are inattentive housewives.

Viewers' critical responses can also be understood as part of the hegemonic process: 'within the existing ideology it appears "obvious" that people are autonomous individuals, possessed of subjectivity or consciousness which is the source of their beliefs and actions. That people are unique, distinguishable irreplaceable identities is "the elementary ideological effect" ' (Belsey, 1980: 58). So ironically, while through their expressions of critical interpretation, viewers may feel themselves to be at their most individual and autonomous, it is at these moments that the ideological effect may be most successfully working. And yet, in her discussion of productive critical practice, Belsey draws on Barthes to argue that while expressive and classic realisms work to construct the reader as consumer of the text, other, deconstructive texts may work to construct the reader as producer of the text, according to the following set of oppositions:

consumer	producer
passive consumer of meaning	active producer of meaning
readable text	challenging (writable) text
trance	alert
spectator	critical
labour is mystified	labour is made visible (textuality)

While this is intended to apply only to high culture, we may ask whether some of the audience's responses to popular culture also move between these oppositions, occasionally fitting those on the right as well as those on the left. Maybe audience discussion programmes, by challenging any straightforward mode of interpretation or involvement and by posing so many classificatory problems for the viewer, also challenge the notion that critical response is an essentially elite privilege.

CRITICAL RECEPTION AND INVOLVEMENT IN VIEWING

Viewers' evaluative and interpretative responses affect their involvement in the genre in complex ways. Liebes and Katz (1990) map out some common-sense connotations of critical and uncritical:

critical	*uncritical*
conscious	unconscious
oppositional	hegemonic
creative	normative
aware of production	window on the world
cool	hot

However, as they later make clear, critical readings need not imply that viewers are less involved or more distanced than when making referential readings. Rather different patterns of involvement between viewer and programme occur. As we have seen, those who make critical interpretations but feel positive about the public service aims of the genre may feel very involved in their analysis of the conventions or forms according to which the programmes are constructed and may care considerably about whether these aims can be brought off on television. For others, an awareness of the programme as product, especially if one endorses the entertainment view of the programme, may lead to the experience of distance rather than involvement. Conversely, some may make referential readings and feel very distanced from the representation of the world – people's opinions are indeed trivial, everyone has their own opinion and sticks to it and nothing ever results from mere talk, while some may make referential readings and feel highly involved, adding their own experiences and opinions into what they feel to be a valuable exchange of views. Clearly, this analysis of critical readings and viewer involvement depends crucially on the analysis made, usually implicitly, of the genre itself.

If critical responses are not necessarily the opposite of involved or participatory responses, then at least two dimensions describe the viewer's relationship to the programme, critical/accepting and involved/distanced. This may have different consequences for persuasion (Petty et al. 1981). Liebes and Katz (1990) propose four categories of viewer involvement:

	referential	*critical*
hot	moral	ideological
cool	ludic	aesthetic

Each form of involvement may be conceived as a form of opposition to the text and hence as a defence against media effects:

> Moral defense is based on giving a program standing and, thus, deeming it worthy of argument. Ideological defense is vulnerable because it is based on automatic transformations, as if to say that the opposite of the message *is*

the truth. Aesthetic defense risks letting the ideological message slip by, while the playful escape of ludic defense may fail to return one to the ground.

(Liebes and Katz, 1990: 129)

Unfortunately, this classification confuses evaluative and interpretative notions of critical, implying, for example, that ideological readings are negative and that ludic readings are positive. As discussed above, those who are involved (hot) and also critical may be those most concerned about the positive public sphere aims of this genre and so be most concerned with establishing how best the genre can achieve these aims. Similarly, those who make cool, referential readings may have little inclination to play with the ideas expressed, rejecting the programmes as trivial or boring. As the moral readings suggest a positive orientation and the aesthetic imply a neutral/ negative orientation, we still have implicitly in Liebes and Katz's scheme the assumption that referential is accepting and critical is distancing rather than a recognition of the independence between these dimensions which can be seen in viewers' responses.

CRITICAL RECEPTION AS SOCIAL ACTION

Being critical, whether understood in evaluative, interpretative or political terms, is not so much a cognitive mode of response as a social one. Speakers and hearers, programmes and audiences, accept a social responsibility to generate meanings which can withstand scrutiny. For example, hearers have a social responsibility to evaluate what they hear and to be ready to discuss their criticisms in other social situations (including a focus group discussion). Speakers have a social responsibility, as Grice (1975) has noted, to be relevant, cogent, parsimonious, and, we might add, to ground their claims, not abuse their authority, entertain their audience, and so forth.

As these different orientations to the programme, or different interpretive strategies, are always expressed in a social situation (here, the focus group), they have rhetorical aspects (Morgan, 1988). Most obviously, social desirability works to support critical comments as clever, impressive self-presentation. Critical comments may also defend against the power of the media. Further, critical comments themselves act upon the world, for in making one's interpretation, one re-presents the discussion in a certain way, making it real for the present audience through one's own voice.

People's critical judgments draw on social knowledge: they depend on a shared discourse of production/genre knowledge (itself largely promoted through popular culture), a shared representation of expertise and ordinariness, and a shared set of values about the public sphere and public interest and about the place of commercial interests and private experiences. Social norms and morality, social prejudices and stereotypes, are all used as a resource when orienting to television, whether positively or negatively, critically or referentially, acceptingly or subversively.

The products of critical response are also social. Through their responses to television, people generate social identities for themselves and others. Moreover, the discourses and social representations which underpin these responses are themselves reconstituted through use. In the case of audience discussion programmes, the discourses of democracy, public interest, privacy, expertise and rationality are reproduced through talk about television. Nonetheless, we can only suggest here that critical response positions viewers as public citizens rather than private consumers, and so may result in a critical public opinion, with consequences for the involvement of ordinary people in public argument and public policy making. Nava (1991) points to the political and economic consequences of consumer movements such as green consumerism or the boycotting of South African goods. In relation to the media, some argue that viewer and listener organizations affect the conduct and regulation of broadcasting. Generally, 'the world is intelligible only through discourse: there is no unmediated experience' (Belsey, 1980: 61). Politics occurs within a shared, though diverse, discursive context in which public opinion, shared knowledge and common-sense assumptions are central, and public scrutiny of state and economic practices is ever more pervasive, if not intrusive.

Chapter 5

Media constructions of expertise and common sense

RELATIONS BETWEEN POPULAR AND EXPERT CULTURES

Compared to expert, scientific knowledge, ordinary or common-sense knowledge has long been derogated, and its supposed deficiencies have been used to justify the institutional separation of science from everyday life:

> Severing civil society from science, Hegel contends that subjective views and opinions have nothing to do with science . . . The opinions of the multitude are degraded to common knowledge.
>
> (Holub, 1991: 5)

Positivist science generally castigates common knowledge as superficial, ignorant and full of error, emphasizing scientific discovery as counter-intuitive findings, rejecting old wives' tales in favour of masculine science. Yet this modernist separation of scientific rationality from everyday thinking has led to a crisis in legitimation such that scientific and other forms of expert knowledge become so separated from ordinary thinking they can only be legitimated through claims to authority. This is ironic both for institutions used to making claims of validity in terms of logic and truth claims and for the public whose problems of the life-world, framed in ordinary language, can no longer provide an agenda for expert concern:

> The relationship between 'art' and 'life' is just as problematic as the relationship between 'theory' and 'practice' or between 'morality' and 'ethos' is for philosophy. The unmediated transposition of specialized knowledge into the private and public spheres of the everyday world can endanger the autonomy and independent logics of the knowledge systems, on the one hand, and it can violate the integrity of life-world contexts, on the other.
>
> (Habermas, 1987a: 340)

Bell also criticizes modernism's blurring of art and life through the 'democratization of criticism' so that 'the touchstone of judgment is no longer some consensual agreement on standards, but each "self's" judgment as to how art enhances that "self" ' (1990: 323). Asking then whether modernism has been co-opted, as the critical theorists claimed, Bell argues that the crisis in legitimation undermines any co-option or commodification:

> A societal order is shored up by its legitimations, which provide the defenses against its despisers. But the legitimation of the culture . . . is the quest for self-gratification and the expression of 'personality'.
>
> (Bell, 1990: 327)

Lyotard also takes up the crisis in legitimation, for 'the postmodern condition' hinges on a new incredulity toward metanarratives, such as religion, science, knowledge, in which legitimacy once resided. Once we understand science as a language game on a par with all others, where 'someone always comes along to disturb the order of "reason" ' (Lyotard, 1990: 335), knowledge no longer legitimates action, science cannot lead to emancipation or be seen as superior to other forms of knowing. For both science and ordinary understandings, there can be no universal consensus: knowledge can only be provisional, local and heterogeneous.

The crisis in legitimation of expertise stems both from developments in scientific rationality and from the increasing separation of expertise from ordinary understanding. While Habermas would disagree with the post-modern argument that knowledge is provisional and discursive, he develops Weber's characterization of cultural modernity as the separation of reason into the three autonomous spheres of science, morality and art, legitimated by criteria of truth, justice and beauty respectively. Habermas is concerned with the institutionalization of these domains, for specialized professions have emerged for each domain, with their own expertise and specialized languages:

> As a result, the distance has grown between the culture of the experts and that of the large public. What accrues to culture through specialized treatment and reflexion does not immediately and necessarily become the property of everyday praxis. With cultural rationalization of this sort, the threat increases that the life-world . . . will become more and more impoverished.
>
> (Habermas, 1990: 348)

One expert participant in an audience discussion programme noted: 'it made me aware of the closed nature of the academic world and of how little expertise does seep into the general public . . . as an expert you rarely come into contact with the public' (expert 2, psychologist).

Once expertise has been institutionalized, the public are no longer involved in criticism of established power as they had been in the public sphere. The disintegration of the bourgeois public sphere occurs as:

> With the mounting bureaucratization of the administration in state and society it seems to be inherent in the nature of the case that the expertise of

highly specialized experts would necessarily be removed from supervision by rationally debating bodies.

(Habermas, 1989: 233)

Although pessimistic about the ability of ordinary people to become involved in institutionalized forms of debate, Habermas suggests that the reception of art and, by analogy, of morality and scientific knowledge, may be one solution: while the ordinary consumer of art may not receive it as does the expert, he or she will appropriate it, relating it to his or her own life problems and so creating a new language game different to that of the aesthetic critic:

> The project aims at a differentiated relinking of modern culture with an everyday praxis . . . the life-world has to become able to develop institutions out of itself which set limits to the internal dynamics and to the imperatives of an almost autonomous economic system and its administrative complements.

(Habermas, 1990: 352–3)

Thus, through the active reception of communications from established power, ordinary people may enrich the public sphere, countering institutional forms of knowledge production and control by establishing their own interpretative institutions in everyday life.. To prevent the fragmentation of criticism into individual matters of taste, Habermas proposes forms of collective criticism emerging from the life-world. Others, such as Fraser (1989), suggest that ordinary people can best constitute a public sphere which escapes state control through the dispersal, fragmentation or disruption of expert communication rather than by constructing public institutions which oppose established power:

> If the contemporary 'public sphere' were reconceived . . . as a plural, provisional, and multi-layered concept that includes rather than excludes the disciplines and that disperses its debts and obligations rather than concentrating them in a single totalizing instance, then fears of bullying might be appeased, while the authority to which such fears refer might take a more concrete oppositional form.

(Robbins, 1990b: 115)

In the work of Foucault (1970), which anticipates much of that of postmodernism, the various ways in which power is dispersed among social institutions can be contrasted to both positive and Marxist conceptions of power as residing in rational and economic processes respectively. This dispersal of power is reflected in expressions of diverse interests through discourse, so that, in contrast to the attempt to construct a consensus with which to challenge established power, discussion should give free rein to difference. In this sense, proponents of the oppositional public sphere are postmodern: proposing that an institution could provide a context for diverse voices, representing different subject positions with different power bases, to generate a discourse as part of the social dispersal of power. This contrasts with Habermas's proposal for the institutional development of a critical voice within the life-world so as to produce a consensual and reasoned challenge to established power. In this vein we can regard the audience discussion programme as a particular form of public discussion institutionally mediated by television. The role of the television might be regarded as attempting to provide an organized representation of rational consensus, as corrupting the life-world through institutional power, or as giving a voice to diverse subject positions and allowing the negotiation of meanings and compromises. In each case, there is a repositioning of the media's construction of the relationship between expertise and common knowledge from the dissemination of critical, elite knowledge to a presentation or management of public opinion. Certainly, through its dissemination model, the media can be seen as part of the legitimation crisis of modernity, offering the laity only the powerless subject position of receivers of ready-existing expert knowledge, thus further fragmenting and marginalizing the life-world. But, we suggest, this is not a 'natural' and inevitable characteristic of the broadcast media. The recent emphasis on participatory programming repositions the media and constructs a different relationship between established power and laity.

THE PROCESS OF POPULARIZATION

If we see social institutions as constructing expert knowledge as a form of social control then the dissemination of knowledge for popular consumption plays a key role in this process of control. We have linked the tradition of public service broadcasting to the legitimation crisis as it encodes institutionalized critical positions and constructs a discourse which positions the laity only as receivers of knowledge. Garnham (1990) identifies a confusion concerning expert knowledge within the ethic of public service broadcasting between the functions of information-giving and political advocacy. Politicians and journalists use the media for dissemination of knowledge, thereby making claims to objectivity and neutrality which tend also to be applied implicitly to advocacy: 'it is a perennial and justified criticism of journalists by experts that journalists themselves decide the agenda of what is relevant, and at the same time too often garble the information for presentational purposes' (ibid: 112). Robinson (1982) notes that experts on talk shows frequently offer implicit value judgements as well as factual statements. Garnham proposes that expert organizations (research bodies, charities, pressure groups, etc.) should receive airtime for information broadcasts under their own control in a manner akin to the oppositional public sphere in which representatives of local, plural, internal public spheres come together for information, advocacy and debate.

The dissemination of expert knowledge can be seen in everyday discourse. Linde (1987) showed how the explanatory systems implicit in the ways people tell their life stories draw upon expert explanations from psychoanalysis, behaviourism, or astrology. Similarly, Moscovici (1981) shows how psychoanalytic theory has filtered into popular understanding. Thus, popular understanding represents a transformation of expertise. Linde notes three features that characterize the relation between popular and expert explanatory systems: first, the popular version uses only a small, selected subset of the concepts present in the expert theory; second, the concepts remain isolated, rather than interconnected into a theoretical system, as in the original theory; third, those concepts that are incorporated into popular thought supplement but do not contradict other popular theories.

We can identify two processes by which expertise filters into ordinary understandings – through journalists and through popularizing scientists. Moscovici showed how the adoption of psychoanalytic terminology by journalists has encouraged the adoption of such terms into common sense. In scientific popularization, which itself increasingly occurs via the mass media, scientists or other experts propound their views to a popular audience. The discursive constraints of both journalists and popular scientists match Linde's three features of ordinary explanatory systems, for both are selective in their use of concepts, both neglect theoretical integration in favour of discrete facts or points, and both are careful not to encourage disfavour by contradicting common-sense beliefs. In these ways, knowledge is transformed rather than mediated, and new popular explanatory systems are established, to be used in new circumstances and for other purposes. Processes of popularization are thus unlikely to resolve the legitimation crisis through their particular linking of expertise and common knowledge, for the expertise is still generated independently of the issues in the life-world.

The practices of science clearly differ from the practices of popularizing science as each draws on different rules, conventions and skills. For de Certeau (1984), the increasingly common expectation that experts should speak in the public, nonspecialist domain – to popularize, to be accessible, to disseminate, to be accountable – inevitably results in a loss of expertise. As specialist knowledge cannot be communicated in a public, nonspecialist domain without significant transformation and impoverishment, their only qualification to speak is based on the authority granted them because of their specialist knowledge, rather than on that specialist knowledge itself. There is a danger that the media might, unintentionally or otherwise, deconstruct the expert as a repository of knowledge (Klonoff, 1983). For example, to present a media debate among experts rather than a single and hence authoritative talking head might undermine the credibility of expertise, as each contribution is relativized and each expert questions the status of the others (for example, see Tulloch and Chapman, 1992). As we see below, experts are often not perceived as such when deprived by the media of their expert discourse, technical paraphernalia and peer group context.

As the ordinary person becomes not only hearer but also speaker, through participatory programming, it becomes apparent that, ironically unlike experts, the ordinary person can communicate in an ordinary way to an ordinary audience, and indeed, they are becoming better communicators on television as they gain in familiarity with the media. Of course, they can only communicate ordinary knowledge in this manner, not expertise. Thus as ordinary people participate in public debates on television, the discourse changes: expertise is undermined and lay discourse is elevated. For some, this is an improvement: making a similar argument to that of grounding expertise in the life-world, Friedrich argues that putting policy decisions into practice depends on everyday understandings which are 'related in manifold ways to the prevailing folkways of the community. For effective functioning and execution, such decisions require integration with these folkways' (Friedrich, 1950: 114).

If speaking in ordinary language is a problem for sustaining the expert position, members of the public may have difficulties in speaking in public and maintaining authenticity. The participation of private individuals in public debates, on television or elsewhere, draws upon two key opposition: expert/ lay and public/private. As we argue below, participatory forums prioritize the lay over the expert, requiring the expert to talk in lay terms and making the expert accountable to the laity. They also, necessarily, prioritize the public over the private, bringing the private into public view, using private individuals to illustrate public issues, and demanding that private people be transformed into public citizens. As experts belong, in Habermas's terms, to the system, while the laity belong to the private domain of the life-world, these forums break with cultural traditions, and attempt a reconstruction of both expertise and lay knowledge.

One way in which science is popularized is through myth or epic adventure, as in the scientific documentary, where the scientists are constructed as heroes searching for knowledge and truth against all the odds (Silverstone, 1984). The audience is drawn into this mythic drama and, along the way, tends to accept that there are such things as facts which can be sought through scientific discovery. Following Foucault (1970), we see that this form of representation disguises the devices through which knowledge is produced in established science.

In audience discussion programmes, the audience are admitted into the search (commissioned as a search party?) and the host takes on the hero role, often in opposition to the representatives (villains?) of established power (see Chapter 3). The media reposition themselves to provide a critical forum instead of reifying processes of scientific discovery in terms of truth, thereby moving, in Foucauldian terms, from a regulatory to a discursive institution which includes rather than excludes the laity.

THE CHALLENGE TO EXPERTISE FROM PARTICIPATORY PROGRAMMING

> A face is a face. An expert asks an opinion, and then someone else asks an opinion. And the expert counts for nothing, or no more than the person who was just expressing an opinion. (D4.150)

Observing the behind-the-scenes production of *Kilroy*, a journalist noted, when two medical experts for the programme are introduced to Robert Kilroy-Silk, that 'Kilroy has a well-known aversion to pundits, so these last are introduced rather apologetically' (*The Radio Times*, 19–25 March 1988). Kilroy-Silk elaborates this, when asked how the programme has changed in its first five years:

> The audience is different. At first it was assumed it would be mainly housewives, but a large chunk are university students. Many viewers are unemployed or disabled, and there is an enormous number of shift workers. In the beginning, the producers used to stack the show with experts. All the real people were put in the back row. The BBC were very distrustful of *real* people: they didn't think they could talk. I knew they could and would. People can be very articulate about things that affect them. Now we do shows with no experts at all – I don't like them. If we're covering cot death I want to talk to women who've experienced it. The best parts of *Kilroy* are when real people talk to each other. You don't see that anywhere else on TV.
> (Interview by William Cook in *New Woman* magazine, November 1991)

Public access to and participation in the mass media represents a challenge to expertise, a challenge reflected in a broader public anxiety and ambivalence about expertise, education, science and intellectuals in society (Ross, 1989). The increase in participatory programming and particularly the positioning of ordinary people and experts together to talk as equals could intensify public scepticism and distrust of established power. Not only is just such access now being given, but the form of television talk is changing in the direction of the conventions of lay discourse; the discourse of 'real' people rather than the artificial discourse of experts. Television is increasingly conversational and informal in style, even in current affairs and news programming (Heritage et al. 1988). As formality is lost and chat takes over, the expert has problems in managing his or her image and in presenting complex arguments or scientific evidence. Experts are pushed into either oversimple arguments or a reliance on their status as their source of credibility (Hovland et al. 1953) rather than on the quality of their arguments and evidence. Undoubtedly, experts are regularly frustrated in their desire to draw comparisons, pursue analogies, identify complexities and moral difficulties, locate arguments in their historical or cultural contexts, and so forth.

This has potentially important consequences for the perception of expertise, setting up a cycle of disrespect whereby the representation of experts is ever more downgraded (Ross, 1989). One lay speaker on *Kilroy* attacks the experts: 'I'm terribly sorry but you are ostriches. You've got your heads buried deep in the ground and you can't get them out again.'

Experts who participate in television programmes (for example, politicians, academics, pressure group representatives) place themselves in a new, more accessible, relationship with ordinary people. Consequently, ordinary people become accustomed to making critical comparisons between their own experiences and expert knowledge, to seeing ordinary experiences being accorded time and respect, and to seeing experts in conflict both with each other and with the lay public.

> This programme was about people not trusting experts, wasn't it? You can always get two experts that disagree with each other. (D2.99)

Experts may try to undermine each other's expert status: the Tobacco Advisory Council representative on *The Time, The Place* says of an anti-smoking speaker, 'she is a nutritionist not a medical expert'. Hosts may also undermine experts: 'I've got two medical experts and I know they are going to argue' and 'I know you could go into deep medical arguments but that wouldn't get us anywhere' (*The Time, The Place*).

Few programmes dispense with experts or expertise altogether, as traditionally they have played a key role in maintaining a critical public sphere (Tuchman, 1988), yet their role is changing. The pedagogic role of informing and advising the laity is being supplemented, if not replaced, by a role in which they are contrasted with and held accountable to the laity who are themselves constructed as authentic (the real 'experts'). Kilroy forces one expert to answer a tricky question by saying to the lay speaker, 'ask your question again' until she gets, or in some cases publicly fails to get, an adequate answer. Yet experts who cannot communicate cannot be held accountable, and an uninformed laity cannot hold them accountable:

> They should be made accountable to ordinary people but what the experts should be striving to do and what they don't get an opportunity to do in this situation is to thoroughly explain and make sure that the people they are explaining to understand what is going on in this particular field so that they have a thorough grounding in what the expert believes is going on and then if the public or whoever happens to be in opposition wants to set some questions to the expert based on that then that's fine, that's accountability, that's OK. If the expert can't answer it then he knows he's got some work to do.
>
> (Jack, studio audience)

Undoubtedly, the very terms 'expert' and 'lay' or 'ordinary' are problematic. Many who are called experts resist the label and many 'ordinary' people claim specific domains of expertise. Different elites – political, intellectual, scientific, moral – claim different power-bases and different epistemologies through which their expertise is justified and expressed. These categories are in part media constructions. In interviews, 'experts' worried about whether they fitted the social representation of an expert (for example, male, not young, bow tie):

> I don't actually like calling myself an expert but it is an area in which I am called an expert. It was the BBC that first called me an expert on an awful lot of things that I don't believe myself to be an expert in.

> (Expert 4, academic in international relations)

> Experts? I think you have to wait until the end of the programme before you draw any conclusion about who the experts are. I think that people who Kilroy thinks are going to act as the experts don't always turn out that way. You often get much more useful information from the ordinary person in the studio who happens to be very good at communicating and has some significant thing to say. What you tend to get from experts is you're reminded of the same things, you often don't get new perspectives from experts. But what you do get from Kilroy's programmes is new perspectives, from for example the young offender himself. When he says absolutely I will go out and reoffend unless I'm locked up, you can't really argue with that. No matter what an expert's opinion is, this is the kind of thing that really matters.

> (George, viewer)

Audience discussion programmes, in their challenge to expertise and populist valorization of the laity, further problematize the distinction. Let us then take the terms as inherently problematic and becoming more so: we use them primarily to identify the social roles used by the audience discussion genre. The social role of expert in audience discussion programmes may be filled by a variety of people – academics, politicians, pressure group representatives. They gain their authority from different sources and have different rights and responsibilities to speak in public debate. How can we identify the experts? In the programmes, some people have visual labels on the screen, but in a programme on social class, these labels served to identify the upper classes. Some people have throat mikes rather than waiting for the boom mike, but these include ordinary people with pre-planned stories to tell. Some sit in the front row. Some have institutional affiliations. As the programmes prioritize any member of the studio audience who offers 'good television', they become the experts in the sense of having the right to pronounce and pre-identified experts may be marginalized.

There are two forms of audience discussion programme which encode different attempts to relate expertise and laity. In *The Oprah Winfrey Show* and *Donahue*, the studio audience are seated in stalls seats while the invited guests and experts are placed on the stage. In *Kilroy* and *The Time, The Place* the experts and guests sit among the studio audience, although often in the front row. The American programmes elevate ordinary people with personal experience of the issue to the expert position by creating them as lay expert on the stage. In contrast, the British programmes reduce the status of the experts by placing them in the studio audience among the lay people. The American programmes make ordinary people into experts for the day or famous for fifteen minutes whereas the British programmes bring the experts down to earth as one of us.

The social role of 'ordinary people' is also problematic. It may be filled by those who volunteer after seeing programme advertisements, by students bussed in *en masse* to fill empty seats (and who thus do not know the topic in advance), by so-called experts telling a personal story rather than giving an expert account, and by discussant 'seeds' with known contributions who are planted in the studio audience by the production team:

> Basically, they keep asking me back for the same issues, it's always the 90s new man's view on sex is what I'm supposed to be putting forward. They've got me typed as (a) as a new man and (b) as someone who is quite prepared to open their mouth about their and other people's sex lives.

(Tony, studio audience)

THE MEDIATED LEGITIMATION OF ORDINARY EXPERIENCE

> On the television, the doctor is on an equal footing with any of his patients, just as the Archbishop of Canterbury is with a pop star and yet in real life that is not so. People are not equal in society, the little girl who works in the back of the shop is not on equal footing with a professor of Greek, and yet on the box, everyone is the same, and maybe it is good that this should be so. The telly is a great equalizer, a leveller if you like. (D4.148)

Audience discussion programmes and various other access and participation programmes offer a celebration of ordinary experience by constructing a particular relationship between lay and expert participants. Both are presented as interested parties but as knowing different things in different ways. The media organize expert/lay relations through particular rules and rhetoric which specify whose discourse is adopted, what counts as a good argument, what evidence is needed to ground claims, and what resolutions are valued. Following the modernist separation of expertise and common sense, with the former becoming increasingly specialized and privileged while the latter is degraded and personalized, television genres which involve both expertise and ordinary experience (for example, documentaries, current affairs) have traditionally valorized the expert by opposing experts to the laity thus:

Lay	Expert
subjective	objective
ungrounded	grounded in data
emotional	rational
particular	replicable and general
concrete	abstract
motivated	neutral
supposition	factual
obvious	counter-intuitive

For Habermas, these connotations of lay knowledge reflect the undermining of the life-world, while the connotations of expertise represent the triumph of the system. For Foucault, these oppositions construct a way of knowing which establishes a particular group as powerful. One challenge to this relation of knowledge to power is to celebrate alternative ways of knowing. Some recent research would reverse the evaluations of these two kinds of knowing, suggesting that the ordinary person also lays claim to a particular epistemology which should be revalidated: see, for example, research on narrative thought (Sarbin, 1986); on communal morality (Gilligan, 1982); on lay reasoning (Heider, 1958; Lunt, 1988); and on contextual/rhetorical understanding (Billig, 1987). Audience discussion programmes adopt an anti-elitist position which implicitly draws on these alternative epistemological traditions, offering a revaluation of the life-world, repudiating criticisms of the ordinary person as incompetent or ignorant, questioning the deference traditionally due to experts through their separation from the life-world and their incorporation into the system, and asserting instead the worth of the 'common man'. The above traditional oppositions are challenged and an alternative (or additional) set of oppositions is posed:

Lay	Expert
authentic	alienated
narrative	fragmented
hot	cold
relevant	irrelevant
in depth	superficial
grounded in experience	ungrounded
meaningful	empty of meaning
practical	useless
real	artificial

The formal arrangements of the genre support this recasting of the expert/lay relationship. Experts are seated among the studio audience, rather than sitting on a raised platform facing them. There is no formal structure of, for example, questions from the studio audience and answers from the experts. The programmes often begin with a discussion already under way between host and lay audience, while the experts take second place, awaiting their cue, often having to fight for space to get a word in edgeways. The hosts may ask experts harder, more hostile, or more demanding questions while addressing the studio audience members in a more intimate, courteous and sympathetic manner ('go on, love'). For example, when a politician responds to a lay speaker's question by asking a question of them, Kilroy intervenes:

> Kilroy: Don't you do that, don't you do that. Typical politician. You asked him a question, make him answer your question. David [Member of Parliament], he asked you a question, how do you define poverty? It's a good question.

He then insists further that the politician answers the question: 'hang on, David, you were asked a question by Mike the chef,' and he defends a member of the studio audience, saying 'we've got to be fair to Betty'. Hosts often act to protect or speak for the lay participant:

> Kilroy: Ask your question again, you started with a question to Chris [expert], ask him your question again.

And again:

> Kilroy: Do you doctors recognize yourselves? All the doctors are sitting very quiet aren't they, but I know where you all are (laughter) . . . all very . . . no doctors want to respond to all this? Doctor, do you recognize yourself, looking at your watch when they walk in, giving prescriptions without listening?

Experts also attack each other:

> Expert 1: On your own government's figures, you know that the numbers in poverty have increased by 55 per cent since 1979. That is a terrible . . .
>
> Expert 2 (politician): John Moore was not saying that if you have a colour television you're not poor. He was not saying that. Let me finish, let me finish. He was just enabling – perhaps older people who remember very difficult times, so that they can understand that the poor, the people in difficulties these days do have these consumer –
>
> Expert 1: But now David, these very difficult times are certainly back now . . .

The host may also clarify the expert contribution for the benefit of the lay:

> Kilroy: What the minister is saying is that if you've got, or what

the argument is, if you actually possess a colour television there's no way you can be described as being poor.

In contrast to the order which experts would usually expect of a debate, all participants engage in questioning, answering, challenging, interrupting, recounting and emoting. People may resist each other, struggling for space. A lay speaker says to the host, 'no, I didn't mean it like that. You're putting words into my mouth'. Hosts too can resist the laity: Kilroy insists, 'no, you should answer the question that's just been put to you'.

Hosts often give priority to the revelation of personal experience and showing impatience at the citing of statistics or scientific findings: 'in debate the authority of the expert is replaced by the authority of a narrative informed by lived experience' (Carpignano et al. 1990: 53). When someone cites a statistic on *The Time, The Place*, claiming an ever-decreasing representation of working-class students in higher education, 'and that's a fact', Mike Scott answers, 'well, that's one view, are there any others?'.

The ordinary, anecdotal account of everyday life is repeatedly prioritized over the expert, scientific or abstracted account. The implication is that discussions must be grounded in everyday experiences, not expert abstractions:

Woman: I've got colour TV, I've got everything. For me to maintain what I've got, I get up early in the morning and do cleaning. Why, because people like tie and suit don't give us a chance because we've got kids when going for a job interview. Also when your kid's sick, who looks after your kid? So when you're saying I should sell our TV that's nonsense. When we sell our TV, what are our kids to do? Go out and cause trouble.

Similarly, expert definitions such as the definition of poverty are subordinated to people's right to define their own lives:

Woman: I now am severely invalided, and I live on £40 a week, but I think I live a very rich, rewarding lifestyle. I don't live in poverty. My spirit is not impoverished.

Indeed, as experts have often no personal experience of the issue being discussed, their contributions may be rejected:

Man: The gentleman [an expert] down in the front is saying get your priorities right. . . . Have any one of them ever lived in a bed-and-breakfast for more than two minutes? Have any of them ever stood in a queue waiting to get their money and said, right £52 is your lot?

We need, then, to hear from those who have direct experience of the issue:

I watched the one the other day about people offending while they're out on bail. I found it very interesting that Kilroy managed to get a chap into the studio and interview him about his own feelings and why he did it, his own reactions, and I thought he was totally honest, it just came glaring through that he was totally honest about his own feelings and views on it. And I thought this was immensely useful. However one may disapprove of a young man who offends eight times mostly while on bail, it has to add to our knowledge and understanding of these issues.

(George, viewer)

Even for protest groups, pressure groups, self-help groups and other organizations whose aim is to represent the ordinary person in political debate, these programmes will seek to substantiate the account of such a representative with the personal story of an individual who has experienced the problem under discussion. On a *Kilroy* programme about wearing fur, an anti-fur speaker says, 'I think it is patronizing to suggest that people stop wearing furs because they feel intimidated', Kilroy replies, speaking for a pro-fur speaker, 'she's not being patronized, she's talking about her experience'.

Analytic categories are often resisted: in a programme about computer games, a psychiatrist's talk of 'addictions' and 'obsessions' was rejected as inappropriate or meaningless. On a programme about smoking, when the representative of the Tobacco Advisory Council questions the use of the term 'addiction', the host anchored the term in personal experience rather than in expertise, thus legitimating it, 'I don't know about the dictionary definition but I know I was addicted'. Further, direct analysis of contradictory opinions is often avoided, simply stacking up lay opinions side by side: 'I believe in a mandatory jail sentence to knock some sense into people' (victim of drunk driving on *The Oprah Winfrey Show*) is followed by 'Jail is not the answer for everyone' (drunk driver on *The Oprah Winfrey Show*).

Thus expert abstractions are frequently questioned or rejected, and people are constructed as individuals not subject-matter for analysis. On the doctor–patient communication programme (*Kilroy*), one doctor instantly lost audience sympathy when he responded to his lay challenger, 'people like you . . .'. Classifying people into groups is a legitimate aspect of expert, but not lay, discourse. Another expert, on the poverty programme, became very unpopular when he responded to one hardship story with an abstract policy argument: 'I don't think it was ever envisaged that social security was designed to pay mortgages'. Again, an expert shocked the audience (indicated by an audible intake of breath in disapproval) when he asserted general concerns over personal ones:

What I would like to say is that Michelle who is in bed-and-breakfast, that is a grim situation because you don't have a home of your own. And the important thing is that you are costing the tax-payer a vast amount of money.

One problem for experts is that in a fast-moving debate where contributions are necessarily brief it is easy to make false inferences. One expert made a disastrous assumption that a speaker claiming poverty had a car. In putting him right she strongly returned audience sympathy to the ordinary person:

> No, I have a motorbike, which I drive and I've been driving right through my pregnancy because it's the only way I can get to work, I'm a student nurse.

A member of parliament, made an assumption, easily turned against him, that a homeless speaker had unreasonably turned down an offer of a council flat:

Expert:	What do you define as a decent offer?
Lay speaker:	I'm saying I was offered once a place in Ealing on the fifth floor without any lift to take a double pushchair up, washing, shopping, whatever I have. There were no shops nearby, there was no transport nearby . . .

Hosts may explicitly prioritize the ordinary over the expert. Kilroy encouraged people to talk about their experiences of buying things they don't really want in the sales, saying 'if I have, you have, because we're all normal, by definition'. Similarly, Mike Scott, discussing council support of homosexuals on *The Time, The Place*, wants the argument to 'get somewhere, not nowhere' through the discussion of 'concrete examples' not abstract talk. Discussing how to deal with sexual harassment, Kilroy puts the 'common man's' view: 'surely you just say "sod off", don't you?'. Later, he ignores an expert's account of the hidden costs to the victim of complaining by saying that women should complain, 'quickly, clearly, no problems about that'.

The experts who appear on these programmes are often those who 'espouse theories based on practical knowledge . . . [as] it is in the nature of the show to discourage the use of data or theories that are not immediately explicable and plausible' (Carpignano et al. 1990: 52). Thus expert discourse, which is seen arrogantly to distance itself from common sense through the valorization of the counter-intuitive, is attacked. On the *Morton Downey Jr. Show*, 'they [the experts] are to be the object of derision. The working class is going to have its day' (ibid: 53). This programme provides 'a forum for the disenfranchised', fitting with the oppositional public sphere advocated by Fraser (1989, 1990) and others, and the expert is reduced to just another audience member. From the point of view of the ordinary person, 'it probably makes it easier to communicate if everybody is on an equal footing' (D4.163); doubtless the experts would disagree.

EXPERT AND LAY CONTRIBUTIONS TO AUDIENCE DISCUSSIONS

In order to understand the sequencing of expert and lay contributions more generally, 35 episodes of discussion programmes were analysed for order and type of contributions throughout the discussion (see Appendix 2). Looking first at programme openings, the majority of *The Oprah Winfrey Show*, *Donahue* and *The Time, The Place* episodes began with a general issue (e.g. sibling relationships, gambling obsessions, public schools). On *Kilroy*, around half of the programmes began with a two-sided debate rather than a general issue (e.g. fur coats: we should versus should not have the right to wear them). The vast majority of all programmes ended with no conclusions. Typically, discussions are cut off in mid-flow with the host announcing 'that's all we have time for, see you next week', except in *The Time, The Place* where, while over half the programmes ended with no conclusion, many ended with advice or decisions offered to the home audience. The American programmes, then, fit the forum rather than the debate model, inviting all to contribute with no opening or closing structures, while the British programmes incorporate elements of the debate model, *Kilroy* in some of its openings, *The Time, The Place* in some of its closings.

A variable number of ordinary people tell personal stories on these programmes. When defined as anecdotes revealing at least three 'facts' about the speaker, anywhere between 2 and 24 people told their story on each programme, with an average of 10 people, and no real differences across programmes. The number of experts who appeared varied similarly, from none (in only a few cases) to 9, with an average of 3. The British programmes invited more experts (4 on average) while the Americans tended to include only one expert in each programme. Moreover, the American experts tended to be either authors of books or psychologists/therapists who could offer advice and discuss the 'normality' of activities being discussed. In the British programmes, the experts varied widely in status. A representative from the British Medical Association and the Director of the Medical Advisory Service appeared on *Kilroy* to address doctor–patient communication problems; a consumer rights advisor, a representative from Shelter (the homelessness charity), a junior minister for housing, a representative from the National Association of Estate Agents and the shadow housing minister appeared on *The Time, The Place* addressing the problem of housing repossessions due to mortgage arrears; and a furrier, a fashion designer, representative from Lynx (the pressure group campaigning against fur for fashion), and a representative from the Fur Education Council appeared on *Kilroy* addressing whether we should wear fur coats.

On the British programmes (in 28 episodes), the experts were labelled thus: 35 people who worked in the profession or occupation relevant to the topic (for example, community policeman, doctor, boxer), 26 representatives from charities, pressure groups and self-help groups, 13 spokespersons from professional, union or industrial organizations, 9 members of parliament, 6 academics and authors, 8 psychologists, therapists and counsellors, and 3 media personalities/journalists. In terms of the public sphere, the participants were drawn from the economy, the life-world and the state. More are directly involved in the topic, through their work or through representing those involved, than are distanced commentators and analysts. Many were of high status – government ministers, charity organization directors, medical consultants. Many were selected to oppose each other – a government minister and a shadow minister, the headteacher of a public school (i.e. private) and the headteacher of a state school, a pressure group to stop smoking and a representative from the Tobacco Advisory Council, a pro-euthanasia and an anti-euthanasia expert.

In over three-quarters of programmes, the first speaker is an ordinary person telling a personal story. Rarely are experts given the first word, rarely do discussions begin with the expression of abstract opinions. An exception was an episode of *Kilroy* about Yugoslavia, where the expert was given an initial platform to describe the situation: maybe the host feared that the home audience's ignorance is such that they might turn off the programme unless filled in on the political situation.

> I was just told would you sit there, this is the person you are sitting next to, we've reserved a spot for you at the beginning, we'd like you to talk for about two, two and half minutes putting the whole issue into perspective and then we'll take it from there.
>
> (Expert 4, academic in international relations)

In nearly as many cases, the second speaker is also an ordinary person telling a personal story, although occasionally the second speaker may be an expert or an ordinary person expressing an opinion to support the first speaker. Experts generally have to wait some time before their first chance to speak: on average, ordinary people make a significant contribution before an expert is invited, or gets a chance, to comment. This allows the lay speakers to set the agenda, guided and facilitated by the host.

The final word also comes from an ordinary person in over half (*The Time, The Place*) to over two-thirds of cases (*Kilroy* and the American programmes). The discussions are thus anchored by ordinary people's experiences at beginning and end, with experts playing a role only in the body of the discussion. Experts who do get the last word attempt to draw conclusions or give advice, and *The Time, The Place* often attempts to steer the discussion towards this end, but generally, the programmes tend to end on ordinary people not so much failing to draw a conclusion as being cut off in mid-discussion.

Kilroy:	One way to help get rid of poverty is to find jobs. If there were jobs you wouldn't have poverty.
Woman:	Exactly, but . . .
Kilroy:	Wish we could find a few more jobs! See you in the morning.

The genre implies that rather than holding a debate in order to reach a conclusion, we have been given a glimpse into an ongoing discussion which started before the programme opened, indeed which really is always restarting as people live out their everyday experiences, and which continues long after the programme has finished – supposedly both in the studio and in the living room. One episode of *The Time, The Place* ended by interrupting a story to say 'sorry, you can tell me in a minute, because I have to say "goodbye" to them [the home audience], [host turns to home audience] thanks to everyone for coming . . . .see you tomorrow, same time, different place tomorrow, do try to join us, till then goodbye. [Host turns back to interrupted speaker] Tell me again . . . [title music]'. The impression, then, is that television is not hosting this debate, but merely opening a window onto a real-life debate – an impression which, of course, television fosters in other genres too, most notably the news. Assuming the home audience is interested and wants to follow up on the discussion, addresses for further information and support are sometimes provided at the end of the programme (e.g. on euthanasia) or a help-line phone number displayed throughout the programme (e.g. for hayfever, for sun-tan dangers, for stopping smoking).

THE EXPERTS' EXPERIENCE OF POPULARIZATION AND PARTICIPATION

Verwey's (1990) analysis of commercial Canadian radio call-ins suggested that they have 'performed the positive function of making political candidates more widely available than most other alternative methods' (ibid: 233). However, for other experts, the format of the call-in may be problematic: 'the subject-matter of a scientific, technical or academic guest is not readily adaptable to the call-in "split" format. For some of these guests the call-in format has negative rather than positive consequences' (ibid: 234). All invited experts accept this element of risk, for 'not only can the moderator frustrate the guest, but some callers deliberately try to do so' (ibid: 234). She argues that noncommercial call-ins (e.g. Radio 4's Tuesday Call) intentionally provide a public service which 'adds authority to the expert, professional or academic guest, who seems to get much satisfaction out of servicing his many grateful callers' (ibid: 235) as well as 'disseminating useful information in a specific field' (ibid: 235) and providing an 'effective public complaint service' (ibid: 237).

Experts regularly appear on audience discussion programmes and other media genres and they give behind-the-scenes advice for many more (Robinson, 1982). Why do they do it and what kind of experience is it for them? We formally interviewed seven academics who had appeared on audience discussion programmes and talked informally to many more. Undoubtedly, experts have difficulties in managing the genre successfully and yet they also consider that their appearance offers them significant advantages.

Experts often found it difficult to present a complex or integrated argument because of the conversational format:

> You had to be careful because you couldn't speak unless you were supposed to be speaking, and so the cues had to be extremely clear, otherwise you just get a free-for-all.
>
> (Expert 1, psychologist)

> It has the enormous drawback for any expert or indeed for anybody who wants to put a rather long structured argument. Effectively you're reduced to about 30 seconds I suppose. Maybe you might take a minute but really you'd feel you were hogging it if you took a minute so you couldn't develop a really coherently structured argument. That's slightly awry to the academic temperament.
>
> (Expert 5, academic in government)

> It's very difficult to do anything other than present a very simple view which is then very easy to knock down obviously.
>
> (Expert 2, psychologist)

Experts feel they have contradictory demands placed on them because of the discursive structure of the programmes:

> You certainly didn't get a chance to say what you wanted to say because it tries to fulfil two roles. It tries to get across expert opinions plus having real people so to speak trying to express their views, which is equally valid but they don't necessarily integrate with what the experts are saying or the direction that the discussion might go in. So it doesn't achieve an awful lot, it's a very frustrating type of programme.
>
> (Expert 1, psychologist)

> On the one hand they were wanting me as the expert . . . yet I was in the audience and I had to vie for space to speak with the rest of the audience . . . I was very much an equal member of the audience. And the audience would disagree with what I was saying but from a personal perspective as opposed to an expert perspective, and so I felt it was a very ambiguous situation because I didn't want to engage with them on a personal level because I felt I was there as the expert and yet my expertise was being undermined.
>
> (Expert 2, psychologist)

The problem of vying for space to speak is considerable: even when the host explicitly signals an expert to speak, they do not necessarily successfully keep the floor and they may be rapidly interrupted by a persistent lay speaker. The camera will generally, though sometimes with some reluctance, follow those who speak most loudly and clearly rather than those explicitly cued to speak. Difficulties also arise from the common frustration of experts' expectation of a fact-finding inquiry or analytic debate; rather debates are confrontational:

You were brought in in order to be confrontational, because that's his style. He tries to make it confrontational I assume because he thinks it's going to be better television.

(Expert 1, psychologist)

It's all a set-up because they get two experts who disagree with each other and they tell you that's what they're doing beforehand.

(Expert 2, psychologist)

Also undermining is the way in which experts are not always allowed to retain their expert status but rather are pushed towards the personal:

It's very difficult to apply general research perspectives to one individual . . . it's taking expertise out of context and applying it in a way which isn't appropriate.

(Expert 2, psychologist)

It was very difficult because all they were interested in was my personal experience, and in a sense that was the reason they were there, to talk about their personal experience, and why shouldn't I talk about mine?

(Expert 2, psychologist)

A lot of other reporters don't seem to bother about that sort of thing, just go, yeah, yeah, we know you're a scientist and all this, and just brush it off, but what do you really think?

(Expert 6, psychologist)

Some experts relish the involvement of the lay studio audience. One compares *Kilroy* to a predecessor programme, the *Dimbleby Talk-in*'s. In the latter:

You have your experts facing your audience out in front. Here we were in the front row in a semi-circle. That made it harder to have informal interchanges with them [the other experts] without involving the whole audience and the formal interchanges were minimised except occasionally Kilroy juxtaposed a couple of us, what do you think of that point? . . . On the whole he was rather careful to make sure it didn't become a discussion simply between the experts with comment from everybody else.

(Expert 5, academic in government)

For this expert, the point is to participate in a joint construction of meaning; the role of speaker is distributed rather than individual. In Goffman's terms, the author and animator may be separated, so that others – including the laity – may speak for him:

This one [*Kilroy*] was freer, much more real interchange, I think it worked better and although I'm quite conscious of many other points I would have liked to have made, some of which were made by the studio audience, mentally you would tick off actually somebody's made that point, it's right and I'm not going to challenge it.

(Expert 5, academic in government)

Certainly, the format may be managed by some experts with sufficient motivation and/or experience of broadcasting:

The secret is to be able to encapsulate your thoughts very quickly . . . [and] to make your points at reasonably short length

(Expert 4, academic in international relations)

I believe you can nearly always get quite a complex point over so long as you don't use too erudite language.

(Expert 5, academic in government)

I was worried that they would try to make me say things that I didn't want to say or trick me into saying things that I shouldn't say . . . so I'm always very wary when they're questioning me . . . I still think that, yes, go and talk to the media, I mean it's up to you to not lose anything by speaking in lay persons' terms or whatever.

(Expert 6, psychologist)

What do experts have to contribute to audience discussions? For some, they feel that they have useful information for the general public:

Because my research areas concern public health basically. It's information that people can use.

(Expert 6, psychologist)

Others see themselves as providing an objective, factual basis for discussion:

I made the assumption that I was effectively to be the kind of neutral exponent of which of these varied claims was actually going to be right . . . I didn't have any impression that they had any particular interest in one side or the other, they really do want to achieve a good discussion and what they really wanted from me was – Kilroy was the referee – it's really somebody who will say that claim is a bit over the top, that one is about right, have you thought of that?

(Expert 5, academic in government)

I was simply asked if I would put the thing in context, and I said yes, that was what I was asked to do and that's what I did and I interjected several times during the programme in order to put some balance into what I thought was becoming unbalanced.

(Expert 4, academic in international relations)

Yet, this last speaker, talking about the political problems in Yugoslavia, found that while a Serb acquaintance found 'I wasn't sufficiently pro-Serb, I think she [a second acquaintance] found I wasn't sufficiently pro-Croat' (expert 4, academic in international relations). Another expert had similar problems with his audience:

It was interesting talking to some people afterwards, some thought I'd been pro- some thought I'd been anti-. In fact actually I have some support to arguments from both sides. I saw myself as a kind of factual check.

(Expert 5, academic in government)

Some experts hope to raise the standards of a discussion or contribute a valuable point:

It's quite interesting to be able to try and put your ideas together in a way that makes sense to other people in front of a reasonably large audience. It's an opportunity I think – if you've got something you think might be of value or are able to contribute to a discussion, then clearly doing it on television or on radio is a valuable thing to do.

(Expert 1, psychologist)

Others felt that, despite being 'one of the best-placed people to talk about it', they are being used by rather than using the medium, and certain extreme cases may become known in academia and the media as 'academic tarts':

To me partly it feels a bit like academic prostitution, to talk on anything, and it's very seductive to be phoned up and asked, will you appear as the expert, quite flattering.

(Expert 2, psychologist)

There are many reasons why experts agree to appear on audience discussion programmes, from public sphere concerns to those of promoting one's profession or oneself:

I was very pleased because I want my work to be known to the public; I don't see any point in doing lots of research and having it published in academic journals where the general public are never going to hear about it. Particularly in the sort of work I'm doing, I think it is very much related to the everyday person and it's the sort of thing I feel they should be aware of and know of so I was very pleased about that. And I also felt it would be good to get that sort of publicity in relation to contacts and possibly getting funding to do more work of the same sort. And then also the whole thing about going on television was quite exciting, so it was nice.

(Expert 6, psychologist)

I regard it as a challenge to go on a reasonably popular programme and put in fairly simple language what is a complex issue. So I did it because it was a challenge and I did it because I think it is an important issue which I think has been rather misunderstood by the press and I thought that if I could do something to correct some of the misapprehensions I would be pleased to do so.

(Expert 4, academic in international relations)

I suppose going on television as an expert is one way of contributing to what I hope is an improved public debate.

(Expert 5, academic in government)

In order to influence politicians you have to appeal to the public . . . you don't necessarily always succeed but it's one way of trying to do it . . . I agree that lobbying from the scientific community has to happen as well but why shouldn't the public be involved in it?

(Expert 6, psychologist)

In relation to the participation framework established by expert contributions, one can ask who these experts were speaking to when they appeared on such programmes. As with the lay participants (see later), there was a primary focus on those in the studio:

I don't think it makes very good television if you're aware that there might be an awful lot of people watching it.

(Expert 1, psychologist)

Nonetheless, the audience is recognizably plural:

I suppose in the studio I was really talking to two or three people each time, the person who'd made the point I was replying to and two or three others round that I was crucially aware of. I think you have a sense of a slightly wider group but it's shadowy. I think that works for the people at home as well . . . my sense is that what works in the studio with modern camera work is also the right way to think of the audience at home.

(Expert 5, academic in government)

I was addressing Kilroy because Kilroy looks at you and asks the question and obviously one doesn't look at the camera . . . but in answering him I also looked at the audience there and I was also talking to a much wider audience which at that time of the morning would for the most part not be a very well-informed audience.

(Expert 4, academic in international relations)

The audience, however plural, is conceived of as a lay audience: a specific protagonist, the lay studio audience, the lay home audience (generally and inaccurately supposed to be composed of housewives; see Chapter 3), one's students or one's family. All these audiences justify the use of simple language and an avoidance of complex argument. To think of one's academic peers is to become aware of the compromises made when communicating in this way:

It's quite easy to think that nobody's watching it, because you're in this hot studio which is very very small and you get lost in the debate . . . if I thought all my colleagues were watching me doing it I couldn't do it, I'd be so embarrassed.

(Expert 2, psychologist)

What consequences are hoped for from such programmes? For those who prefer not to appear on audience discussion programmes, there is little to be achieved, and the costs to both oneself and one's profession or expertise may be considerable:

I really dislike going on television for anything, but I hate all this trivializing and slickness.

(Expert 3, psychologist)

I felt that there wasn't enough time, which was quite frustrating, and that's one of the reasons why I wouldn't do it again.

(Expert 2, psychologist)

Similarly, another expert felt 'very wary' (expert 7, psychologist) about going on the programme; indeed, she arrived at the studio and then decided not to appear after seeing 'the way they were covering it', feeling that appearing on television is 'quite a risky thing to do' as the media are 'likely to twist your words'. Indeed, many experts have stories to tell of being misquoted or quoted out of context, particularly by the popular press.

But for those experts who appear, some useful purpose is hoped for, and several drew a comparison with teaching: 'it's another form of teaching really' (expert 5, academic in government):

I suspect that some people who were not aware of some of the potential risks of things they do were made aware of them. So raising awareness, and raising awareness of strategies and simple safety precautions that people should take. It's a way of getting information to them and not just to the people who might be taking the drugs or might be the victims but also people who can help, for example, politicians.

(Expert 6, psychologist)

I thought this was a perfectly serious conversation. We actually got a surprising amount of material into the debate, I would have thought we did actually leave anybody who had a modicum of interest (a) probably slightly better informed and (b) with a feeling that they might actually want to take it further.

(Expert 5, academic in government)

While most experts felt that their contribution was strictly one-way (except in so far as they felt they learned about the workings of the mass media), at least one expert, talking on Scottish Nationalism, felt that he too gained from the programme:

There was a straightforward gain to hearing Scots talk about their own problems in their language. Some were very well informed indeed, others less informed, yes I think I gained an enormous amount in terms of feel for the programme and some knowledge, some information but feel above all and a sense of what was important, that I think was pure gain.

(Expert 5, academic in government)

Overall, a consensus emerged on the limitations of the genre as a forum for the dissemination of expert knowledge, but there was disagreement about whether such limits were excessive. Those more experienced in broadcasting felt that the genre could be managed and valuable points could be made. Those less experienced in broadcasting, or those speaking off their expert territory, tended to feel threatened or undermined by the medium. They recognized a loss of expertise through discussion with the general public in this way: is it appropriate to call all technical terms 'jargon' or to be expected to summarize all research findings in two minutes? The topic is also significant: if the lay people have more emotional experiences to recount it is harder for experts to argue a different position. On some topics, the laity are more informed than on others. Further, on some topics, expert and public opinion are in harmony, for others they are in conflict. The fate of the expert on the programme will vary accordingly.

THE ORDINARY PERSON ON TELEVISION

It is not obvious why ordinary people go on television and little research has addressed this question. Programmes may include a certain amount of discussion of 'why I came on the programme was . . . ' and 'what we're here to discuss is . . . '. The public sphere answer is that people participate so as to generate rational discussion. As a lay speaker says on *Kilroy*, 'we've all got to respect the wishes of a rational person in society'. Interviews with studio audience participants suggest a mixture of motives, combining contributions to a perceived public sphere with self-glorification (see also Chapter 7).

When asked what he had to contribute to an audience discussion programme, Tony replied: 'only a reasonably intelligent perspective, I suppose, I mean I don't think I had any special expertise . . . but at the same time I like talking so . . . '. He also makes the public-sphere point explicitly:

You are conscious of the fact that there is an audience out there then, that people are listening, however many there may be and that you might be able to make a very small difference to this issue that you care about if you can put it cogently enough that these people and the person you are actually making it to directly understand.

(Tony, studio audience)

Similarly, Alice took part in *The Time, The Place* 'because I've written endless letters prior to that to the local council complaining bitterly about the litter problem in the neighbourhood, so I'm a bit of a campaigner'. For Alice, appearing on television is an extension of her everyday protest activities, although she also says, 'I was very flattered and excited at the prospect of having being earmarked as being a guest speaker'. For Margaret and her friends, participating was a bit of a joke: 'they just said it was a laugh, a chance to get on TV, and because you got a bit of food and wine afterwards, they just went along for that aspect of it'.

Who do they think is listening, who are they talking to? Tony recognizes the multiple audiences for his speaker role:

> Obviously you are directing your comments in the first instance to whoever it is you are disagreeing with. You'd hope obviously the rest of the people in the studio were listening. There is a certain consciousness that you are talking in front of cameras, but I found that I forgot that fairly quickly. I wasn't sort of saying, 'hello mum'.
>
> (Tony, studio audience)

For Ruth, being aware of her mother watching made her extremely nervous:

> I was very conscious of making a fool of myself really. And also I was very aware that my mum knew I was going to be on it, so I knew certain people knew I was going to be on the show, so that was . . . how I felt.

Martin also was aware of the home audience: 'I think I was talking to a cross-section of people, I was talking to people like me who find it very difficult to get kickstarted in the morning.'

AUDIENCE PERCEPTIONS OF EXPERT AND LAY PARTICIPANTS

The ways in which expert and lay people appear on the programmes invites certain questions from the home audience. We suggest that the following questions are invited by the representations of ordinary people: is the account authentic, is it a good story, did their emotional expression validate their account, and can we learn from this experience? The programmes also suggest, we have argued, that expertise should also be assessed in lay terms rather than by reference to expert, scientific or philosophical criteria (such as internal coherence of the argument, scientific reputation, validity of evidence, generalizability of findings, usefulness of key concepts, and so forth). The programme thus invites the audience to ask whether the experts are credible, helpful to ordinary people, comprehensible, trustworthy, attractive, in tune with ordinary experience, and so forth. Broadly speaking, the viewers are thus invited to identify with the studio audience and to be critical of the experts. Two-thirds of focus group respondents' evaluative comments about the experts who appear on audience discussion programmes were highly negative. Generally, they were seen as having to say little that was original and as saying it badly. It seems that, if an expert cannot communicate to a lay audience, their very expertise is questioned:

> I don't think he was much good at all . . . . He didn't even seem to make a good job of what he was trying to say. (P1.105)

> Looking back, I can't remember anything that he said. If you have an expert, you should at least come away with something. (P1.111)

> I hardly noticed them, I must admit, they didn't impress me at all, because I thought that whatever they said would be so predictable I switched off, mentally. (P2.210)

> I thought she was really rather irrelevant. (F1.37)

Nearly one-third of expert evaluations were positive, although not necessarily critically appreciative:

> I thought he was excellent, he was sensitive. (D3.105)

> Sometimes he has experts who really are very informative on programmes. (SC.178)

> Except for the one with pebble glasses, I thought they were really nice. (D4.37)

In contrast to the many critical comments made about experts, few evaluative comments were made by focus group discussants about the lay studio audience. Most comments were fairly neutral, though some were positive, and those comments which were negative tended to focus on disagreements with the content of what was said rather than the manner of presentation or the person who said it:

> I thought that the way they discussed things showed a reasonable level of intelligence. (P4.22)

> There was that stupid suggestion that somebody should sell off their washing machine and their television to help pay off the mortgage. (P1.192)

Some comments recognized the constraints under which ordinary people appear on television:

> I think that what one must remember is that these people are amateurs, they are people brought in off the street. It's like us going into a studio without any preparation whatsoever, and just being asked to bring forth our ideas, and to me that is entirely different to just watching professionals who are used to bringing forth their ideas. (P4.85)

> You get used to seeing bland, sort of professional people who are schooled to cut off at a certain point. These [lay] people are not cut off, they will keep going and say what they have to say. (P4.129)

In contrast, only a few respondents considered how the difficulties of the programme format made life hard for the expert:

> Did you react that way to him? I thought he was in a corner. I didn't think that he was selfish at all. (D2.20)

There were differences in the perceived motivations of experts and lay people for appearing on audience discussion programmes. A few explanations of experts' motivations were in terms of personal motives:

> I would have thought it was for personal glorification. (P2.75)

Rather more concerned the demands of public accountability:

> But then if the Minister of Sport refuses to comment, that puts him in a bad light, because his public voted for him. (P2.80)

> They are the official representatives, they had to go in, that is part of their job. (D2.60)

> I suppose if you go into politics then you expect to be shot at. (D4.183)

Respondents were very concerned about the representativeness of the lay participants. If ordinary people are to provide the grounding for claims, the validity-testing for generalizations, and the justification for social action, then who these people are and why they choose to speak are key questions. Before people can accept the implicit invitation to participate in what is constructed as a public space, identifying with particular positions, they should be, and indeed are, critical and wary. Among our respondents, there was a debate about representativeness, with around one-third of comments arguing that the studio audience did indeed represent the general public:

> They were ordinary people, ordinary people who watch television. (P2.14)

> It's a cross-section, in fact. (P3.67)

Twice as many comments suggested that the selection criteria were problematic, thus undermining the discussion:

> I thought they had chosen a group of very extreme cases. (P2.202)

> I wondered why when you looked at the people you had the token black faces there. (P4.23)

A studio audience member comments:

> what was quite strange was that from our school they did sort out who sat where and what faces sat where, because there was a group of four West Indian girls, four black girls sitting together and they separated them and dotted them around.
>
> (Ruth, studio audience).

This debate about representativeness was encouraged by the lack of information provided about the selection of the studio audience. For a public debate, we must know the criteria by which some have access and not others. What procedures are used to bring people into the public arena: where do the programme producers search, how do they check if they have the right people? Such questions were of considerable concern, and respondents did not uncritically assume that the studio audience are representative of the general public (or indeed, that they are a biased misrepresentation).

> I would have liked to have known a bit more about how they choose the people they did, did they advertise it, did they have any stipulations about who could come and why? You weren't told anything about why the people were there, how they found out about it. (P1.11)

Those familiar with the production procedures were inclined towards a more positive, open access view of the genre:

> Well, they all ring up and volunteer, and then they are quizzed on the phone. (F1.88)

> I have a friend who has actually been on the programme, she did say they are very good, they select you on the telephones, a lot of conversations to make sure you are actually going to give something of yourself on the programme. (F1.16)

This does not, however, guarantee representativeness:

> You don't know whether that is the norm or the general mix, it is purely at their convenience that they press their views on you of those people. You don't know whether that is normal. (P1.27)

> But do they weed out the people for any special reasons? I mean they might, mightn't they? I mean, one needs to know that. (P1.165)

Two notions of representativeness are relevant here. First, does the range of positions represented correspond to a statistical distribution? People seem to refer to this notion, yet to do so incorrectly, for extreme positions were seen as invalidating statistical representativeness while the normative positions were applauded. Yet a statistical normal distribution must contain a few extreme cases as well as many average ones, and, having included them in a discussion, they might well be expected to dominate.

The second notion of representativeness is that implied in the oppositional public sphere: as no-one can speak for humanity in general, all subgroups or plural publics must be separately represented. Respondents also expressed concern here: maybe those without doctor–patient communication problems did not volunteer, those who lived in rural areas were missing from the poverty programme, and those who didn't want friends were not seen on the friendship programme.

Some were concerned about the consequences of representing particular groups in particular ways. For example, one group discussed why, on the programme about poverty, the studio audience of 'poor people' were all well dressed and presentable. Was this how the poor looked? Had those who could not dress well chosen not to respond to the programme advertisement? And what about the implications for viewers' representation of the poor?

> Wouldn't it be dangerous to confirm the stereotype image of poverty by having the studio full of people who look like down and outs? (P1.166)

Some thought the studio audience was selected not for the content of their contributions but for their communicative skills, not a point made about the experts: communicative skills are assumed to be present in all experts, and so much criticism centred on experts, but not on all ordinary people.

> I would suggest that they [studio audiences] are selected on their ability to get over a point. (P4.51)

This communicative skill in ordinary people may indicate their unrepresentativeness:

> How did they manage to find a group with so many stories to tell, because I don't think most people would be like that. (F3.07)

Let us also consider the motivations for which people supposedly go on these programmes. These concerned, in roughly equal measure, the public sphere, making complaints, and self-publicity:

> Because you feel that you have something to say in public, either for or against whatever the subject happens to be. (D2.58)

> If your relationship with your GP is satisfactory, then you don't write in. (D4.14)

> I think it does say something about someone's character if they actually, well most of them, seem very keen to air their own personal experiences, so obviously have some desire to have everyone listening to these experiences. (F1.75)

Another major concern was with lay participants' style of interaction and comportment on the programme. This discussion is inevitably connected with respondents' analysis of the host's management of the programmes (see Chapter 4). Considerable concern was expressed that the conflictual and heated atmosphere prevented good points being made:

> Every time he made a point of view he was shouted down. (P1.106)

> I don't think the audience were listening as much as they should do. (F1.14)

> Some people spoke very sensibly and they only got two sentences in. (SC.127)

Some were concerned that the nature of the programme changed people's contributions, making them more dramatic, or allowing more dramatic characters to dominate:

> At one point they did seem to be competing with each other for hard luck stories. (P1.96)

> It was simply that everyone wanted to put their own horror story forward. (P2.23)

How do respondents think that experts act when they appear on audience discussion programmes? That this genre is live is seen to enhance its 'public sphere' character:

> Mostly when you see politicians it is all pat, it has all been worked out. But the thing about this is that they can be caught on the hop. There is a chance that it is perhaps a bit more realistic. (P3.179)

One consequence is that experts may lose their impersonal facade and show their emotions. While live television may reveal experts' genuine opinions and undermine deceit, experts are expected to retain their professional public manner and not reveal their private emotions:

> He is a doctor. Right or wrong, I think that they are on a plane above. They should hold their temper, especially in public. (D1.196)

Yet respondents recognize that high expectations are placed on experts:

> I think people expect too much from their doctors, they expect them to be absolutely perfect, and yet they are people with emotions. (D1.13)

While experts are there to represent their profession or organization, some were observed to extricate themselves from criticism by claiming to be exceptions ('I can only speak from my experience'), thus undermining the accountability function served by appearing:

> I felt that a lot of the doctors took the same attitude, they said 'oh, I don't do that in my practice, what I do is . . . '. (D3.21)

They were also sometimes seen as patronizing:

> It was the BMA representative who came out with 'the patients expect' sentence, which I thought was quite revealing. The doctor telling the patients what they expect! (D3.39)

Experts didn't always play the role they could have done:

> She could have come in towards the end and given more of a summing up towards the end. (F2.151)

Viewers want experts to act as critical representatives in the public sphere, as do the experts themselves. They should be clear and memorable in their arguments, draw conclusions, be genuine rather than concealing, accountable rather than evasive, public rather than private. To the extent that experts fail in these requirements, notwithstanding the difficulties of the medium, viewers are highly critical. But inevitably, the viewers evaluate experts in lay terms, not in expert ones, and the critical comments outweigh the appreciative. Arguably, certain genres, such as the documentary, try hard to establish professional or expert criteria for audience use, providing experts with considerable discursive and visual support. In audience discussion programmes, experts are very much on their own in an alien environment. Maybe viewers are overcritical: the following summary of a programme, although cast in a negative light, could be considered a reasonable achievement for a 40 minute programme:

> The only three things that came out of it were, there is no redress for the people who have been struck off lists, . . . there are other agencies that we could go to, and the BMA chappie said, that they are now getting better, learning how to treat customers, patients, communication skills, to me, that's all that came out of it. (D3.181)

While people were concerned about the value and manner of expert contributions, they were concerned about the genuineness of the accounts given by the lay participants: were people exhibitionists or were they honestly struggling to express themselves? Despite being critical of the competitive and heated style of the discussion, many but not all felt that the contributions were genuine:

> I just felt that it was all rather self-indulgent and self-pitying. (P2.25)

> But a lot of their reactions were so strong that I believed that it was true. (P2.195)

> I think that they were all honest. (P3.103)

> Some people after all were quite nervous. (D3.197)

Focus group respondents commented little on the effects on participants of appearing on audience discussion programmes. Half thought appearing would be good for people, particularly through gaining a flexible awareness of other people, and half thought there would be no effects at all, for participants would not change their opinions after appearing. Very few thought the effects would be actively harmful.

> I think that through talking it out and talking to people, some of those people would have gone away – from both sides – not quite so rigid in their viewpoints. (P1.94)

> At the end of it actually, I don't think that anyone really learnt anything from it. I think that they all came in with the same ideas and they all went away with exactly the same set. (P2.103)

> None of those people went away from that programme learning anything, there was no advice for them as to how they could cope. (P4.142)

In generating a participation framework through which to understand the programme and position oneself as party to the communication, viewers use clues within the discussion to situate the speakers in their real lives. One respondent used her everyday experience to question a speaker's account:

> I thought, OK, well the lady in the bedsit, what is her husband doing? She said that he has been out of work for X months. I don't care, you could always get a job, even if it is washing up. (P3.149)

Another inferred that, because one woman 'wouldn't allow her husband to go out at all', that:

> That's because the woman is insecure. She felt that her relationship with her husband wasn't strong enough. (F3.15)

Another worried about the relatives of studio audience members, to whom they must return after the programme:

> Her parents must have seen her, so what did they think? (F3.66)

Sometimes, imagining particular others in the studio audience member's life is a means of reinforcing one's own beliefs:

> There was one comment by a blonde youngish lady about her mother not having the right treatment, because of lack of communication, and I think that this is very important with older people, it takes a lot of expertise for a doctor to get through to a patient. (D3.99)

While the expert is denied an identification with the world of expertise and science, through a lack of respect and the imposition of lay discourse, the studio audience gains impact through an identification with the home audience – the general public. The home audience is invited to identify with the studio audience, allowing the studio audience to stand in a metonymic relation to the general public. When introducing the friendship programme, Kilroy elides 'us' as everyone, the general public, including host, home audience and studio audience, with 'us' as the people in the studio who can directly answer his questions:

> Good morning. A lot of friends of mine here this morning obviously, and at some time most of us need a friend to turn to. But who makes the best friends? Men or women? And what makes some friendships so special they can last the whole of your life? Who has needed the help of a friend?

The studio audience exemplify and reify the subject position of the viewer, constructing the viewer at home as an 'ordinary person' or as a relevant party to the issue under discussion. The viewer may be constructed as a parent whose children may yet be victims of a drunk-driving accident, as taxpayers who should or should not support welfare benefits, or as an elderly person concerned about declining morals. The host easily moves from 'most people here think that...' to 'most people think that...'. The lay audience too moves easily from 'I found that ... happened' to 'and then you find that ... happens'. The studio audience may also feel that they represent the public: 'I was there representing an agitated member of the public and that was my role' (Alice). Viewers too may accept this: 'in most of the shows there's at least one person who says something that clicks with me that I'm thinking all along and so I think that's why viewers keep watching it, they're thinking yeah, that's right' (Marie). Occasionally, the studio audience and home audience are directly compared, for example, by ending the programme with a yes/no phone-in vote which may or may not confirm any studio consensus.

However, this invitation to identify is risky and depends on the reception process. The audience at home may be sceptical of the representativeness and motivations of the studio audience. They may have expertise or experiences of their own which distance them from what is said. Further, the home audience is a contested resource, as different sides in a debate lay claim to knowing what 'the public' or 'the taxpayer' thinks or wants. It is unclear whether members of the studio audience are heroes, revealing triumph over tragedy, baring their hearts, speaking out for the rest of us, or whether they are fodder for debate, objects of discussion, exemplifying problems, providing evidence for expert claims. Consequently, it is unclear whether the home audience is constructed as subject or object. No single subject position is offered to the viewer as the studio audience is diverse in composition and often contradictory in its contributions and, while sometimes a representation of public opinion emerges, more often the debate is left wide open.

AUDIENCE PERCEPTIONS OF COMMON KNOWLEDGE AND EXPERTISE

Some comments from our respondents revealed their perceptions of the nature of expertise itself, rather than of the role of experts. These noticeably stem from the discussions on doctor–patient communication, as the GP is probably the expert with whom people have most everyday dealings. This may then be generalized to other domains of expertise. For example, people assume that doctors act reasonably, despite apparent criticism:

> You wondered whether you had heard the whole story. Obviously there was more to it than that, because doctors wouldn't just cross you off their lists like that. (D2.27)

We need to trust experts, because they have power over us:

If you are going in for an operation, you tend not to think about the fact that they might make a mistake, otherwise you would never go. (D2.77)

On the other hand, this power causes its own problems for ordinary people:

Before you even walk in you are on the defensive. If you do have an unsympathetic doctor then it must be a battle because you are in such a vulnerable position and he is in such power and you are really at their mercy. (D2.61)

Part of this power inequality between the expert and the lay person is related to social class:

The doctor is a highly educated, university trained chap and somebody who is not educated goes to see them and they feel at a disadvantage. I don't know whether the doctor is aware of that, possibly he wouldn't be, but the patients are very aware of it, it is the first sort of toff they have been face to face with and they feel at a disadvantage. (D4.43)

The doctor is one of the very few professions where they use their title in everyday life. And I think that they have put themselves on this pedestal and now they are starting to object because people have assumptions of them. (D2.110)

Experts are seen to have replaced religion as the source of certainty:

People think that everything is fixable, mendable, there is no chance for a hazard or death, they are looking for a thing in the doctor like what the church used to be. (D2.108)

However, experts are not uncritically admired, and they are only trusted within their acknowledged sphere of expertise:

Now the doctor seems the first port of call for all the upsets [not just physical] and really it is something else that you need to get off your chest, and then the doctor is having more and more responsibility when perhaps he isn't equipped. (D2.109)

Clearly, experts are known to be fallible, for as Giddens (1991) notes, social science findings have filtered into everyday knowledge of, among other things, expertise:

GPs, experts – the fact that alcoholism and suicide rates are well above normal, well, the word expert I mistrust anyway. (D2.100)

Indeed, experts may be very bad at certain necessary skills at which ordinary people are quite competent, such as emotional expression:

One has only got to briefly look to realize that doctors are terrified of any expression of feeling. You know, people are worried that they may have got a serious illness and the average doctor just retreats, because they can't stand it. (D3.105)

Qualifications alone may not make the expert, contrary to the argument that status and credibility are all that matters:

> I wouldn't use the word 'expert' in a narrow sense, I would use the word 'expert' in the sense of someone who we respect and are interested in, not just someone who may have just a form of qualification. (F1.110)

Whether expertise can be translated into policy is also a question on which respondents have reservations:

> I don't think that the social services should be permitted to suggest that people should sell their goods to get themselves out of poverty. (P1.200)

People have expectations not only of expertise and its boundaries or limitations but also of common knowledge and ordinary experience. For some, lay accounts are valid because they are grounded in experience:

> Unless you have experienced or know of people and that type of thing, it doesn't mean a thing. (P1.51)

> Well, life is the greatest teacher. (SC.212)

Lay accounts do not attempt to generalize, and thus stay with what can be validly said, for after all, 'we are all individuals' (F1.136):

> It is very difficult indeed to make generalizations because so much depends on your personal experiences. (F2.26)

> You never have a right to say what is right or wrong, only for yourself. (F3.72)

> At the end of the day it is still the personal things that count. (F3.119)

This lack of generalization may of course be regarded critically, for some prefer to receive generalized facts from the experts:

> People cannot see beyond themselves. (F3.112)

> Is that what poverty is – it seems so different to different people. (P1.114)

> Everyone's ideas of what is right can be so different. (P2.163)

> Actually nothing is there except people's attitudes. (P4.06)

While for some, the facts are indeed established by hearing of personal experiences: 'I think that it is a fact of life that there are many desperate people who are living in this sort of hostel accommodation' (P4.48), for others, little of value is said because 'a lot of them were speaking about their individual problems' (D1.09). Such speakers hold the traditional valorization of the expert over the ignorant lay person:

> You can't have a balance between people who don't know and people who know. You can learn an awful lot when an expert talks on a subject they know very well. (SC.193)

What we need is a return to the old days:

> Those of us who would like to be Lord Reith and have television completely under their own control, would feel very frustrated by the bilge that sometimes gets churned up. (SC.317)

Despite the critical rejection of much that ordinary people may say, ordinary accounts are sometimes valued for being unbiased, and so more representative than the views of elected representatives. Lay accounts are also credible because they are spontaneous:

> I suppose you are more inclined to believe it because they are not reading a script and because in our daily lives we tend to believe what people are saying. (P2.186)

After all, we do not routinely question people's truthfulness in everyday life. Yet:

> I think that a lot of what people say in life is not what is going on, you know. You often say things and it's a habit, you say things for so long that it is no longer true. (P2.192)

The respondents also believe ordinary people because they are talking about familiar things, they can be checked, and they can be identified with:

> Everyone has been through that, haven't they? I can understand, because after being a student after leaving school, I was very short of cash. (P4.104)

The lay studio audience after all, are 'just like us' and even in their faults we can say that 'that's human nature, isn't it?' (P4.116). Yet ordinary people know different things, depending on their experiences, and are not simply examples of a generalized humanity. There was a certain amount of talk about how people from different social classes, ages or genders, have different things to say: the working classes are seen as less articulate, but not necessarily less insightful, women are supposedly more sensitive and so their observations are more perceptive, younger people are more open to new ideas and yet are more extreme, while older people are more tolerant of alternatives and yet more rigid when it comes to accepting such ideas themselves.

THE ROLE OF EXPERTS AND LAITY IN THE PARTICIPATION FRAMEWORK

While traditionally, the expert has both status and knowledge, audience discussion programmes imply that while the expert still has status, the laity have knowledge. There is an implicit promise that if the laity speak to the powerful, telling them their personal stories and persuading them of their authenticity, then their knowledge may influence social policy through the expert's use of power. Ordinary people can say, 'this is what's wrong and this is what I want to see done about it', but experts cannot manage their own accountability by saying 'leave it to us' or 'we know best'.

The traditional expectation of expert-speaker and lay-hearer is challenged when the public appear on television. Ordinary people, as speakers, receive a legitimated knowledge position from which to speak, while experts, listening to the public, become hearers. The audience at home, who are represented by the studio audience and who engage in parasocial interaction with those represented, become speaker as well as hearer (Horton and Wohl, 1956). While the programme host is speaker, this is often in Goffman's (1981) sense of embedded speaking, for the host speaks for the studio audience or the public to help them articulate their position or challenge experts. Speakers speak to each other, for in Goffman's terms, they are the ratified and addressed hearers, and yet they also speak to the home audience, who are ratified but not directly addressed, and may be hearers or overhearers.

The subject position of 'ordinary person' is created when the studio audience 'tell their own story'. They construct the folk category of speaker in which animator, author and principal are the same, and so gain communicative power through the construction of authenticity. As the experts frequently speak for other experts, they are thus reduced to a mouthpiece, the animator, who speaks for another expert (author and principal) or, more nebulously still, speaks in defence of 'expertise' or 'the profession'. As one respondent noted, this can be done differently:

> Winfrey would have got the doctor and the patients together in pairs and she would have confronted each one, and that works quite well. You see a personal relationship there in front of your eyes, so you can actually see the way they relate to each other, and then she says to the doctor, 'why won't you listen?' (D1.184)

In general, however, the doctor about whom a complaint is made is not the doctor on the show making the defence, and so the expert participant loses authenticity as a speaker, as does any lay speaker who, despite discouragement, speaks not from direct experience but on behalf of 'the general public'. For experts, the speaker is inevitably separated from the principal – the role, profession or institution – being defended. If the expert presents the findings of a report or popularizes the conclusions of a government debate, the animator is separated from the author. The host, speaking from a privileged position, may speak on behalf of the public, but still must attempt this by selecting a studio audience member to stand in for the public. In sum, experts speak for others while the audience speak for themselves. Thus it is difficult for experts to construct an authentic and credible persona on the screen, and yet, authenticity and credibility rather than, say, intellectual argument or verified evidence are, simultaneously, being constructed as the rules of the discourse. As experts are trained to develop arguments carefully, at length, citing supporting evidence, rebutting refutations and noting qualifications, they are doomed to failure in discussion programmes. They appear fragmented rather than whole, cold rather than warm and alienated rather than authentic.

Some experts adapt by taking on the media version of ordinary discourse prioritized by the genre, but then they face a different problem, for it is near impossible to offer expert knowledge in a personalized voice:

> That's very clever, to talk in the same language as they do, smiling and getting to know the names, and they all have their own technique. (F1.185)

On *Kilroy*, one expert answered a general question briefly and quickly moved on to a personal anecdote, saying 'if it's anything like my household . . .'. A psychologist describes his research interviews in informal terms, saying 'I've talked to people and . . .'. In a *Donahue* programme on divorce, the expert discusses his own divorce. Similarly, a therapist couple discussing marriage problems included their own experiences:

> So they had the expert view but at the same time they were giving their own story, and it did focus on them for quite a long time. I found it faintly annoying actually, because they were telling their stories, but the guy was saying in such an authoritative way, making out that this is the way to do it.
>
> (Margaret, studio audience)

Different genres establish specific epistemologies or forms of knowing. The documentary can visit the scientific laboratory to observe the evidence which grounds a claim, it shows a speaker's poverty directly, it graphs the crime figures whose increase is of concern. The classic debate can pursue a complex argument without interruption, pitting opposing sides against each other, giving each equal space to speak, demanding answers to potential refutations, uncovering the logic of an argument. The soap opera gradually makes real and believable its claims about, say, the hardships faced by a single mother, by portraying the unfolding of actions' causes and consequences through a realistic dramatization of everyday life.

The discussion programme can do none of this. Its strengths lie in the revelatory retellings of personal experiences, using the credibility of the source to validate the message. The display of spontaneity, self-disclosure and direct experience are vital for grounding the argument, and if animator, author and principal coincide, the speaker is seen as credible. Evidence counts only if it can be produced in the studio. On the doctor–patient communication programme (*Kilroy*), both the problems with communication and the unreasonableness of some doctors and patients were displayed rather than reported:

It was great that it was a discussion about the lack of communication [between doctors and patients] and there was some fantastic lack of communication there. Especially when you had two or more people talking at the same time. (D2.19)

That came out on the programme. I should imagine that some of those GPs were tearing their hair out, if she just goes down to have a chat, if she has no friends to talk to. (D1.42)

If a mother is to speak about her son's illness, she must reveal her own suffering rather than dwell on his. If a widow of a drunk driver victim appears, she instead is constructed as the victim so that the principal can after all be present. If a wife discusses her marital problems, it is best if her husband is also present, not so that we may hear his side also, as in a documentary, but so that we may directly witness their disagreement, for she cannot report on his views without separating animator from author and principal.

If the evidence displayed is inadequate, the arguments they supposedly ground can be rejected. There was some concern among focus group respondents that the studio audience, especially in their appearance and clothing, for the programme on poverty had not looked poor enough:

I saw the woman in the leather jacket and she said that she hasn't got enough money to buy her food, well, where did the leather jacket come from? (P3.09)

There was another lady who was rather fat, and I thought that she certainly wasn't underfed. (P2.33)

However, once evidence is displayed and agreed, wider conclusions can be drawn. Thus, when *Kilroy* hosts programmes on the Israeli–Palestinian conflict, or the Serbian–Bosnian conflict, whether or not reasonable discussion can be achieved between opposed groups in the studio is taken metonymically as evidence of whether such discussion is likely to take place outside, in the real-world political negotiations: Kilroy says, 'here you see, this is the Middle East in miniature'.

CONCLUSIONS

We have suggested that new forms of relationship between experts and laity, as part of changing conceptions of expertise in society, are encouraged by audience discussion programmes. This argument counters the general criticism that the media are conservative in the sense of generating forms of knowledge that reproduce established power relations, supporting the elite and passivizing the laity. According to this criticism, established knowledge is handed down to the laity in a form that disguises the institutional processes which constructed it, leading to fatalistic acceptance by the audience. We suggest that there are problems with extending this account to the audience discussion programme and that the existence of such programmes on television affects the meaning of common sense and expertise as represented by other media genres. Schlesinger (1978) argues that there is a 'missing link' in understanding between news producers and audiences. Yet in the audience discussion programme, experts and lay people are put together, setting an agenda of social issues and offering both established elites and ordinary people the opportunity at least to discuss the lived experience of current-affairs issues in relation to expert solutions. In this context, it is interesting to observe the spread of the audience discussion format into other genres, such as news, documentary and current affairs.

Chapter 6

Media management of argument and rhetoric

Central to the study of argumentation and rhetoric is the opposition between positivist and discursive views of reason and rationality. These different conceptions of rational discussion – a positive view of progress through procedural rationality and the discursive expression of diversity, opinion and local practice – underlie the bourgeois and oppositional conceptions of the public sphere respectively. Rationality is also central to relations between the public and private: what persuasive, educational and rhetorical processes connect ordinary people with bureaucrats, experts and politicians and how are conflicts between private individuals and institutions played out through public debate? We argue that audience discussion programmes express not one or other of these views of rationality but the oppositional tension between them. Similarly, they do not express one relation between the laity and the experts, or the life-world and the system, but rather they problematize their mutual interpenetration. If the audience discussion programme represents at least a candidate for the public sphere – and after all, even though the place is odd and the conditions strange, people still turn up to participate and to argue – then we must ask what kinds of arguments are held within them. More generally, we can ask what place there is for rational discussion in the mass media.

PHILOSOPHICAL DEBATES OVER THE NATURE OF ARGUMENT

The dominant philosophical notion of rationality, derived from deductive logic, holds that there is a set of formal reasoning procedures that express tacit inference rules concerning the truth or falsity of assertions independently of the content or context of utterances. On this view, much lay reasoning is fallacious. Yet, in everyday discussion, people regularly generalize from the observable and consensual. Following Wittgenstein (1958), recent theories of argumentation are developing an alternative, conventional, situated account of rational discourse.

Toulmin (1958) suggests that informal reasoning should be regarded as meaningful activity rather than as fallacious and chaotic. The rationality of ordinary reasoning lies in an underlying ideal structure of argument-in-context. Toulmin's central concept is the claim, where the pragmatics of staking a claim concern its clarity or ambiguity – a real issue in the cut and thrust of conversation. The person making the claim bears a social responsibility to present it clearly and unambiguously while the recipients of the claim are responsible for questioning and clarifying it. In audience discussion programmes, these social responsibilities are distributed in particular ways: some are invited to make claims, others compete to do so; some question the claims made by others; and prioritizing some claims over others is the responsibility of the host and studio audience.

For Toulmin, the grounds for a claim – the data or evidence offered in support – also involve social responsibilities. Grounds are established not by logical principles but according to the varying conventions for appropriate evidence used in different types of argument – such as those of business, law or science. In audience discussion programmes, these conventions privilege anecdotal and personal evidence over the abstract, expert or general. The warrant of an argument justifies the inference connecting grounds and claim by reference to some general principle. Claims are warranted through generalization, formula, rule, law or principle, experience or exemplification. In audience discussion programmes, warrants based on experience or example are especially valued. Warrants can be contested in terms of their backing (is the warrant based on a valid generalization?) and arguments may be qualified against possible criticisms or rebuttals.

In this account of argument as structured relations between a set of elements, there is an implicit narrative; starting with making, choosing, challenging and refining a claim, then seeking and criticizing its grounds, discovering and testing the warrant for the grounds through critical examination of the backing and the scope of the warrant, qualifying the argument and anticipating possible rebuttals. The more thorough this narrative, the better the quality of the argument and the less likely the reasoning is to be fallacious.

Some philosophers would go further in moving argument analysis away from the discovery of a general form towards the analysis of social context. Walton (1989) argues that the basic unit of analysis is the dialogue. Here at least two people are parties to a goal-oriented task which involves them in various obligations, including those which concern the conduct of the argument. While Toulmin proposed a general schema of practical reasoning in which elements and relations are modified according to social conventions, Walton characterizes different dialogues in terms of the social roles of participants. Social context does not simply restrict the set of choices within the overall structure of argument, for the rules governing forms of argument are constitutive of social situations rather than caused by them. For Toulmin, the social rules matter little if the underlying argument structure is satisfactory; for Walton, the social rules make the argument. Walton differentiates kinds of dialogue – the quarrel, debate, critical discussion, inquiry and negotiation – by their social goals, conventional obligations placed on participants, and legitimate means of achieving the goals. Each kind of dialogue has its place in the audience discussion programmes, and this analysis of argument as social action connects with the participation framework.

Quarrels are characterized by intensity, emotional expression and a commitment to assert one's point at all costs. The opposite of the disinterested ideal of rational argument, Walton characterizes the quarrel as a personal attack which lacks strategy. As psychoanalysts note (for example, Bion, 1967), residual aggressive impulses from childhood anxieties erupt into adult disputes. Even for sophisticated adults, arguing is a frustrating business involving regressive feelings of persecution that undermine the development of the argument. A common criticism of audience discussion programmes is that the discussion rapidly degenerates into an emotional quarrel. Although emotions need not preclude a satisfactory argument, they tend to undermine it in practice. The host must tread a difficult line between encouraging emotional expression so as to mark the depth, reality, and authenticity of lay contributors – as required by the implicit valorization of lay over expert knowledge – and placing boundaries around this emotion so that other forms of argument may be sustained.

The debate form of dialogue or argument is characterized by an audience of judges who give a verdict, a set of procedures concerning who can speak, for how long and in what order, and the establishment of two sides to the issue. The goal of participating is to impress the judges with the relative superiority of one's arguments compared to one's opponents' within the constraints of the agreed procedures. While the institutional rhetoric behind audience discussion programmes tends to emphasize the debate form, often the arguments fit this pattern only in a partial manner.

Walton's critical discussion represents the intellectual ideal, expressed in Habermas's model of ideal communication for the public sphere, in which two or more people argue for differing but not necessarily opposed views. They acknowledge that their position may be undermined, and use argument to establish the reasonableness of concessions to be gained or granted. It also fits with the accounts of expert and lay participants (Chapter 5), who see themselves as modifying their position, as trying to modify that of others, as offering an informed argument or a relevant experience. However, other considerations – of emotion, power, status, prejudice – often disrupt the critical discussion, switching it to another form of dialogue.

In the inquiry, the argument is characterized by the accumulation of facts and statements of evidence so as to draw conclusions. Participants are obliged to cite only known facts in a neutral and cooperative fashion for the mutual discovery of conclusive knowledge. In the audience discussion programme, hosts may conduct a kind of public enquiry into a topical issue, enlisting the help of concerned lay people and relevant experts. Having accumulated the evidence, it may be weighed to reach a consensual conclusion. The inquiry may be an effective way of demanding accountability from public bodies, examining the validity of complaints so as to attribute blame where it is due. Verwey (1990) finds that 'call-ins have become something of a daily available protest and complaint medium' (ibid: 234), where people complain anonymously and are relatively uncensored. During 1992, BBC's Radio 4 held a series of programmes, *Call to Account*, in which senior managers from major public and privatized services (the Post Office, electricity, transport, etc.) were held accountable to 'their toughest critics – their customers' in just this way.

The demand for accountability produces a contentious inquiry, in which participants either accuse or defend. Other forms of inquiry aim to generate knowledge according to an agreed agenda. For example, several discussion programmes on drunk driving, which all agreed should be controlled (Livingstone et al. 1992), took the form of collecting social and personal causes of drunk driving so as to understand and prevent this phenomenon. In the discussion, a list of causes was generated by lay and expert participants until they felt a reasonably complete picture had been produced. The list was grounded collaboratively both by personal stories, generally from victims, and by facts provided by experts. Nonetheless, a debate emerged, which cut across the expert/lay distinction, between those who sought personal causes (blaming the drunk driver) and those who sought social causes (blaming society). In the end, the resultant proposals for control were thus still contentious. In both forms of the inquiry, the host plays the role of romantic hero (Chapter 3) undertaking the difficult search for the prize, whether accountability or truth, on behalf of ordinary people so as to restore order and calm to their lives. Fogel (1986) sees the inquiry form more critically as inquisition. In opposition to the debate, he notes how talk show hosts are often assessed by how tough they are, meaning how inquisitorial they are and how well they grill their guests, while the lay participants are often assessed as (mis)representing free public debate.

Finally, in the negotiation dialogue, the aim is primarily to promote self-interest. Negotiators aim for settlement as close to their ideal resolution as possible while confronting an opponent who is also an interested party and who desires a different outcome. The argument is adversarial, characterized by compromises gained by trading costs and benefits through bargaining. Audience discussion programmes offer the significant resource of symbolic capital over which to fight: participants fight for the right to define or analyse a problem in a particular way, to assert particular solutions, to establish the terms of the argument (for example, anecdote vs. statistics), to allow certain people to propose solutions (expert, lay person, host). In the oppositional public sphere, issues of voice, of distributed power, and of confrontation are central, and the hope is that through diverse attempts to promote self-interest, a greater good will result.

For Walton, arguments tend to go wrong when people switch from one form of argument to another. Particularly in practical social contexts, people tend to regress to persecutory and anxiety-ridden forms of argument such as the quarrel, thereby undermining cooler, more complex forms of argument. We cannot fulfil our obligations to the debate, critical discussion, inquiry or negotiation when our main intent is to hurt the other person. Yet in the audience discussion programme, all forms of dialogue and argument can be seen, partly depending on the topic, the participants and the host. More importantly, all these forms occur because argument-switching is endemic to a genre in which different kinds of participants negotiate their ways through an unstable set of conventions and obligations. While one coherent argument does not result, various separate aims may be partially achieved.

Such plural and partial achievements still depend on the general avoidance of fallacies in reasoning. Walton suggests that, to avoid fallacies, arguments – especially, critical discussions – ideally go through several stages, each with its associated rules of appropriate behaviour. In the opening stage the main prohibition is against 'unlicensed shifts from one type of dialogue to another' (Walton, 1989: 17). Here, issues are stated and the type of argument dialogue established: audience discussion programmes typically open with a series of personal anecdotes grounding a claim or evidencing the need for inquiry or accountability. In the confrontation stage the two sides of the issue are elaborated and the main taboo is attempting to change the agenda. In audience discussion programmes, confrontation may emerge at various, unpredictable points. It may even be unclear who are the main protagonists, for this itself is often contested within the discussion.

The argument proper then unfolds. This is much more rule-bound: people must fulfil their obligations, accept the burden of proof, use acceptable inference procedures, make their contributions relevant, ask and reply to questions appropriately and offer definitions of terms if asked. They must not use intimidation, appeal to pity or emotions, attack personal qualities of the opponent, make unreasonable appeals to authority, set up a straw man, beg the question, and so forth. Here we find the viewing audience most critical of the arguments held (see below). Participants too are often frustrated as these rules are often broken and the genre rarely permits criticism of the conduct of the argument itself. In the closing stage, participants must not force a premature closure of the argument and certainly premature closure, indeed closure of any kind, is often resisted in audience discussion programmes.

RHETORICAL APPROACHES TO PRACTICAL REASONING

The study of rhetoric represents an alternative approach to argument in naturally occurring situations (Billig, 1987; Leith and Myerson, 1989). Everyday conversations are seen as essentially persuasive. Rather than opposing the formal, deductive approach to rationality against that of discovering the social conventions for inductive reasoning, one should explore how talk is organized around principles of persuasion. Rhetoric provides a basic interpretive framework which emphasizes the performative aspects of language: language is always addressed to someone; a particular utterance is a reply to another and will be replied to; language is embedded in a stream of arguments; language is characterized by openness or 'play' such that meanings are never complete but open to interpretation and reinterpretation (Leith and Myerson, 1989).

This approach sensitizes us to issues of address, performance and persuasion when analysing audience discussion programmes. Meaning-as-rhetoric reaches out beyond the immediate context to other people, other arguments and other meanings. Meaning is seamless and the imposition of boundaries is achieved not through the structuring of meaning in language (as in Toulmin and Walton) but through the demands and conventions of performance. This focus on practice fits most closely with Goffman's (1981) dramaturgical model of communication in the participation framework: it takes effort to place boundaries on meanings in use and these boundaries come from the social organization of practice. Being a speaker or hearer is a social role with attendant obligations and who says what to whom is a central question in the analysis of argument. The social context is not a selection principle in a schema (Toulmin) and does not constrain the aims, means and obligations of participants (Walton) but rather it puts boundaries on the potentially infinite possibilities for address, argument and play, imposing order on chaos by privileging certain aspects of performance.

Leith and Myerson (1989) explore several forms of performance which variously manage the closure of rhetorical possibilities and so allow meaning to emerge: lecturing, preaching, political oratory and story-telling. Each constructs a different relationship between speaker, hearer and argument. Rather than representing a single, new type of situation, the audience discussion programme provides a place in which people can play out a variety of language games. Thus the participants must manage the rhetorical task of linking diverse forms of address and linguistic conventions.

The lecture represents 'an emblem of the power relations underpinning the formal education system: the lecturer is paid to "know" things and transmit them to an ignorant audience' (Leith and Myerson, 1989: 11). The power inequalities in social roles between lecturer and student are encoded in the physical setting. The language of the lecture is scripted in advance, propositional in nature, declarative in presentation. Pragmatically, the lecturer gives new and relevant information, often intended to attack folk theories. The lecturer is thus in dialogue with imaginary expert and lay voices.

In preaching a sermon, an initial quotation – rhetorically offered for contemplation – is often elaborated through a story, an argument and a conclusion, so that the 'argument offers an interpretation of the narrative' (Leith and Myerson, 1989: 19). Rather than presenting new information, the sermon rehearses fundamental tenets of christianity and relates them to the particular and the contemporary. The audience is invited to reflect and contemplate rather than to acquire knowledge.

In political oratory, Leith and Myerson again emphasize the relationship between the speaker and the audience. In a political conference speech, 'the address of the speech is therefore complex. The speaker holds a dialogue not only with the audience, not only with opposing but absent voices, but also with the previous speaker at the conference' (ibid: 23). Audience participation is based on expectations about having a legitimate voice and a place within the speech to voice it. Persuasively, political speeches work by rehearsing shared political, social and moral values.

The analysis of story-telling shows how everyday, informal conversation can be regarded in rhetorical terms:

> A narrative of personal experience [is] to many people an unlikely candidate . . . for the term 'oratory'. Indeed, such stories seem so familiar and unremarkable that we hardly think of them as *performances*. Stories like this very often simply 'emerge' from the flow of informal conversation.
>
> (Leith and Myerson, 1989: 27)

Story-telling is valued in most societies as the repository of folk wisdom and encoding of moral positions. Since stories often emerge spontaneously from ordinary conversation, they need flagging at the outset ('have I told you the one about . . .?') and wrapping up at the end ('so, as I've always said . . . '). When the story-teller holds the floor she or he is obliged to be interesting and relevant. As stories are valued, telling a story may provide opportunities for self-aggrandizement.

STORY-TELLING IN AUDIENCE DISCUSSION PROGRAMMES

Contributions to audience discussion programmes include mini speeches and expert lectures which position others as hearers and critical discussions or inquiries which position all participants as speakers. However, story-telling is a dominant form in the genre, positioning the lay person as speaker, and the expert and the host as hearers. Rhetorically, stories are both an opportunity to provide evidence for claims and an interruption of critical discussion. The argument demands that they receive space for they offer data that ground claims made by the narrator or others, but as the narrator may regard the story as sufficient in itself he or she is placed under pressure to make the story relevant, informative and brief. Generally, experts develop the argument by providing warrants, qualifiers and rebuttals, although they may attempt stories of their own. Story-telling places particular social obligations on lay participants. They may arrive at the studio with a story worked out and wait for the opportunity to tell it, which may not come. While not responsible for the whole of the communication, they must establish the truth of their contribution through the authenticity and emotion of their story.

Given the competition for the floor, the discussions do not develop neatly, weaving stories into an overall structure. Rather, the argument is built up in a haphazard manner by layering, recursion and repetition, giving participants a chance to add their stories to current and earlier points. Emotionally, the abstract arguments generate a tension which is periodically resolved by touching base with personal experience, punctuating the argument with another story. Thus, story-telling locates a 'place' in the programmes for the expression of emotion – establishing authenticity and relieving tension, thereby channelling it away from other modes of argumentation being used. The focus on diverse individual experiences distracts attention from any contradictions or oppositions between personal stories. Through their diversity and particularity, stories also resist institutional or dominant explanations, bringing together the public and private by asserting the private, the lived reality, over public control and institutional inadequacies.

ARGUMENT AND RHETORIC IN ONE AUDIENCE DISCUSSION PROGRAMME

Many of these points about argument and rhetoric in audience discussion programmes are illustrated through analysing one programme which we showed to our focus groups, an episode of *Kilroy* on doctor–patient communication. From the attempt to apply analytic schemata to programmes, it is clear that no one schema fits neatly. Within the ebb and flow of the discussion, many elements of argument structure, many forms of argument dialogue and many types of rhetorical performance may take place in any given programme: it is the mix of argument style and performance that characterizes the genre.

Programme Opening

This programme begins with the signature tune over visuals of participants talking on previous programmes combined with abstract graphics and leading to the programme title: *Kilroy*. We cut to the studio with a wide-angle shot of the studio audience from a central camera. The host walks down from the back of the studio, through the applauding audience, towards the central camera. As he passes, he says 'hello there' to one and 'nice to see you' to another. He then talks directly to the home audience: 'hello and good-morning. The family doctor used to be the first port of call if you had a problem but some people here this morning would make it their last because they can't communicate with their doctor'. He turns his back on the home audience while a subtitle appears on the screen stating the issue, 'DOCTORS: Trying our Patience?', and addresses the studio audience generally: 'who has problems with their doctor?'. Several participants put their hands up signalling readiness to answer. Kilroy selects someone and holds out the microphone: 'what's the problem?'

Specific forms of argumentation are already being shaped up through the host's performance which demonstrate the complexity of address in these programmes. First, by casually greeting participants on his way to introduce the programme, we are welcomed as overhearers of the private conversation he will have with a group of friends. Second, he demonstrates that the home audience is the primary recipient by purposefully moving towards us and turning his back on the participants to announce the issue for discussion. Third, he couches the issue in terms of the studio audience's personal experiences and turns quickly to the participants, addressing them with a general question while they compete to catch his eye. Fourth, this general invitation is addressed only to the lay participants, cutting out the expert participants (doctors, health officials and academics) to determine that the discussion will open with ordinary people telling of their personal experiences. Rhetorically, this asserts that the two sides to the argument are doctors and patients without any attempt to find out if this is in fact the case. Fifth, one individual is singled out for attention. So, having come towards us to introduce the issue, Kilroy takes us 'with him' back into the studio audience. He opens by prioritizing the revelation of personal, lay experience through story-telling, preventing any initial discussion of the nature and scope of the issue.

First Stories

Having been offered the microphone, a lay participant tells her story:

Woman 1:	I just find him really insensitive. If there's an embarrassing situation he'd like make it worse. Just like a simple thing like a smear test, the doctor would never usually talk to me until I was there with my knees in the air and he's like, wanting to ask me how I was and how the family was. It was just awful, it just made it worse.
Kilroy:	Oh, he was filling in time . . .
Woman 1:	Well, it just made it that much more embarrassing for me.

Initially, the right to take the floor to tell a story requires permission by the host and only the host may be addressed. In this and the next four stories by further speakers, he follows up his invitation to tell a brief story by interjecting with a joke or an aside which makes the speaker wind up the story:

| Man 1: | . . . . there wasn't really time for me to question his suggestion as to what to put the thing in. |
| Kilroy: | It was clean? |

| Man 1: | Oh it was clean – I won't do it again. |
| | (audience laughter) |

This use of the ironic comment or joke also allows a noisy response from the rest of the studio audience, breaking the silence surrounding the story-teller and so interrupting the privacy of the dyad. The host withdraws permission to continue the story by transforming the private space into a public one, reminding everyone of their pressing claims to tell their own stories. The studio audience shift from overhearers like the home audience to individual potential speakers.

The stories must also be controlled not because they become dull but because they are supposed to be moving an argument forward through illustration. While peers often have difficulty stopping an anecdote, the host exerts his or her power, changing from sympathetic hearer (I'm on your side) to one who can, abruptly or rudely if necessary, stop the story. An illusion of equality between speaker and hearer, maintained during the story itself, is broken: the speaker cannot pass on the right to speak to another hearer for the host retains the microphone; the storyteller addresses neither home nor studio audience but only the host; and the host represents the supposed interests of home and studio audience by imposing a judgement of relevance or interest.

These initial stories resemble a soliloquy or soundbite. Unlike spontaneous story-telling, the usual negotiation between story-teller and audience is missing. As the programme proceeds, the host's control is increasingly modified by the studio audience, whose nonverbal or paralinguistic responses may also represent the interests of the home audience and move the discussion onwards. They also become better at gaining the attention of the camera and may begin their contribution without invitation in the confidence that a clear loud voice will draw the host and camera by having already gained permission to speak from the studio audience through their visual attention and relative silence.

Conversation and discussion

From this point onwards, the host interjects less, encouraging the free flow of generally supportive discussion amongst lay participants. First, the host provides a model for this more conversational mode and invites others to join in:

Woman 2:	Yes, the time – doctors that haven't even got enough courtesy not to look at their watch from the moment you enter the surgery, with their kind of checking you in and clocking you in.
Kilroy:	What, your doctor does that?
Woman 2:	Absolutely. Well, he used to, he doesn't do it any more when I visit him.

Kilroy:	I hope he doesn't do it the next time you walk in.
Woman 2:	He's actually a very nice man. Time and attitude – doctors can be terribly patronising, they cannot communicate.
Kilroy:	You're nodding your head there, what would you do? You – when [she] was saying patronising and time?
Woman 3:	The thing is they don't communicate and they do patronize people, especially, they just don't understand when doctors, they just don't understand the less-educated people. You know, like my mother wasn't very educated at all, and they just didn't diagnose her illness in time.

Now there are many interruptions for story-tellers to contend with which generate interaction among the studio audience and allow the host to drop out:

Woman 4:	Doctors will think that you just go in for prescriptions.
Woman 5:	Yeah.
Woman 4:	Whereas you don't, sometimes you just want to have a chat, and you can't talk to your family or your friends, and doctors are the only one, you know –
Woman 5:	And they often won't give you time for a chat anyway.
Woman 4:	No, you can't, because they think you're wasting their time.
Woman 5:	They make you feel guilty.
Woman 4:	Yeah, they do.

Expert contribution

The interaction thus far between lay participants involves anecdotes and supportive points. After a while the host changes the emphasis by addressing the experts in the studio audience as a group:

| Kilroy: | Do you doctors recognize yourselves? All the doctors are sitting very quiet aren't they, but I know where you all are (audience laughter) – all very, no doctors want to respond to all this? Doctors, do you recognize yourself, looking at your watch when they walk in, giving prescriptions without listening? |

Telling them off for their quietness seems a harsh introduction, as the experts had been excluded from Kilroy's initial invitation to speak, illustrating the intimidation that experts often receive in these discussions. The host borrows from the negotiation model, attempting to gain a concession from those cast as opponent. Not surprisingly, the first response is defensive:

| Doctor 1: | In 30 years I've never looked at a clock during a consultation, or indeed during the surgery. |

The multiple stories of doctors' incompetence and insensitivity laid down in the early part of the programme are an accusation which grounds the host's initial claim for doctor–patient miscommunication. The multiplicity of stories also acts as a warrant: many people have these experiences, it is therefore a common problem, and so it has generality beyond any one person's experience. The point of the programmes is not that doctors should address individual complaints but that they should be held accountable for a general problem affecting the public and made aware of the problems they cause by listening to patients' complaints. The accusation is also personal: the host suggests that these problems surely apply to doctors present. How can the doctors respond to this challenge?

Kilroy: How do you respond to the kind of things that are being said? Do you recognize any of it in you?

Doctor 1:   Not very much, no, I'm afraid. I think they've been very unfortunate.

Kilroy: So you're a good doctor then?

Doctor 1:   I hope so.

It is problematic for the host that this doctor personally denies the accusation, refusing the subject position implied by the argument.

Expert/lay interaction

The expert's response provokes an interesting intervention from a lay participant:

Woman 6:   I've been dying to say something, because my GP is fantastic. I've been quite seriously ill recently, and he's had all the time in the world for me. I went back when I knew what my diagnosis was, he spent about three-quarters of an hour with me, he had as much time as I particularly needed then . . . we really had a very very good service. And he's always been like that.

The doctor is not slow to grasp this opportunity:

Doctor 1:   That's right. I think, really, I mean I've gone along for nearly 30 years now and I've felt you give a patient as much time as they need.

This development cuts across Kilroy's initial definition of the problem of doctor–patient miscommunication as the fault of doctors and as an opposition between experts and ordinary people. He responds by simply using his power to ignore the emerging line of argument and tries to get back to blaming doctors by switching his attention to other lay participants, inviting more personal experiences. This time, however, he does not ask the open question but focuses on a particular problem doctors may cause patients, specifically asking those who earlier complained about doctors:

Kilroy: Do they give you enough time? Do doctors – time, a lot of people complained about time.

Man 2:   It's like being on a production line.

Kilroy: Talk to the doctor.

Man 2:   You're straight in, he has a few words, and then he sends you out again, straight away. He don't seem to want to spend the time with you because he's got other patients waiting outside. I think there's allocated a time limit per patient.

Doctor 2:   Yes, yes, it can –

It seems that Kilroy would rather promote a personal quarrel than redefine his earlier direction, placing boundaries on a potentially open critical discussion by inviting people to attack doctors in a specific way. In fact, a negotiation dialogue is sustained: as the opponent will not accept the most general form of the argument, try a more specific and clear-cut case as a compromise. The expert is offered a way out of the quarrel if he concedes this specific criticism. As we saw, the doctor accepts this, conceding that patient allocation systems can be problematic. We thus see three of Walton's argument types working here – the personal quarrel, the critical discussion and the negotiation dialogue.

In terms of address, it is significant that Kilroy directs the lay participant to 'talk to the doctor'. Until now, the host has addressed the lay participants separately, mediating between them and the doctors. Having failed to get the general concession he wanted, he invites the lay person to make the complaint directly to a member of the elite group – and it seems to work. However, this doctor's concession is a limited one, and one that holds dangers for the host and lay participants because the representation of patients as victims may now shift to one of doctors as victims. The first doctor seizes his opportunity to suggest that doctors are under considerable time pressure. The problem becomes one of dealing with patients' unrealistic expectations of unlimited consultation time rather than one of doctors':

Doctor 1:   Well, somewhere along the line, you see, if you've got a list of around 2,000 patients, and you're going to see three or four of them times that many every year, clearly there's a pressure on you to see patients. If you only had half a dozen patients to see every morning and half a dozen afternoon, wouldn't it be lovely, you could give them all half an hour?

This contribution is notable for the introduction of statistics, shifting the argument from a personal anecdote about particular surgeries to a problem facing doctors in general. He uses his newly gained position of strength to refuse Kilroy's game. Rather than trying to undermine the claim grounded by the series of personal stories just heard, he contests the issue more fundamentally. He thus avoids attacking the lay people, and redefines the issue as political or structural rather than interpersonal or communicative. A lay participant supports the doctor's reframing of the issue:

> Woman 7:   Yes, don't you find there's so much paper work to do that the doctor is no longer a GP any more, he's really a, you know, administration office?

This redefinition to a political rather than interpersonal debate raises a new threat for the programme, for the epistemological strength – of demonstrating the problem directly in the studio through displaying actual doctor–patient miscommunication – is lost. The debate may become a conflict between the political left and right rather than between lay and expert, a debate which audience discussion programmes are ill-equipped to sustain. The doctor who originally conceded needs no further encouragement to strengthen his weakened position by more firmly shifting the focus to politics:

> Doctor 2:   Well, you have to organize all that, and you have to find time to do it, and we are worried under our new contract we may have less time with patients, which is another concern . . . but I think also there are all sorts of questions there. But also there is the point that I think the GP can be trained to use his time properly.
>
> Woman 8:   Yes, I –
>
> Doctor 2:   – perhaps by using other people in his team as well.
>
> Woman 8:   I agree. I think it would help if the doctor had a nurse, when you phone up for a call-out, a house-call, which I'm afraid in our area we very rarely get. And if you want a house-call, I mean I know someone who had a fracture last year and for six days she was in great pain and she could not get a doctor for six days.

The success of the doctor's effort is that a patient's complaint is now offered as support for rather than a challenge to the doctor, evidencing problems with the system not the doctor. The earlier attempt to assert that doctors are victims of patient's unreasonable expectations is taken up by the patients themselves, albeit in a modified form which also questions doctors' expectations:

> Doctor 2:   What is interesting –
>
> Woman 9:   It all boils down to expectations.
>
> Doctor 2:   Yes, I think that's right.
>
> Woman 9:   What the doctor and what the patient is expecting out of the consultation.
>
> Doctor 2:   I think what's interesting is –

Host's management of the discussion

Interrupting the doctor's attempt to make a point, Kilroy now supports the lay speaker, temporarily conceding this change of argument direction in order to reassert himself. The doctor again intervenes, strengthening his case by redirecting the lay speaker towards the problematic expectations by patients and away from collusive expectations between doctors and patients:

Kilroy: What do you mean, your expectation?
Woman 9:   Well some – there is a myth about, between doctors and patients, they both collude in it, that whatever the patient comes up with can be cured, you know. That's why there is pressure behind the doctor.
Doctor 2:   There is an expectation, there's always a strong expectation, that still comes from many of my patients that when they come in to the surgery, they actually want to leave with a prescription, you know, I mean that is something I often have to explain is not necessary.
Woman 9:   Yes, yes. There's an education process that you've got to teach patients to expect something different from the doctor.

This is too much for Kilroy and having reasserted his role he returns the argument to its initial claim, blaming doctors' interpersonal style for the problems they cause patients. He manages this by appearing to accept the present turn of events, but then turning it on its head to assert that patients' expectations are reasonable rather than unreasonable. A third doctor, slow to realize what has happened, responds as if the argument still concerned excessive institutional pressures on doctors, a mistake for which Kilroy ridicules him. Through this ridicule, he brings the studio audience back onto his side:

Kilroy: What, what have we got to expect? Hang on, hang on – what have we got to expect different? We just expect civility, time, courtesy, someone who will listen, and deal with the problem. Is that too much to expect?
Doctor 3:   Yes it is.
Kilroy: It is, is it? (explosion of noise from the audience) Hang on, hang on, I thought I was asking for the least, is this too much to expect?

The argument shifts very quickly and the lay studio audience follow Kilroy's lead, shifting their support. The host has reasserted the idea that doctors give a poor service, denying patients time and courtesy. He has also divided one doctor against another, for the ridicule levied at the third doctor can be extended to reject the first doctor's hitherto accepted statistics on pressure on surgeries. Thus the doctors' strength as a professional group is undermined and the possibility is reopened that the other criticisms made of doctors in the initial story-telling phase are also, after all, reasonable.

A lecture

The course of the discussion is again changed when a doctor now puts a more detailed case which, while conceding some patient complaints, again explains these in terms of the institutional and political pressures on doctors. His use of lecture mode slows the argument down by positioning everyone else as passive hearer instead of turn-taking speaker. The lecture mode is itself established through an initial style of self-interruption which prevents space for any other interruptions:

Doctor 3:   Hold on, hold on just a moment. What happens now – and part of this is the profession's fault, and is now going to be the government's fault, as in the case of the appointments system – now I speak quite openly, I don't have an appointment system, because my patients unfortunately are not bright enough to know in advance when they're going to be ill. And if they're ill I want to see them. I don't want to see them two days later, I mean, this is a criticism which I have heard about appointments systems. Now the thing is, no-one with the best will in the world, all my colleagues here, we go into the surgery hoping and anticipating, trying to listen to all the patients. But to hear them one after another, what happens is after a while one develops a technique, if you like to use that word, a technique of listening to a patient, hearing what they say, and sort-of half listening, and suddenly they mention something and the alarm signals go up, we say aha, this is something serious here, what's going on. And anybody – can I just say this final thing – anybody who thinks going to their doctors, say, for the appointments system, at the last appointment of the day, that they're going to get a long consultation – if they get a long consultation, either the doctor is a saint, or the doctor's having matrimonial problems of his own.

The doctor tries to draw the patients in the studio and at home onto his side by inviting empathy for his difficulties. His lecture includes a glimpse into a professional dispute over the appointments system and into a professional technique for managing patients: he reminds us that for doctors, we are addressing a professional issue, while for patients, the problems are personal and private. If doctors' real arguments are among themselves and with the government, not with patients, the personal, patient attack on doctors is defused. In the programme, the rights of host and lay participants to determine the claims for which personal stories provide the evidence is challenged and, as data underdetermines theory, the claim to be drawn from the stories is contested. Rhetorically, the doctors are playing a different game, publicizing their professional problems rather than addressing the interpersonal debate established initially by the programme.

Developing the arguments

The discussion then develops certain arguments, such as that of time management in patient care. Doctor 2 offers a consistent opinion on appointments systems, reiterating his points. While the discussion is back on track in terms of attacking doctors, it retreats from critical argument towards the recounting of personal stories – as encouraged by Kilroy.

Doctor 2:	I think an appointments system is something you actually have to run very very carefully, and if you have an appointments system that simply doesn't give enough space in the day it will just get –
Kilroy:	Is five minutes enough space?
Doctor 2:	No it's not, no, no. The best appointments system is one that actually has built-in gaps in it, and that actually works a lot better.
Woman 10:	And why do doctors – the doctors in my area, work only the office hours, 9 till 5.30. They don't make any provision for people that are working, or have young children who cannot be found –
Doctor 2:	Well, the majority of GPs will be doing surgeries right through to 6, 6.30 in the evening, the majority will.
Woman 10:	Yes, they will, but the last appointment stops at half past five, and you can't make an appointment for any later than that.
Kilroy:	Now hang on, hang on my love, go on.
Woman 11:	I have actually lost a student's placement because I've had to take so many afternoons, so many days off to go and see my GP. He does have a surgery to 7 o'clock but I don't finish till 6 and I don't get there till 7, and he won't see me for five minutes after 7 o'clock.
Woman 12:	I mean, at my surgery there's three doctors, one you can go in and he's got his pen poised as soon as you go in, and there's two other, lady doctors. And one of those lady doctors will give me 20 minutes, and she will sit there and listen and I've argued with her for three months and I'm now going to see a specialist, but I've had to fight for three months to see the specialist.

Doctor 2:   If you do have that sort of flexibility in the system it does allow you to give that extra bit of time without too much detriment to other people.

Other issues are also now developed, including medical training, patient responsibilities, male versus female doctors, and the gate-keeping role of the receptionist. The programme moves freely from one topic to another in the manner of a group word-association game, airing issues for the cultural forum, but offering little development of sustained arguments.

Despite the attempt by the host to address the doctors as a group, the doctors have responded in different ways. The first uses personal experience to assert the tradition of general practice, amateurish but dedicated. The second doctor is the representative of the British Medical Association and skilfully constructs a case for doctors which accepts the need for changing work-patterns and training but argues against proposed changes in doctors' contracts. This is the institutional voice of the medical establishment: careful, prepared, and best able to hijack the argument. The third doctor states his opinions in extreme form, thus making him most vulnerable to the host's attack. Similarly, the lay participants also resist the attempt to form a coherent patient group against the doctors, for they express variable support for or criticism of doctors, depending on different personal experiences or analyses of the problem. The original depiction of the debate between two opposed sides, doctors and patients, keeps getting lost and instead a more open-ended discussion involving a variety of voices is underway.

Maybe the abstractness of the developing discussion becomes dull or stressful, for at this point, a critical discussion about the receptionist's role is transformed into an emotional personal quarrel between a doctor and a lay participant, thus reasserting the opposition of expert versus lay and also, in the process, stripping the expert of his professional demeanour so that the lay person emerges as triumphant over the expert.

Doctor 4:   But you basically need common sense. If you remember, those who are old enough to remember Dr Finlay's Casebook, Janet was the receptionist, she knew them all, I don't accept all these regulations. When we advertised in our practice a few years ago for a receptionist, I wrote down clearly, ability to deal with the public, sense of humour more important than knowledge of paper work, and we've got two super receptionists. But they've got no qualifications. It's almost as if qualifications are meant to –

Woman 13:   Well, training, as in social skills! I mean a lot of doctors hide behind their receptionists –

Doctor 4:   Yes, but you can't –

Woman 13:   – if they don't want to speak to someone, if they've got a cold or a headache or if they want to go off a bit early because they're taking an MSc or something, they will hide behind their receptionists, and quite often they will listen to the receptionist's opinion of the patient, of the patient's condition. In fact my relationship with my doctor only changed when we had a head to head about the receptionist.

The doctor is frustrated by being denied the floor and commits the error of treating a person as a member of a problematic category of patients, rather than as an individual with citizen's rights. He thus loses the sympathy of the studio audience as they shift from overhearers of the quarrel to supporters of the other side:

Doctor 4:   But, people like you –
             (noise of outrage from the audience)
Kilroy: Anne, Anne –
Doctor 4:   – people like you want it both ways, a lot of people here want it both ways. This colleague here says his surgery goes on for an hour and a half after time, that means the patient is probably not having to wait –
Woman 13:   I object to your saying people like me! Would you explain what you mean by that?

The doctor does not anticipate that the lay speaker will stand up for herself, and he is forced onto the defensive:

Doctor 4:   Well, what I'm saying is that if you have an appointments system receptionists have a timetable to fill up and the rest, and the point is very often –
Woman 13:   Yes, but they've also got manner and attitude, the fact that they've got appointments doesn't mean to say that they turn round and say, we're not going to see you, hard luck, take an aspirin.
Doctor 4:   But the receptionist is part of a team and the team is headed by the doctor –
Woman 13:   Yes! And it's the doctor's responsibility, if he's – I do take great exception to that, people like you, there's an attitude that's revealing. You see, you've just seen me for the first time today, you know nothing about me –

Her annoyance at being categorized as a problem returns to interrupt her argument, maybe suggesting to her that she now has the position of strength from which to win her case – for in a quarrel, one attacks by the best means available. Also frustrated by the quarrel, the doctor compounds his mistake by applying a pejorative and presumptive label.

Doctor 4:	I think you're a very aggressive young lady, if I may say so.
Kilroy:	A very what?
Doctor 4:	Aggressive young lady.
Kilroy:	Aggressive.
Doctor 4:	Yes.
Woman 13:	You see, I have been made aggressive (lots of supportive noise) by circumstances (applause). We respond to the way we are treated (applause). I don't feel as aggressive today as I used to, we have managed to reach a plateau of understanding. But you see, when we're sick, when we're ill, or our children are sick and ill – and I did not used to phone or consult my doctor in an aggressive manner, the aggression was coming at me, you know.

Not believing what he is hearing, Kilroy charitably assumes that he has misunderstood the doctor and asks for clarification. When the doctor restates his position, Kilroy retreats: presumably the doctor deserves whatever comes to him. His opponent turns the label around, reattributing the aggression to the personal and professional practices of doctors rather than to her own problems. By broadening the discussion through references to 'us' as victims – ill, with dependent children – she gains even firmer support from the studio audience. The host now joins the winning side and attacks the doctor:

| Doctor 4: | But you must admit, you must admit that we never met before, and just by watching you, just by watching you and non-verbal communication I can see for myself – |
| Kilroy: | She's not on trial, she's not on trial! No! What about, if we've got this kind of problem, here we've got, whatever it is, whatever the reason, there's a problem here of not being able to communicate, isn't there? |

He reframes the argument by using the quarrel as evidence for the claim of the critical discussion – that doctors and patients miscommunicate. Maybe, he implies, we can now return to a considered discussion of the causes of this problem. Unfortunately, the doctor refuses this reframing and persists with his analysis of the patient as problem. Again, Kilroy wants to be sure what the doctor (David) is saying and so prevents Doctor 2, the representative from the British Medical Association (Mike), from rescuing the situation:

Doctor 4:	Oh no, I don't think so at all.
Kilroy:	Hang on, hang on Mike. David, not at all?
Doctor 4:	As far as I'm concerned there's no problem at all.
Woman 15:	It's you telling her, she can't tell you what –
Doctor 4:	As far as I'm concerned, as far as I'm concerned I communicate very well.

Kilroy invites a lay speaker (Tina) to convince the doctor. Another lay speaker tries a new reframing so as to draw more abstract conclusions. Kilroy, resigned, suggests that this quarrel has gone too far for such resolutions:

Kilroy:	Did you hear what Tina said, did you hear what Tina said?
Doctor 4:	No, what was that?
Tina:	There's no problem in you telling her how you feel about her, but you're the doctor, you're meant to be able to listen and hear what she says. There's a difference between listening and hearing.
Woman 16:	May I just interrupt here a second. I think there are three things that would help patients to use the health service better –
Kilroy:	They can't hear you.

Concluding section

The programme eventually returns to the issues discussed in the body of the programme. As the programme approaches its end, the British Medical Association representative attempts to sum up:

Doctor 2:	There are two points that we've discussed throughout the programme. One is communication, and from what we've all heard, it sounds as if people do need training in communication. But David here pointed out that one of his patients asked him how long he was going to be in hospital, and he didn't know. Another very important fact is that the NHS, although cost-efficient, etc., etc., is progressing, it's developing new techniques and new ideas time and time again. And there doesn't seem to be the training, both for GPs, to update them on the new technologies.

Just as he originally tried to construct doctors as baddies and patients as goodies, Kilroy (below) attempts to redirect this bland conclusion, suggesting that doctors must still improve. Doctor 2 resists this interpretation and, as Kilroy refused to allow the professional/political perspective to stand, he instead exploits the genre's use of individual stories. He relativizes any conclusions one might draw, rather than concede the anti-doctor perspective. The host winds up the discussion with a joke which both terminates the discussion and asserts the superiority of the mass media ('we') over other professionals (doctors):

Kilroy:	Are you, having listened to this, Michael, all these, do you

	think doctors – have you learnt anything today about how you're going to –
Doctor 2:	Yes, what I've learnt is what in a way I already knew, that a consultation is a terribly personal thing, and some people will be happy with their individual GPs, and not every patient will be happy with the same doctor. What I think everybody is saying –
Kilroy:	And you're not going to be happy with me when I cut you off here, but we do try to listen! See you in the morning!

In the end, the host returns to the opening claim, that experts/doctors cause problems for their lay patients, and asks whether making doctors listen and be accountable to patients will provide a solution? For this reason, rather than in deference to the expert, Kilroy gives experts the last word.

COMMENTARY ON THE TEXTUAL ANALYSIS

By managing a social occasion in which experts and laity publicly discuss their conflicts, the programme cannot lose: if the doctors admit their culpability and change their attitudes, then the discussion has achieved its goal; but if they do not, then the programme constructs the doctors as unreasonable and thus establishes the validity of its analysis. While a critical discussion was needed for achieving the goal, a personal quarrel may still succeed in this latter task of supporting the programme's analysis. Both these aims can only be achieved if the discussion is steered away from an argument in which experts and lay people together find a common enemy – the government.

The arguments of this programme are socially distributed. The host sets out the claim and invites the studio audience to supply the grounds and, through their numbers and implied representativeness, the warrant. The doctors attempt some qualifications. However, after a lay speaker has supported her doctor, the argument exceeds the programme boundaries by demanding some estimate of the frequency of positive versus negative experiences. The warrant – that the stories just heard represent a generality, is questioned. The programme tries to offer more backing for the argument by hearing further personal experiences which support a more specific claim. However, following a struggle over the definition of the two sides, the claim is itself contested, and the argument shifts many more times over the course of the discussion.

These shifts and struggles are managed by altering the performative and rhetorical modes of the discussion, drawing upon elements of the critical discussion, story-telling, the lecture, the quarrel and the debate, in order to realign arguments and participants. This plurality of argumentative and rhetorical forms is constitutive of the genre and through this plurality, relations between media and audience, expert and laity, speaker and hearer, are asserted and contested. The participation framework which connects participants in joint communicative action is reframed as the argument shifts, for different performance modes cast participants variously as speaker – speaking for themselves or as representatives of others – and as hearers, overhearers, ratified or nonratified hearers, and so forth. Each recasting alters one's rights to speak or hear and one's responsibilities to contribute in particular ways, and so the argument moves on, if not forward. People are often clumsy in their attempts to renegotiate the positions in which they find themselves, but nonetheless, this renegotiation is important to them. This socially distributed argument establishes particular public identities for different categories of participants – an ideological and epistemological enterprise whose conduct arouses strong feelings.

THE AUDIENCE RECEPTION OF TELEVISION ARGUMENTS

In our focus groups we asked people about the nature and quality of the arguments in the programmes they had just watched. Respondents had much to say about the arguments used (see Chapter 4 and below), and were especially concerned about how programmes covered the issue or omitted relevant points. They also commented on the argument as a debate, on the worth or quality of the argument and on the absence of closure. When invited to judge the arguments, the majority of comments were negative, in contrast to comments on the social value of the programmes, the worth of hearing ordinary and expert participants, the host's management of the programme, and so forth (discussed in other chapters), where the mix of positive and negative comments reflected a debate about the merits of the genre. Clearly the actual arguments were generally felt to be poor and respondents reacted with some frustration:

> Yes, it was left up in the air at the end, there were no conclusions, well nothing was really followed through, you just got the beginning of the story, and I wanted to know, I wanted to ask questions, how did you come to be that way? (P3.95)

Topic coverage was the first question which we put to the focus groups in order to provoke discussion, but respondents returned to this theme over and over again, for it raised an underlying issue of bias. Omissions of political perspectives, certain categories of explanations or varieties of experience were criticized:

> I think that the programme was given entirely to the monetary function of poverty, and a lot of the poverty is relative to people, governed by whether they have an illness or misfortune. (P1.116)

> When you have these married couples being unfaithful, nobody seemed to see any fear of bi-sexuality, that wasn't mentioned at all. (F3.148)

> They didn't mention rural poverty at all, did they? There was nobody who had no transport, no shops, no jobs. (P1.30)

Nobody seemed to mention alternative medicines. (D3.95)

Many points were not omitted but were undeveloped, again slanting the argument. While the studio audience had time only for brief contributions, a satisfactory argument should include critical responses:

He seemed to think that drinks and cigarettes should be included in what they are giving, or the possibility of buying that sort of thing should be allowed. Which is again, very contentious. But nobody picked him up on it. (P1.112)

Because viewers only saw the participants in the studio, they received no direct view of their personal circumstances outside the studio:

I would like to know more about why they found themselves in these circumstances – especially the able-bodied ones. (P1.10)

You don't hear enough from each individual. This doesn't give enough detail for anyone to get a real idea of what their life is like. (P1.60)

You wondered whether you had heard the whole story. (D2.27)

Some issues were unclear and basic terms often went undefined, encouraging misunderstandings:

They said that you should have holidays, and nobody defined what sort of holidays, you know, how expensive? (P3.110)

I think the problem wasn't defined in the first place. (D2.08)

They are using the word 'friend' and 'friendship' in different ways. (F1.52)

Some questioned the premises of certain arguments:

I didn't think you could sell a washing machine second-hand. (P1.194)

The other thing is that it varies with time. People's expectations were different in the 1930s, and no doubt, you know, people's expectations in the year 2,000 are going to be different again. So the definition is going to change. (P3.11)

In general, many demanded more detailed information to be satisfied with the arguments offered:

But with this programme you didn't get enough information. (D2.25)

For some, the variety of information offered undermined rational discussion:

He started off with so many different things that it was almost pointless to discuss it in the first place, it is utter nonsense, you know, you can't do it. You are starting with so much different material that you can't compare it. (F1.51)

Others saw this more positively, for the diversity of opinions and lack of linear argument structure gives viewers more freedom to form opinions:

> At least in this you can, you know, you have got at least more possibilities for making your own mind up, in an unbiased sort of sense. (P3.98)

The debate between respondents about coverage reflected the underlying debate about the value of ordinary talk: either ordinary people are seen as offering a diversity of views from which one makes up one's own mind or as offering a series of biased and blinkered accounts which fail to add up to a coherent whole:

> But all we hear on this kind of programme was what people think of their own situations, and presumably it can be very biased. (P3.99)

Some were concerned that if diversity is valued, it becomes difficult to place boundaries on relevant contributions and to screen out the irrelevant:

> It was irrelevant really whether there were colours or white, they were poverty stricken, and this is the point. (P4.29)

Sometimes these concerns may mask other, more ideological concerns about relevance:

> But nobody mentioned the fact that the expectations of poverty are very much raised by what we are led to believe we should have, by advertising, the media. (P1.117)

Offering diversity also undermines the depth of argument:

> Yes, it's not an in-depth thing, it's just airing people things, full stop. It's very very shallow and one can't expect a great deal out of it. (P4.136)

> I wonder if it is that nobody is really doing any thinking. Even the people in the programme were asked to answer some very simple questions. (F1.132)

The lack of argument development was also attributable to the host's strategy:

> People were tending to go on, and he was stopping them at the initial question. He wouldn't let them develop it and go onto a second stage, which as far as they were concerned was probably the more important question because they were trying to develop the argument. (P1.180)

> Obviously the main concern of the presenter was to get in as much case history and people, presumably because this is what the viewers are going to find interesting. And any philosophical sort of points would barely apply and were brushed aside. (P3.30)

Yet discussions are not always easily managed. Certain individuals may dominate, undermining diversity without necessarily adding depth:

One or two people were allowed to dominate the discussion and not allow other people to speak when they had a different point of view to put. (P2.03)

If very broadly defined, some topics are simply 'too big' for the available time and resources:

I think that you are covering an enormous subject, in quite a short space of time really. There were so many reasons why you were poor, why they were landed in that situation in the first place. (P4.38)

And, inevitably, time is limited, which some felt undermined the breadth and depth of arguments:

The scope of the programme was very limited, the time was limited. (D2.155)

For some respondents, these combined problems resulted in a general lack of credibility, or even a sense of unreality which made one lose confidence in the arguments:

It was like something out of Monty Python, those two women who used to read in the launderette. (D2.29)

I think sometimes they give a sort of phoney look of well, that it's all above board and legit, give it a bit more authenticity. (SC.183)

Argument coherence was generally of less concern than argument coverage or depth. Coherence, for our respondents, referred to the broad problem of order versus chaos, rather than to aspects of argument structure:

These sort of things, well it was mumbo jumbo, and I find it difficult to select the important things to go into the mind. (P4.132)

Unfortunately you always get that on those sort of programmes, I just get lost, there is so much banter going on that you lose eventually what is being said. (D4.66)

One comment, however, suggests that a good argument should move from the evidence of individual cases towards general conclusions:

I felt that they personally talked about 'when I was in hospital I had this terrible thing', which is fine, but you expect them to do that, but I think I'm right in saying practically none of them went beyond that to generalise about problems with the Health Service Constraints, government policy, the pressures on GP's which are enormous, etc. (D3.13)

For others, a good argument was one they agreed with, one which reflected their own opinions:

There was something in what she said, that the quality of life for her children was quite important. (P2.31)

People often used themselves as the measure of the worth of the programme: had they themselves been convinced or moved by the arguments:

> I don't know, it didn't really do a lot for me, the programme, I had no faith in either side of the argument. (P4.29)

There was considerable interest in the way that arguments were concluded. The frequent absence of conclusions can itself be regarded positively or negatively, depending on respondents' implicit notions of programme worth:

> Now what he says is, so we can do this or do that, but there is no ending to the programme. They are all the same, and in the end I think that they get boring. (D1.56)

> Towards the end I was thinking, I wish they would just resolve something! Just tell us one thing that they think would be better that they could do constructively. (D2.186)

> You are left to draw your own conclusions. I think that it is just getting the best out of people and encouraging them to give their own opinions, which is a strong point of the programme I think. (P4.12)

People's attitude towards the lack of conclusiveness depends also on their understanding of the genre: if it is seen as a debate, conclusions are expected:

> I don't think it really is a form of debate, because there's no drawing together of conclusion or, one side of an argument and then the other side of an argument. (D3.55)

But if programmes are seen as providing a forum for informal discussion, then the imposition of rules of procedure as in formal debates would be inappropriate:

> Nobody there is in a position to say, 'well, it should be this way,' or the other way. It was just a discussion with people saying what they think, isn't it? And nobody can actually say, 'well yes, it should be, or shouldn't be'. (D4.147)

Judgements of argument quality depend, then, on the perceived genre of the programmes – on the perceived social context for the argument. Viewers may compare the discussions with the formal procedures for argumentation in the debate. Or they may see the argument as an informal conversation. Different argument forms presume different criteria for their validity claims – crudely, critical appraisal of how well the rules for procedural debate are followed compared with assessment of the involvement and expression of diverse voices. Moreover, these would have quite different social functions in the public sphere: one is related to the public criticism of the system world; the other to the public expression of diversity in the life-world and to a view about the possible social effects of discourse.

CONCLUSIONS

In his theory of communicative action, Habermas (1987b) draws upon a universal pragmatics to contend that all utterances include implicit validity claim to truth, truthfulness and appropriateness as well as comprehensibility. The cognitive use of language has propositional content, thus making the claims to truth (the rationality of which lies in the rules of argument, assertion and proof) into a lay epistemology which can be checked against the experience of the listener. The interactive use of language constructs interpersonal relations, thus making claims to rightness or appropriateness, whose rationality lies in the rules of justification and social norms. The expressive use of language reveals the speaker's intentions, making sincerity claims, whose rationality lies in the obligation to demonstrate truthfulness. Rationality, then, lies in the potential for testing and criticizing these various validity claims.

In our analysis of both programme discussions and viewers' reception, these three concerns focus our assessment of the rationality of the arguments. First, studio and home audiences repeatedly check statements against their own experience and knowledge, and they are critical when the grounds are inadequate to substantiate the truth of the claims, when qualifications are not answered, and so on. Second, through the rhetorical justifications offered by participants and viewers, we see how the arguments raise difficulties for the management of social identities, where different social identities draw on different justifications to establish their truthfulness – the knowledgeable and professional expert, the authentic and experienced lay person, the controlling and skilful host, and the alert and perceptive studio/home audience. Third, only if this construction of social identity is successful, if the epistemological justification for one's contribution is accepted, can one assume the right to speak, the appropriateness of one's contribution, and the right to be attended to and taken seriously: those who speak out of place are roundly criticized.

More problematic is Habermas's opposition between communicative action, seen as oriented towards reaching a consensus about what is true, truthful and appropriate, and instrumental action which aims at controlling or manipulating people. Insofar as the audience discussion programme escapes Habermas's fears about the institutionalization of public discussion, this is not because the programmes achieve some ideal form of communication, such as the critical discussion, but rather because the programmes act communicatively as a forum for the expression of multiple voices or subject positions, and in particular, because they attempt to confront established power with the lived experience of ordinary people. In this they are, undoubtedly, extremely flawed, and viewers are highly critical of the arguments offered by these programmes. But the viewers are operating with Habermasian ideals, expecting to hear a rational discussion leading to a critical consensus.

The programmes appear more successful if we judge them by other criteria: they express a diversity of views on an issue and sometimes reach a compromise, as the oppositional public sphere model demands; as in the cultural forum, they place accounts of lived experience in the life-world alongside official explanations in order to expose the limitations of the regulatory/surveillance aspects of established power; and they attempt this demonstration of the practical difficulties the system creates for ordinary people without using institutionalized forms of expert–lay communication such as public opinion research, which rationalizes lived experience as mass opinion for the benefit of established power. In these ways, they address concerns over the relations between the system and the life-world.

Chapter 7

Studio discussions, social spaces and postmodernity

INTRODUCTION

We have suggested in this book that audience discussion programmes can be understood as part of social space, as places where people congregate for public discussion, even as a 'forum'. What kind of space is the audience discussion programme and what are its social implications for participants and for public discussion more broadly? Any space has an internal set of rules, roles and procedures and is constituted through the particular accomplishments of the actors. Furthermore, social spaces are also embedded in, and so constitutive of, the wider community. Their boundaries may vary in permeability over space and time: some spaces are genuinely public and offer open access to anyone, others are closed to all but a few. Some spaces are heavily rule-governed and restrict opportunities according to criteria of status or power, while others are more open to negotiation and flexibility. The constitution of a particular space, with particular rules of access and opportunity, also affects the meanings of other spaces.

Different societies may be characterized by the presence or absence of certain kinds of spaces, with implications for the understanding of citizenship, or the public, in these different societies. For the bourgeois public sphere, the space must offer equal access and equal opportunities to participants, and to the extent that it does not, it has been refeudalized: according to Habermas (1989) there is no space for the development and expression of critical consensus in contemporary society.

In this chapter, we consider audience discussion programmes as social space. For participants, we ask what kind of experience it is to appear on television. For viewers, we explore the idea of watching television as parasocial interaction – viewing 'as if' it were face-to-face interaction with the characteristics of primary social experience, asking whether the viewer is involved in the constitution of the audience discussion programme as an imaginary community and possibly as a public sphere. But, however far one takes these arguments, audience discussion programmes remain mediated spaces, subject to institutional control and management by the mass media.

AUDIENCE DISCUSSION PROGRAMMES AS CONVERSATION

At the centre of audience discussion programmes are conversations between ordinary people and representatives of established power. The public sphere depends on these conversations being genuine rather than manipulated, with rights of access and opportunity being institutionally protected rather than undermined, and resulting in critical rather than false consensus. Interestingly, both face-to-face conversation and television can be unfavourably compared with print media in that their speed and intimacy prioritizes trust and credibility over critical thought (Petty and Cacioppo, 1981; Pfau, 1990).

How can we analyse the conversations that occur on television? Schudson (1978) outlines five criteria for the American conversation ideal: continuous feedback between two people in a face-to-face setting; multichannel communication (hear, see, touch); spontaneous (and thus unique) utterances; each person is both sender and receiver of messages; norms of conversation are egalitarian (both follow same rules). Avery and McCain (1982) argue that these criteria are not met by 'conversation' on the mass media, even in talk shows and call-ins. Callers may be cut off and humiliated, they avoid calling shows where they disagree with the host's perspective, they lack visual information, and so forth.

However, while participation programmes fall short of these conversational ideals, so too, frequently do face-to-face conversations. There is a danger of idealizing everyday conversation and comparing that idealization to the realities of mass-communicated communication. In everyday conversation, feedback is not continuous but problematic, subject to misinterpretation, especially when more than two people are involved. A telephone conversation, which lacks both touch and vision, is generally regarded as real conversation, while television discussions provide both sound and vision. While on one level, all interactions are spontaneous and unique, conversations are highly rule-governed, frequently repetitive, and commonly used to repeat handed-down or unoriginal ideas (i.e. common sense).

In many conversations, the roles of sender and receiver may be unbalanced – it's hard to be the sender when talking to a 'gossip'. More subtly, textual theories of communication challenge the roles of sender and receiver, for senders take into account the anticipated responses of receivers, even on television, and receivers may make creative and diverse interpretations of messages sent. In practice, interpersonal and mass communication interact: the receiver of a television message may be the sender in the living room who then alters the interpretations of other receivers who may then in turn shout back at the television or turn it off. Finally, the ideal that sender and receiver should be bound by the same interactional rules – who can interrupt, or make jokes, or disagree – does not occur in many face-to-face conversations. Conversations where participants are differentiated by gender, generation, status, or power, all place different demands on the participants, who speak with different voices reflecting a variety of subject positions.

THE EXPERIENCE OF APPEARING ON AUDIENCE DISCUSSION PROGRAMMES

Let us begin our analysis of audience discussion programmes as social space by exploring the experience of ordinary people on these programmes. People are sometimes confused about the experience of appearing on television; after all there are few cultural representations with which to frame their experience. Not all participants are naive and overwhelmed:

> I've done quite a lot of public speaking of one description or another so I think I managed to get the point across. I don't think I made very good studio audience material because I talk too fast, but I think I made the point that I wanted to make.
>
> (Tony, studio audience)

Tony is aware of the skills required, but is mainly concerned with making his point in public. Although 'British people are becoming less and less nervous about what they say on television' (John Stapleton, host of *The Time, The Place*, speaking on TV Weekly, ITV, 19 November 1992), some still experience difficulties:

> I chickened out really. It was towards the end of the show when I bubbled up enough to think 'yeah, I ought to say something, this is ridiculous,' but it was literally within the last five minutes of the show and I put my hand up to speak as he was coming down but I deliberately didn't look at him so he didn't pick me which was a bit stupid so I chickened out basically. I was too scared basically, the sweat was pouring out of me.
>
> (James, studio audience)

Some studio audience members appear on the programmes not intending to speak: 'I automatically assumed that I wouldn't be speaking, so I didn't really think about the topic at all' (Ruth). Others try to find a way into the discussion and may not manage what the experts also acknowledge to be the difficult task of timing one's intervention, catching the host's eye, getting a microphone, speaking to the point, not being cut off or interrupted, and so forth. The lay participants are given some encouragement and instructions about the rules before the programme:

> Mike Scott said 'we like a lively debate, please don't be too polite, it makes good television if people are actually a bit rude and forget their British reserve and actually just push in, talk on top of each other, so please don't be typically Brits, don't be reserved, if you feel strongly then please speak up'.
>
> (Alice, studio audience)

Kilroy said 'just relax, and just say what you want,' and he said he apologized in advance that if he pushed anyone by trying to get round the studio don't take it personally, 'if I try to sit down beside you and shove the microphone across you don't get offended'. He said 'if you've got a point to make just say it and hopefully I'll hear you and come running round,' and he said 'just speak freely and try to join in as much as you want'.

(Margaret, studio audience)

The floor manager had said about carrying on the conversation, making sure that we didn't trip him over, making sure that we didn't shout over anybody else, put our hands up and were nice and polite about the way we carried out the discussion. I think he said something about swearing, that we shouldn't swear too much because the audience wouldn't like it. He was trying to portray the idea that he was facilitating a discussion amongst the audience and that he wanted us to address points to each other rather than to him.

(Martin, studio audience)

We asked people what they gained from participating in a studio-audience discussion. They differed in whether they felt the interaction to be genuine:

I think if I hadn't already known a number of 'media people' I would have learnt something about what media is about and how artificial the whole thing is but I knew that these shows are rigged and I knew the way the audiences were set out and this sort of thing so I think personally I didn't learn very much.

(Tony, studio audience)

I'm glad I had a chance to say it, because even if it doesn't make any difference to the litter problem at least I've vented my spleen and I feel I've done something, I've got my anger and frustration out on television and who knows it might do some good in the long term.

(Alice, studio audience)

Margaret did not go with a particular aim in mind, rather she was just making up the numbers but things still worked out in such a way that she made a contribution:

It just happened it was really apt with my particular situation at the time, and I had a lot to get off my chest in a way. And so, it just happened at the beginning they were talking about marriage, and I didn't feel quite that what I had to say would be relevant, and then it just happened that there was an opportunity where what I had to say was fitting and part of it.

For Margaret it was not a matter of changing the world but of gaining social support for herself, which she felt to be successful. For some, the occasion was too nerve-racking for any contribution:

Every time I went to say something or . . . I didn't even muster up enough courage because every time I went to say something my heart would have gone bump, bump . . . I started getting very nervous, so I didn't actually, I felt 'oh no, it's too much stress to actually say something,' because I was very aware that I was on camera.

(Ruth, studio audience)

Participation is clearly an emotional experience:

I leant forward and just made a comment because he was sitting right next to him and it couldn't be avoided and then he came and sort of sat round next to me and we had this conversation for maybe three or four interchanges and I just felt really angry, I was almost shaking with anger from what he'd said because he was talking about morals and ethics and young people and being incredibly patronising and didn't know what he was talking about and he obviously wanted to be sensational so I can remember sitting there and thinking 'how can I look threatening?' so I sat there and went '. . .', like that.

(Martin, studio audience)

For James, *Donahue*'s topic of toyboys was experienced through his feelings about his parents' divorce:

I have personally had my family break up over, not over a toyboy as it goes, but over affairs and things like that which I wasn't too happy about. But then if somebody had come along and said 'do you think people should be able to work at a marriage they can't stand and live together in a hostile environment for even longer?' I'd obviously turn round and say 'no, it's silly,' the idea of making two people who can't stand each other live together is absurd, guaranteed to lead to violence and animosity so it was that sort of outlook which I didn't have at that time and nobody on that panel really offered that, otherwise I would have perhaps thought about it a bit more after the show, it was all sort of running round the bedroom having a good laugh sort of thing and that we should all live with people and have a good time.

SELF-DISCLOSURE ON TELEVISION

Nonviewers of discussion programmes are often concerned with the invasion of privacy which may result from expressing personal revelations and emotions in a public place. However, viewers were unconcerned: they felt all topics were legitimate, and focused more on the value of personal expression for the public sphere and for heightening the sense of involvement and authenticity. As discussed in Chapter 5, viewers are more concerned that studio audience participants were representative, so that valid conclusions could be drawn from their contributions. Nonviewers interpret the programmes as offering isolated accounts of personal experience in the context of a chaotic chorus. For viewers, the programme is experienced as an integrated whole so that from the retelling of a series of personal stories, significant results may emerge – the construction of public opinion, the expression of the repressed or culturally invisible, the valorization of lay experience, etc.

The issue of public self-disclosure is complex. One can distinguish between revealing consensually defined 'personal' facts or taboos about oneself (concerning sex, relationships, illness, money) from revealing facts which, for whatever idiosyncratic reason, are emotionally difficult to say. The difficulties – and the thrills – audiences may experience on hearing self-disclosure by others may result either from hearing taboo issues aired in public, which even though readily volunteered by the speaker may be difficult for the hearer, or from hearing facts which the speaker finds emotionally difficult to express. Self-disclosure may thus arouse emotions in the hearer or may make the hearer bear witness to emotions in the speaker.

REFLECTIONS ON PARTICIPATION

Reflecting on their participation after appearing on television, studio audience members differed in whether they felt the conversation to have been genuine. For some, the end of the programme was by no means the end of the experience:

> So we went back in the lift down to the reception area and they had orange, wine, peanuts, light stuff. But people were talking about it. Because by the end of the programme, more people were wanting to join in. In fact the whole programme came to life, so people were still on a bit of a high and still wanted to talk about it, and pick up on some of the comments they'd heard other people make. And so I had a couple of people say 'ah, you've gone through a bit, I went through a similar thing' or, you know, I made a couple of comments to people like 'that's really good the comment you made'. It wasn't as though the programme finished therefore the discussion finished – it continued.

> (Margaret, studio audience)

Others felt that the constraints of the genre prevented spontaneous interaction:

> I felt that we were placed there a few minutes before, we hadn't really had time to settle in to the surroundings, to even discuss or talk to people before hand. I felt as though I knew no-one there. And so it wasn't like a real discussion, because no ice was broken, so to speak. Even the way it's set out you have the seats facing cameras, every one is facing forward. To talk to someone you have to look over the other side of the audience, it's not like any other situation we're usually in really. Whenever we're discussing

something you're sitting opposite someone and you're in a much more informal situation.

(Ruth, studio audience)

It felt very artificial to me, I don't usually have conversations with someone sitting in front of me with their back to me. Apart from anything else it gives you a very strange, peculiar kind of experience.

(Martin, studio audience)

As 'we didn't have any introduction to anyone' and 'we'd had very little information about what they wanted us to do' (Martin, studio audience), participants were playing by unknown rules. Nonetheless, this meant that both experts and lay people entered the discussion without advance planning of their contribution beyond possibly a general sense of the main point(s), resulting in a sense of involvement in a real conversation where their contribution emerges spontaneously out of the discussion:

You had more of a sense of real conversation, real interchange and I thought therefore that it was probably serving an educational function . . . There was no barracking, there was a sense of a real attempt of arguing with each other. I thought Kilroy induced that quite deliberately and also quite successfully so in a sense he switched the conversation around but he'd try on the whole to keep things going, he got people to make points that were germane to what was under discussion so it was very much more like putting business structure into what could actually have been a bar room brawl but actually became a bar room conversation. Not totally dissimilar to the sort of conversations that do from time to time take place in bars, but with more structure and slightly more discipline. Very much less artificial than from having politicians talking and I thought that politicians actually began to behave slightly differently in that atmosphere.

(Expert 5, academic in government)

Participants do not always stay involved: 'after that I felt "oh right, great, I've had my say" and I switch off then, I thought "right, let everybody else get on with it" ' (Martin, studio audience), but of course this can also be true for face-to-face interaction.

This level of spontaneity attests to the informal character of the audience discussion programme as social situation. It is a place where people go to become involved in a personal conversation in a public space, where self-disclosure and argument intertwine in a tournament that privileges a private voice for a brief time. Corner identifies the 'radical revelatory' consequences of the documentary, where viewers are 'put in touch with one another by revealing infrastructural relations of interdependence' (Corner, 1986: x). To the extent that a conversation is generated in the studio, this radical revelatory aspect is surely all the more powerful in the audience discussion programme, where ordinary people are put in touch with each other in a direct, immediate and spontaneous manner.

PARASOCIAL INTERACTION

In parasocial interaction (Horton and Wohl, 1956), the audience has the experience of face-to-face communication when watching television. This 'intimacy at a distance' is such that people count television characters, especially television personas such as talk show hosts, amongst their friends and family: '*Oprah* viewers, for example, feel quite comfortable greeting their favorite host with comments on her current hairstyle, clothing or weight' (Cerulo et al. 1992: 120). The informal, ritualized and interactive style of talk show hosts encourages this – a conversational style of speech, a direct gaze at the camera, giving the audience an apparent role in an 'interaction' (M. Levy, 1982). The audience know what to expect, they have a role to play, and as neighbourhood ties are reduced, 'parasocial' interactions become an increasing source of intimate bonds:

> The para-social relationship develops over time and is based in part on a history of 'shared' experiences . . . .the daily 'visit' of the newscaster is valued by the viewer, perhaps because the news persona, like a friend, brings gossip.
>
> (Ibid: 180)

The rapid technological changes in electronic media (fax, car-phone, cable and satellite television) challenge us to characterize primary social relationships in terms of their functions for the individual rather than their institutional forms, in part an artefact of particular technological forms. Primary social groups must be defined not only in terms of their psychological functions but also in terms of social space and social relations. Recent institutional and technological changes in the mass media may, it is argued, enable them to play a more positive role in constituting social relations rather than being a mass of isolated individuals:

> Technological and cultural developments in the structure of the mass media – developments fully implemented during the 1980s – have drastically changed the nature of a mass communication. These changes have enabled the mass media to become a new source of primary group affiliations . . . that provide social members with a sense of identity and purpose, strong and enduring emotional bonds, and a source of immediate social control.
>
> (Cerulo et al. 1992: 109)

Audience discussion programmes may substitute for coffee mornings, chats with friends or gossip and, 'with regular viewing, combined with the call-in capability of such shows, the common interests and opinions of both host and audience members become crystallized. As a result, people become identified on the basis of their talk-show affiliations' (ibid.: 115–16).

IMAGINARY PLACES

There is a sense in which the social world is transformed as social relations are removed from public occasions and institutions and placed in the private living rooms of viewers. The informal organization of the social world is transformed from a 'real' to an 'imagined' community (Anderson, 1991) and community involvement changes from public participation to private consumption. In *No Sense of Place*, Meyrowitz (1985) suggests that 'the evolution of media has decreased the significance of physical presence in the experience of people and events' (ibid: vii). Mass communication collapses space and time such that we can witness events which are distant from us or which would previously have taken time to communicate and the traditional barriers and spaces of social life – both public and domestic – have been penetrated by the broadcast media:

> The family home is now a less bounded and unique environment because of family members' access and accessibility to other places and other people through radio, television, and telephone.
>
> (Meyrowitz, 1985: vii)

The decoupling of space and time in modern mediated communication (Giddens, 1985) also detaches psychological experiences from specific contexts and locations, breaking down traditional social structures and relations. Social space is no longer constituted through physical settings but rather through imaginary communities which mix physical and mediated situations and, consequently, mix interpersonal and mass mediated communication. While traditional social structures were enshrined in different communicative contexts for people from alternative social groups, generations and genders, this mapping of the social onto different locales has been blurred particularly by the broadcast media.

For example, Meyrowitz draws on Goffman's (1981) concern with overhearing by multiple audiences to note that adopting mass mediated forms of communication disturbs our ability to communicate strategically to different audiences. Children have access to 'adult' conversation, men may listen to women's issues discussed on 'women's programmes', politicians cannot say one thing to one constituency and something else to another. In the audience discussion programme, a media event occurs which would not have occurred in any other space–time dimension and so the space created is unlike any other. It is inconceivable that the meetings we see daily on audience discussion programmes would have occurred spontaneously during the course of unmediated social interaction.

Following Alexander's (1990) analysis of the role of inconsistencies in social progress, we suggest that one consequence of these new media events (Katz and Dayan, 1985) is that the media do not establish shared meanings so much as make visible inconsistencies in meaning across particular locations or material conditions. For example, through accounts of ordinary people's experiences, audience discussion programmes express inconsistencies in current social arrangements, showing how existing institutional categories fail to accommodate lay concerns. The expression of such inconsistencies is part of the dialectic relationship between institutionally encoded meanings and everyday experience – representing not the legitimation crisis but a moment in the unfolding relationship between theory and practice.

SOCIAL SPACE

The physical limits of the human body place a set of spatial and temporal constraints on the social construction of place and on the social actions possible within it (Giddens, 1985; Hägerstrand, 1967).

> Time–geography is concerned with the infrastructural constraints that shape the routines of day-to-day life, and shares with structuration theory an emphasis upon the significance of the practical character of daily activities, in circumstances where individuals are co-present with one another, for the constitution of social conduct.
>
> (Giddens, 1985: 269)

Hägerstrand shows how the trajectories of individual actors over different time periods intersect in 'time–space maps'. Thus in audience discussion programmes we see that the participants are each on very different paths and they have to influence the joint accomplishment of the social occasion as best they can to fit in with their plans. Consistent with notions of the oppositional public sphere (Fraser, 1990), participants with different life projects negotiate the relationship between their interests and those of others. Whatever the outcome, participants then return to their own life projects (Giddens, 1985, 1991).

The studio discussion has characteristics both of proximate forms of communication, based on all members being co-present in the same locale and engaged in traditional face-to-face communication, and of new, distanced forms of communication across locales through the transmission of the discussion to a mass audience. The space is defined by the relations established between different categories of participant – home and studio audience, expert and laity, host and guest. Giddens appropriates Goffman's (1959) distinction between front and back (or public and private), together with that of disclosure and enclosure (the covering up or open display of information), to analyse the boundaries used to organize social spaces.

In audience discussion programmes, the space is partly organized so as to manage and integrate the disclosure of personal experience and official analysis, getting people together who in the unmediated playing out of social life would never talk to each other. In what other public space could a mother living in bed-and-breakfast accommodation talk to a member of government? Where else could a patient with a grievance discuss it with a representative of the British Medical Association?

The programmes are ostensibly constructed as the 'front', 'where the action is', the place where the laity can publicly express grievances and bring officials to account, where interest groups can contest the definition of social problems, and where official bodies can publicly display the positive aspects of their organizations. This management of disclosure controls public and official access to information and expression. By such outrageous juxtaposition of representatives of established power and the laity the media offer themselves as both a forum for contemporary society and as an implicit critique of existing social arrangements.

However, as in any television programme, the view presented to the viewer hides the mechanisms of production. The viewer gets a partial view of the space in which the discussion takes place. The 'front' that the viewer sees disguises the 'back' which contains all the means of production of the image. Here the front/back distinction maps onto the space as perceived by the viewer and the space as part of the media institution, limiting what is disclosed to the viewer. Disclosure/enclosure is also mediated through time: there are various activities before and after filming, some of which take place in ante-rooms and some of which take place 'off camera': switching on the cameras transforms the space into a public sphere visible to all.

The space created by this genre is also constituted through its relations with other genres and other spaces. In the audience discussion programme, we have a bounded region of access. As ordinary people and representatives of established power demand access, the media make available a backwater, a trivial and unimportant realm of television. People can now be said to have a say in the production of television but that say is strictly bounded and therefore contained from spreading and polluting the rest of the broadcast media. Thus the managed show of participation is partly achieved by locating participation in a particular region of television. The programmes are liminal spaces through which citizens pass, form temporary coalitions and then return to their social identities.

Analysing the space created by the programmes requires us to consider these programmes both as regions of television and as constituting a locale of their own with regional division within the programme. Multiple comparisons of front/back and disclosure/enclosure are possible when analysing occasions that have 'traditional' authenticity in terms of the product (a conversation, a critical discussion) but which are constructed and disseminated in a very 'modern' way (with distributed and shifting locales, with communication at a distance).

Thus the programmes are both locale and region, front and back, private and public, disclosing and enclosing, communicated through co-presence and through distance. They exemplify what Harvey (1989) terms 'time–space compression', a central characteristic of the organization of social space in postmodern or late-capitalist society. Just as the problems of mass production (Fordism) and Keynesian economics demanded the speeding up of turnover time and a relaxation of economic regulation, so too is the media under similar pressure. Audience discussion programmes suit this change: they are cheap to produce and respond quickly to changes in current affairs. They represent the postmodern version of public debate, claiming the advantages of broader participation and relevance but vulnerable to the criticisms of being fleeting and superficial.

LIMINAL SPACES

Television is part of popular or 'low' culture, and cheap, daytime programmes are its 'lowest' form. As a space it therefore has the characteristics of marginal or liminal spaces – spaces which have 'a history of transformations between being margins, near-sacred *liminal zones* of Otherness, and carnivalesque leisure spaces of ritual inversion of the dominant, authorised cultures' (Shields, 1991: 5–6). Audience discussion programmes are marginal spaces both in the sense of being low culture and because they too offer a carnivalesque opposition to everyday life. Placing together ordinary people and representatives of established power in the same space and with similar rights is, if not an inversion of authority, at least a suspension of it.

This social space has the potential for both the reproduction of existing beliefs, representations and practices and the transformation of traditional social forms through the construction of a public sphere which mediates between established power (via argument and accountability) and everyday experience (via story-telling). The cultural significance of constructions of social space, mediated or not, is complex. Following Bakhtin (1981), Shields suggests that social space is in dialogue with its audience (including the researcher). While we are familiar with the idea of television programmes treated as a dialogue, 'as Bakhtin has shown, dialogic processes proliferate in any complexly represented discursive space . . . . Many voices clamour for expression . . . monophonic authority is questioned, revealed to be characteristic of a science that has claimed to *represent* cultures' (Clifford and Marcus, 1986: 14–15).

Thus the communicative relationship between researcher and object of research is incorporated into the discursive structure of participatory programming. The relationship between the text and the audience is now a dialogue which may expose the claims of media to represent reality and disseminate information. On another level, the media offer space for a dialogue between representatives of established power and of the life-world. For Shields (1991), these dialogues challenge traditional distinctions between theory and observation or between social representation and social practice. As with critical hermeneutics, the participatory programme encodes a critical position which attempts to overcome the insular concerns of established power and the life-world. For Habermas the dangers of opening a dialogue between representatives of the life-world and the system world are those of colonization and corruption, refeudalizing the public sphere and transforming publicity into public relations. However, this dialogue may also afford opportunities for accountability, the identification of contradictions between policy/expertise and everyday life, space for ordinary people to generate and validate common experiences, and so forth.

MEDIATED SPACE AND POSTMODERNITY

Any attempt to explicate unambiguously the political and social functions of the genre of audience discussion programmes must be doomed. Following Giddens we have emphasized the multiple levels of influence in the production, accomplishment and transmission of audience discussion programmes and in their relation to social structure. Fraser has emphasized the complexity of an oppositional public sphere dedicated to the expression of multiple voices. Mouffe has shown the decomposition of political identity and protest which results from the different subject positions adopted, we suggest, in audience discussion programmes. Harvey emphasizes the rapid turnover in media products which collapses space and time and makes all ideas available to all of the people all of the time. Our discussion of argument in discussion programmes reveals the plurality of discourses and forms of argumentation used in these programmes, reflecting the post-structuralist focus on the interplay of multiple discourses. Our analysis of the genre of these pro- grammes reveals the shifting influence of diverse conventions – from the debate, the romance, therapy, and doubtless others. Similarly, contradictory assumptions about knowledge, ordinary experience and expertise were found to be in negotiation throughout the interactions observed between expert and lay participants in studio discussions. In the present chapter we have examined the audience discussion in terms of social space, arguing that the relations between studio space and the living room or between front and back are complex, as are the rules which organize interactions within and across these spaces.

In this section, we explore more broadly how audience discussion programmes form part of the popular culture being produced in late-capitalist or postmodern society:

> This landscape of the present, with its embracing of pastiche, its small
> defiant pleasure in being dressed up or 'casual', its exploration of

fragmented subjectivity – all this articulates more precisely with the wider conditions of present reality – with unemployment, with education, the 'aestheticisation of culture', and with the coming into being of those whose voices were historically drowned out by the (modernist) metanarratives of mastery, which were in turn both patriarchal and imperialist.

(McRobbie, 1986: 109–10)

Arguing against the pessimism of poststructuralist writers such as Baudrillard (1988), who see in the rapid expansion of communicative technology into everyday life an imperialistic penetration of everyday life by consumerism, McRobbie (1986), among others, argues that postmodern conditions offer new opportunities to groups previously without a voice. Under these conditions, the media may play a central role, facilitating a plurality of previously repressed voices and subject positions. However, as our empirical observations cannot 'test' the different positions on the emancipatory potential of the media as a public sphere, it remains problematic that giving voice may not affect real decision making and power relations in society, but only give the illusion of participation: participants may act and feel involved, but only as consumers in a managed show rather than as authenticated through processes in the life-world.

We suggest that audience discussion programmes deconstruct the opposition between the expression of diverse voices and the managed show or controlled illusion of participation: they represent a site for the playing out of the postmodern condition. The programmes express many diverse subject positions – personified in the lay participants, experts and host – including the position of the neutral critic, of established systemic power and of the media institution. Thus the studio debates instantiate the broader debate between the post-structural view and that of the crisis of modernism. When we analyse audience discussion programmes we see them to be a result of the clash of the opposition between expression and control, among other oppositions, in a negotiated public sphere: the programmes both exist in a space structured by these oppositions and are a play on them.

The very form of audience discussion programmes is anti-genre and a host of oppositions traditionally used to analyse the mass media are deconstructed by these programmes, including text/audience, production/reception, sender/ receiver, interpersonal/mass communication, information/entertainment, hot/cold and critical/involved. Audience discussion programmes, like most television (Eco, 1990), represent the moving away from reporting of an external reality to a self-referencing and self-constituting system. The audience discussion contributes to this trend by bringing what used to occur in private conversation into the public realm of the media. It is also highly intertextual in its discussion of issues from news and current affairs broadcasting:

The implications of this endless cross-referencing are extensive. They create an ever-increasing, but less diverse verbal and visual landscape. It is these recurring fictions, and the characters who inhabit them which feed into the field of popular knowledge, and which in turn constitute a large part of popular culture.

(McRobbie, 1986: 111)

In the audience discussion programme we observe the media appropriation of conversation, public opinion, protest and political accountability, all tailored to a daily programme slot and thereby intertwined with the rest of popular culture. To the extent that social and political opinion acts as a constraint on political, economic and social decision makers, this process is increasingly managed within popular culture. For example, Sontag (1967) shows how pastiche has been appropriated by homosexual artists as a platform for a more vociferous, politicized gay community. Similarly, even if the audience discussion is in some ways a parody of the serious public sphere advocated by Habermas, it still offers an opportunity not present under post-war political and social civic culture for minority groups, protest groups and ordinary people to gain access to mediated communication.

It is no surprise that access and participation programmes do not fit established generic conventions, but rather borrow from traditional information and entertainment genres: there is little place for the ordinary voice in current affairs, news or sitcoms, but their mixture creates new possibilities. Thus the privileged, elite form of political criticism envisaged by Habermas and the traditional left has been overwhelmed by the growth of popular culture, and the notion of emancipation through an organized public is replaced by the possibility of involvement in the endless mobilization and recycling of ideas, experiences and arguments in popular culture.

PARTICIPATORY MEDIA AND SOCIAL CHANGE

The idea that changes in popular cultural forms have a social and political impact is difficult to accept in an era when politics and welfare have become institutionalized and art is seen as bourgeois rather than revolutionary. Huyssen (1986) discusses how, during the post-war period, the cultural avant-garde has been appropriated and commoditized so as to perform a legitimating function for established power in the face of dissent.

While modernism involved an obsession with the machine analogy – rationalized, standardized and utopian – its early critical position, emphasizing liberation from serfdom, progress and the 'triumph of democracy', had evolved into the alienated and conservative ideology of the civic culture by the 1950s (Almond and Verba, 1980). Postmodernism challenges this through 'a reintroduction of multivalent symbolic dimensions into architecture, a mixing of codes, an appropriation of local vernaculars and regional codes' (Huyssen, 1986: 187). The codes are mixed in space and time and thus represent a schism from the rational progress of modernization. Because they look forwards and backwards, drawing on both abstract/ universal and concrete/local codes, on both high and low codes at the same time, the postmodern style has been called schizophrenic, but we can see how it is in sympathy with the multiple subject positions discussed by, for example, Mouffe and Fraser.

The new avantgarde of the 1960s was defined in terms of the 'technological imagination' (Huyssen, 1986). The concern with technology imbued the images of avantgarde art as well as its production processes. This use of technological images was part of the avantgarde's attempt to destroy the 'aura' of art which had allowed it to become separated from everyday life and thereby from social and political concerns (Benjamin, 1970), although as Huyssen argues, this radical criticism was also appropriated in support of modernism. While Benjamin was concerned with the use of art to shock people out of complacency, the German new avantgarde (for example, Brecht) saw art as having the potential to use critical rationality to demystify the cultural hegemony of bourgeois society.

In the audience discussion programme we can see both the use of emotionally shocking material to disrupt stereotypes and also a demand for a rational account from representatives of the established power. For Huyssen, this reading of the genre may be overly optimistic, for the attempt to disrupt stereotypes and challenge institutional legitimation is easily lost in the cacophony of noises and multiple images that characterize the modern mass media. However, maybe participatory media merely offer a new style of public opinion measurement – through the expression of voices rather than attitude measurement and opinion polls – which reflect the diversification of consumption rather than the devolution of power. As Huyssen suggests it is the culture industry (Adorno and Horkheimer, 1977) rather than the avantgarde that has shaped the landscape of the twentieth century, partly through the appropriation of avantgarde methods of shock and criticism so as to engage audiences.

Certainly, the new forms of cultural criticism which emerged from the avantgarde offered a transformation in social identity by opening up possibilities of political involvement for the ordinary person. Socially, postmodernism rejects the identification of modernism and progress with the white, middle-class male and is linked to a revalorization of popular culture and a celebration of the hidden voices that were seen to have survived in the context of popular culture although denied a place in the landscape of modernism. Being black, working class and female becomes a legitimate cultural subject position. The possibilities of creative collaboration between high and low art and the new profile that minority cultures gained within postmodernism, allow opportunities for a positive role for popular culture.

Yet we should also ask what has been lost by these changes in popular culture. After all, traditional forms of current-affairs programming, although elitist, were often capable of complex criticisms of established power. In Britain, the documentary has often been highly controversial (Corner, 1986). While providing a forum for discussion, the media are moving away from critical exposition and commentary. Letting ordinary people speak for themselves is replacing critically conscious social realism, an aesthetic that has informed much British drama programming as well as documentaries and current affairs (Hoggart, 1957; Jordan, 1981).

Of greater concern is the way in which these new forms of critical discourse can be seen as being rapidly appropriated by established power as part of the increasing penetration of the life-world by the system (Habermas, 1988). Making the elite more accountable to the public fitted with the populist conservative ideology, particularly of Thatcherite Britain and Reaganite America, diluting the power of the elite, making them no longer accountable only to themselves, challenging professional expertise and the power of the liberal middle classes over such diverse social institutions as education, the civil service, the academy, broadcasting and welfare. The backlash against the protest culture and the eclectic expression of multiple voices can be seen in the domination of conservative politics in Britain and America in the 1980s. The coexistence of postmodern culture and conservative politics has led to the cynical reaction of the left to the critical credentials of postmodernism (Huyssen, 1986). Whether or not there may be more radical, although possibly unintended, consequences of these transformations in popular culture remains an unresolved question:

> In an important sector of our culture there is a noticeable shift in sensibility, practices and discourse formations which distinguishes a postmodern set of assumptions, experiences, and propositions from that of a preceding period. What needs further exploration is whether this transformation has generated genuinely new aesthetic forms in the various arts or whether it mainly recycles techniques and strategies of modernism itself, reinscribing them into an altered cultural context.
>
> (Huyssen, 1986: 181)

CONCLUDING REMARKS

Throughout the book we have analysed the ways in which audience discussion programmes cut across various symbolic oppositions which have traditionally been encoded in the mass media as representations and legitimations of the social order. The first of these is the distinction between the public and the private spheres. A key dimension of the crisis of modernity is the problematic separation of these spheres through the creation of elite institutions which have tended to deprive the public of a voice in establishing standards of truth, morality and beauty. According to critical theory, the mass media support this separation and so support elite institutions by diverting the attention of the public from involvement in the public sphere, positioning them as consumers of entertainment.

Information versus entertainment is the principal dimension of television genres, separating news/current affairs from entertainment/drama. In terms of social order, this dimension reflects the distinction between those institutions of established power concerned with the public sphere and with the market. Fraser (1989, 1990) suggests that this distinction can be understood in terms of institutions that treat the individual as part of the public to be governed and those that treat the individual as a consumer to be exploited economically. This is further reflected in the distinction between public-service and commercial television. Habermas (Holub, 1991) suggests that the separation of the political and the commercial into autonomous regions of the system-world is uncritical and, following critical theory, we can suggest that the media have traditionally supported this separation by expressing this distinction as common sense.

Corner has recently suggested that 'critical' audience research mirrors the separation between public and official concerns by subdividing into studies of current affairs (the 'public knowledge project') and of audience involvement (the 'popular culture project'). Research into current affairs is 'concerned primarily with the media as an agency of public knowledge and 'definitional' power, with a focus on news and current affairs output and a direct connection with the politics of information and the viewer as citizen' (Corner, 1991: 268). Corner suggests that the popular culture project

> is concerned primarily with the implications for social consciousness of the media as a source of entertainment and is thereby connected with the social problematics of 'taste' and of pleasure (for instance those concerning class and gender) within industrialized popular culture.
>
> (Ibid: 268)

If we define critical knowledge as the exploration and perception of connections between the separate spheres of established power, then neither television conceived as a whole in the way it organizes its genres nor audience research in the way it pursues either the public knowledge project or the popular culture project constitutes critical knowledge.

The subject positions offered to the audience through information and entertainment genres are the receipt of information or involved emotional expression – reality or escape. Thus the public as they appear on television are traditionally represented as the objects of newsreel footage or as the demented screaming audience and participants of game shows. That audience discussion programmes do not fit into this opposition of information and entertainment casts a critical light over existing approaches to media research. In the audience discussion programme, elements of, for example, the game show and the current affairs programme merge. These programmes are 'intergenre'.

Consequently, distinct subject positions for representatives of established power and the lay public are challenged.

The exploration of connections between the cognitive and the emotional realms of the public sphere and the market is achieved through collapsing the dimension of the system and the life-world. It is by bringing together representatives of the system and the life-world, making each speak to the other, that the separation of established power and the life-world may be undermined. For Habermas, the potential for overcoming the legitimation crisis which results from the separation of the life-world and the system world is linked to the formation of critical consensus in the life-world. Communication between representatives of the system world and the life-world establishes links between those realms and so potentially generates critical knowledge which could overcome the separation of these realms.

The public/private dimension may also be collapsed, in both the system and the life-world, through the processes of story-telling and accountability. Members of the public are invited to tell their private stories in public, undermining the distinction between private and public in the life-world. Similarly, by holding them accountable, representatives of established power are asked to reveal and examine the relations between policy and professional or commercial interests. Through our examination of audience discussion programmes, we suggest that the particular rhetorical forms of story-telling and accountability collapse the public/private distinction both in the life-world (asserting that the person is political) and in the system world (asserting that policy is influenced by interest). To Habermas's call for the establishment of a public sphere which has the potential to generate critical consensus in the public, we can add a call for communicative conventions linked to narrative and inquiry or negotiation which may support a potentially emancipatory public sphere.

Throughout this book, our main concern has been with audience discussion programmes as social occasions. We have characterized performance in such programmes as organized around both the expression of diverse voices and legitimation. The two performative modes of the programmes are story-telling and debate. Story-telling links a variety of themes: expression of personal experience, the personification of social issues and problems, providing relevance, and giving voice to the various, often marginalized, groupings of the life-world. Debate makes established power accountable to personal experience, providing the opportunity for legitimation through consent together with the danger of discovery. The opposition between these two performances reflects those oppositions between the concrete and the abstract, the disempowered and the powerful, lived-in experience and expertise.

Data collection

In these appendices we outline the research methods used in this book. Further details are available from the authors.

FOCUS GROUPS

> The goal in using focus groups is to get closer to participants' under-standings of the researcher's topic of interest . . . Focus groups are useful when it comes to investigating *what* participants think, but they excel at uncovering *why* participants think as they do.
>
> (Morgan, 1988: 24–5, italics in original)

Twelve focus group discussions (69 people in groups of four to eight) were held following viewing of an audience discussion programme in order to explore people's critical response. Eleven groups were held in Oxford during September 1989 and respondents were contacted through the University Subject panel. The twelfth group was conducted in December 1991 in the Outer Hebrides. The number of focus groups was determined by continuing until comments and patterns began to repeat and little new material was generated.

Thirty-nine respondents (57 per cent) were women and 30 (43 per cent) were men. They ranged in age from 18 to 78 with an average age of 46 years. Their occupations were: 46 per cent in paid employment, 28 per cent housewife, 13 per cent student, 10 per cent retired, 3 per cent unemployed. Those in employment were classified according to the Registrar General's scheme: 19 per cent professional (class I), 34 per cent semi-professional (class II), 28 per cent non-manual/clerical (class IIIN), 13 per cent skilled manual/blue-collar (class IIIM), 6 per cent semi-skilled and unskilled manual (classes IV and V). The sample contained a moderate bias towards the middle class and was fairly balanced in terms of age and sex of respondents.

On average, respondents watched two hours and twenty-five minutes of television each day. Between 9 and 11 a.m., when discussion programmes are often broadcast, 28 per cent were generally not at home, 13 per cent were sometimes at home, and 59 per cent were generally at home. On average, they had watched *Kilroy* several times, with viewing habits ranging between those who have rarely or never seen it to those who watch most episodes each week. They tended to watch *Question Time* occasionally. Other discussion programmes (for example, *The Time, The Place, The Oprah Winfrey Show*) were watched by some respondents.

Each group watched a video-taped episode of *Kilroy*. The episodes were on poverty (four groups: can you be poor be if you have a colour television?), doctor–patient mis/communication (four groups: why do doctors and patients so often miscommunicate?), or friendship between men and women (three groups: what makes a good friend?). One of the authors led an informal discussion for 45–60 minutes. In the twelfth group, the respondents and group leader knew each other: they viewed an episode of *Kilroy* on social class (do we still have a class system and why?). These episodes represented the variety and treatments of issues in the genre. Each raised controversial questions on which people generally have opinions and readily become involved.

The groups were kept informal and all discussions were taped and transcribed in full. Focus groups combine interview styles of supportive elicitation and challenging exploration of contradictions and dilemmas. The leader followed a check-list of open-ended questions and otherwise made only minimal interventions, asking: Why do you think people watch programmes like this? Why do you think people go on programmes like this? How well did they cover the topic, was anything missed out? What do you think the host's role is? Why do experts like politicians, doctors or researchers go on such programmes and what is their role? Can you compare the programme to a documentary on the same topic? Are any issues too private to be discussed on television? Do such programmes serve any useful purpose? The purpose of the focus groups was to generate critical response to the programmes, not to continue the television discussion into real life.

INTERVIEWS WITH PROGRAMME PARTICIPANTS

Sixteen in-depth interviews with 14 programme participants and two viewers were conducted following an open-ended interview schedule. Interviewees included seven academics who had been invited experts on one or more audience discussion programmes, seven members of the public who had appeared on audience discussion programmes and two regular viewers. All names were changed for reporting; experts are identified by discipline. Interviews were conducted by one of the authors and were typically conducted face-to-face, although a few were conducted over the telephone. Interviews were taped and transcribed in full.

Appendix 2

Programme selection

A large sample of audience discussion and related programmes was taped over a period of four years (1989–92) for analysis in this book. The issues from one of several consecutive series of recordings are listed here to indicate the issues covered by the genre (Table A2.1).

In addition to the repeated viewing of a wide variety of programmes, 35 episodes (12 from *Kilroy*, 16 from *The Time, The Place*, 4 from *The Oprah Winfrey Show* and 3 from *Donahue*), selected randomly from the total sample, were content analysed for the sequencing of expert and lay speakers by an independent coder (Chapter 5).

Table A2.1: Sample of recordings of audience discussion programmes, showing range of topics covered

Programme	Date	Issue
Kilroy	9/5/89	Being single or a couple
The Time, The Place	9/5/89	Why remember/forget the war?
Kilroy	10/5/89	Jealousy
The Time, The Place	10/5/89	Living on Jersey
The Time, The Place	11/5/89	Is the pill safe?
Kilroy	12/5/89	Infertility and A.I.D.
The Time, The Place	12/5/89	Burglary
Kilroy	15/5/89	Effect of children on marriage
The Time, The Place	15/5/89	Obscene phone calls
Sally Jessy Raphael	15/5/89	Being divorced 3 + times
Kilroy	16/5/89	Doctor–patient communication
The Time, The Place	16/5/89	Public schools
Split Screen	16/5/89	Reporting rape to the police
Donahue	16/5/89	Autoerotic fixations
Kilroy	17/5/89	What is poverty in Britain?
The Time, The Place	17/5/89	Jokes about the handicapped
Kilroy	18/5/89	Friendship
The Time, The Place	18/5/89	Coping with getting the sack
Kilroy	19/5/89	Life support machines
The Time, The Place	19/5/89	Cosmetic surgery
Kilroy	22/5/89	Chastity, sex and marriage
The Time, The Place	22/5/89	Men being waited on by women

Appendix 3

Coding focus group discussions

All focus groups were content analysed according to a detailed coding schedule containing 51 categories using the computer package, TEXT-BASE ALPHA. The 51 categories covered comments about: (1) the respondents themselves; (2) the studio audience; (3) the host; (4) the experts; (5) the topic; (6) the argument; (7) the production; (8) the genre; (9) the public sphere. See Table 4.1 for category labels: full descriptions of categories are available from the authors.

Coding qualitative material is in practice always problematic (Krippendorf, 1982; Weber, 1985). One problem is that of identifying the units to be coded in natural conversation. We chose the conversational turn (or communicative act, 'an individual's single uninterrupted utterance'; Avery, Ellis and Glover, 1978), but decided to code each unit on one or more coding categories where appropriate so as to identify all instances of each category, for one turn may contain several categories. Each conversational turn was assigned a group/ statement code: all focus group quotations in the book are followed by this code (P1–4 = poverty groups; D1–4 = doctor–patient groups; F1–3 = friendship groups; SC = social class group). The 12 transcripts contained nearly 4,000 turns, with an average of 245 conversational turns each (range 183 to 605). Two independent coders were trained thoroughly in the use of the coding schedule. Each turn was then coded in the context in which it occurred. The two coders each independently coded over half of the transcripts and reliability was calculated on the dual coded material (equivalent of one transcript or 8 per cent of the total).

Coding reliability is vulnerable to three kinds of error: type 1 error (mistakenly omitted codes); type 2 error (mistakenly included codes); and explicit disagreements (two coders assign the same unit to different categories). Traditionally, content analysis only calculates disagreements. However, when attempting to identify all instances of categories without specifying in advance how many should be identified (e.g. one code per unit), then the other types of error become important. Consequently, we calculated two measures:

$$\frac{\text{agreements}}{\text{total judgements (agreements + disagreements)}}$$

$$\frac{(2 \times \text{agreements})}{(2 \times \text{agreements + omissions + disagreements})}$$

For the second measure, omissions were defined as categories identified by one coder but not by the other (i.e. types 1 and 2 error were treated as type 1 error on the part of one or the other coder). Disagreements were resolved through discussion. The two reliability measures were 77 per cent and 75 per cent which, for a complex coding task requiring interpretation of the texts in relation to many categories, was considered satisfactory.

References

Abrams, P. (1964) Radio and television. In D. Thompson (ed.), *Discrimination and popular culture*. Harmondsworth: Penguin.

Adorno, T. and Horkheimer, M. (1977) The culture industry: enlightenment as mass deception. In J. Curran, M. Gurevitch and J. Woollacott (eds), *Mass communication and society*. London: Edward Arnold.

Alexander, J. C. (1990) Analytic debates: understanding the relative autonomy of culture. In J. C. Alexander and S. Seidman (eds), *Culture and society: Contemporary debates*. Cambridge: Cambridge University Press.

Almond, G. A. and Verba, S. (eds) (1980) *The civic culture revisited*. Canada: Little, Brown & Co.

Anderson, B. (1991) *Imagined communities: Reflections on the origin and spread of nationalism*. London: Verso.

Andrews, G. (ed.) (1991) *Citizenship*. London: Lawrence & Wishart.

Ang, I. (1985) *Watching DALLAS: Soap opera and the melodramatic imagination*. New York: Methuen.

Arblaster, A. (1987) *Democracy*. Milton Keynes: Open University Press.

Armstrong, C. B. and Rubin, A. M. (1989) Talk radio as interpersonal communication. *Journal of communication, 39(2)*, 84–94.

Austin, J. L. (1962) *How to do things with words*. Cambridge, Mass.: Harvard University Press.

Avery, R. K. and Ellis, D. G. (1979) Talk radio as an interpersonal phenomenon. In G. Gumpert and R. Cathcart (eds), *Inter/Media: Interpersonal communication in a media world*. New York: Oxford University Press.

Avery, R. K., Ellis, D. G. and Glover, T. W. (1978) Patterns of communication on talk radio. *Journal of broadcasting, 22(1)*, 5–17.

Avery, R. K. and McCain, T. A. (1982) Interpersonal and mediated encounters: a reorientation to the mass communication process. In G. Gumpert and R. Cathcart (eds), *Inter/Media: Interpersonal communication in a media world* (Second edn). New York: Oxford University Press.

Bakhtin, M. M. (1981) *The dialogic imagination*. M. Holquist (ed.), C. Emerson and M. Holquist (Trans.). Austin, Tex.: University of Texas Press.

Ball-Rokeach, S. J. (1985) The origins of individual media-system dependency: a sociological framework. *Communication research, 12,* 485–510.

Balter, L. (1983) 'Giving away' child psychology over the airwaves. *The clinical psychologist, 36(2),* 37–40.

Barbalet, J. M. (1988) *Citizenship*. Milton Keynes: Open University Press.

Barthes, R. (1973) *Mythologies*. London: Paladin.

Baudrillard, J. (1988) Consumer society. In M. Poster (ed.), *Jean Baudrillard: Selected writings*. Polity Press.

Beer, G. (1970) *The romance*. London: Methuen.

Bell, D. (1990) The end of ideology in the West. In J. C. Alexander and S. Seidman (eds), *Culture and society: Contemporary debates*. Cambridge: Cambridge University Press.

Belsey, C. (1980) *Critical practice*. London: Routledge.

Benhabib, S. (1992) *Situating the self: Gender, community and postmodernism in contemporary ethics*. Cambridge: Polity press.

Beniger, J. R. (1987) Personalisation of mass media and the growth of pseudo-community. *Communication research, 14(3),* 352–71.

Benjamin, W. (1970) The work of art in the age of mechanical reproduction. In *Illuminations*, Jonathan Cape Ltd.

Benveniste, E. (1971) *Problems in general linguistics*. Miami: University of Miami Press.

Bettelheim, B. (1976) *The uses of enchantment: The meaning and importance of fairy tales*. Harmondsworth: Penguin.

Bierig, J. and Dimmick, J. (1979) The late night radio talk show as interpersonal communication. *Journalism quarterly, 56,* 92–96.

Billig, M. (1987) *Arguing and thinking: A rhetorical approach to social psychology*. Cambridge: Cambridge University Press.

Bion, W. R. (1967) *Second thoughts: Selected papers on psycho-analysis*. London: Heinemann.

Blumler, J. G. (1970) The political effects of television. In J. Halloran (ed.), *The effects of television*. London: Panther.

—— (ed) (1992) *Television and the public interest: Vulnerable values in West European broadcasting*. London: Sage.

Blumler, J. G., Gurevitch, M. and Katz, E. (1985) REACHING OUT: a future for gratifications research. In K. E. Rosengren, L. A. Wenner and P. Palmgreen (eds), *Media gratifications research: Current perspectives*. Beverly Hills, Cal.: Sage.

Boorstin, D. J. (1982) From hero to celebrity: the human pseudo-event. In
    G. Gumpert and R. Cathcart (eds), *Inter/Media: Interpersonal
    communication in a media world* (Second edn). New York: Oxford.
Bouhoutsos, J. C., Goodchilds, J. D. and Huddy, L. (1986) Media
    psychology: an empirical study of radio call-in psychology programs.
    Professional Psychology: Research and Practice, 17(25), 408–14.
Bower, R. T. (1973) Television and the public. New York: Holt, Rinehart &
    Winston.
Brown, M. E. (ed.) (1990) *Television and women's culture: The politics of the
    popular*. London: Sage.
Bryant, J., and Zillman, D. (eds) (1986) *Perspectives on media effects*.
    Hillsdale, N.J.: Erlbaum.
Burke, K. (1973) *The philosophy of literary form: Studies in symbolic action*.
    Berkeley and Los Angeles: University of California Press.
Cantril, H. (1940) *The invasion from Mars: A study in the psychology of
    panic*. Princeton, N.J.: Princeton University Press.
Carbaugh, D. (1988) *Talking American: Cultural discourses on
    DONAHUE*. Norwood, N.J.: Ablex.
Carpignano, P., Andersen, R., Aronowitz, S. and Difazio, W. (1990)
    Chatter in the age of electronic reproduction: talk television and the
    'public mind'. *Social text, 25/26*, 33–55.
Cerulo, K. A., Ruane, J. M. and Chayko, M. (1992) Technological ties that
    bind: media-generated primary groups. *Communications research, 19*,
    109–29.
Chesebro, J. W. (1982) Communication, values, and popular television
    series – a four-year assessment. In H. Newcomb (ed.), *Television: The
    critical view*. Oxford: Oxford University Press.
Clifford, J. and Marcus, C. E. (eds) (1986) *Writing culture: The poetics and
    politics of ethnography*. Chicago: Chicago University Press.
Collins, R., Curran, J., Garnham, N., Scannell, P., Schlesinger, P. and
    Sparks, C. (eds) (1986) *Media, culture and society: A critical reader*.
    London: Sage.
Corner, J. (ed.) (1986) Preface to *Documentary and the mass media*.
    London: Edward Arnold.
—— (1991) Meaning, genre and context: the problematics of 'public
    knowledge' in the new audience studies. In J. Curran and M. Gurevitch
    (eds), *Mass media and society*. London: Methuen.
Crittenden, J. (1971) Democratic functions of the open mike radio forum.
    Public opinion quarterly, 35(2), 200–10.
Curran, J. (1991) Rethinking the media as a public sphere. In P. Dahlgren
    and C. Sparks (eds), *Communication and citizenship: Journalism and the
    public sphere in the new media age*. London: Routledge.
Curti, L. (1988) Genre and gender. *Cultural studies, 12(2)*, 152–67.

Dardis, J. (1992) Discourse analysis: radio phone-in programmes. A gestalt approach. Paper presented at the Second Discourse Analysis Workshop, Manchester.

Dayan, D., Katz, E. and Kerns, P. (1985) Armchair pilgrimages: the trips of John Paul II and their television public: an anthropological view. In M. Gurevitch and M. R. Levy (eds), *Mass communication review yearbook*, 5. Beverly Hills, Cal.: Sage.

de Certeau, M. (1984) *The practices of everyday life*. Los Angeles: University of California Press

Dews, P. (1987) *Logics of disintegration: Post-structuralist thought and the claims of critical theory*. London: Verso.

Dillon, M. (1990) Broadcasting and controversial moral issues: the challenge of public debates on abortion and divorce. Paper presented at the 40th Annual Conference of the International Communication Association, Dublin.

Dryzek, J. S. (1990) *Discursive democracy: Politics, policy and political science*. Cambridge: Cambridge University Press.

Dubrow, H. (1982) *Genre*. London: Methuen.

Eagleton, T. (1983) *Literary theory: An introduction*. Oxford: Blackwell.

Eco, U. (1979) Introduction: the role of the reader. *The role of the reader: Explorations in the semiotics of texts*. Bloomington, Ind.: Indiana University Press.

—— (1990) *The limits of interpretation*. Bloomington, Ind.: Indiana University Press.

Eley, G. (1992) Nations, publics and political cultures: placing Habermas in the nineteenth century. In C. Calhoun (ed.), *Habermas and the public sphere*. Cambridge, Mass.: The MIT Press.

Elliot, P. (1986) Intellectuals, the 'information society' and the disappearance of the public sphere. In R. Collins, J. Curran, N. Garnham, P. Scannell, P. Schlesinger and C. Sparks (eds), *Media, culture and society: A critical reader*. London: Sage.

Farr, R. M. and Moscovici, S. (eds) (1984) *Social representations*. Cambridge: Cambridge University Press.

Ferrarotti, F. (1988) *The end of conversation: The impact of mass media on modern society*. New York: Greenwood Press.

Fiske, J. (1987) *Television culture*. London: Methuen.

Fogel, A. (1986) Talk shows: on reading television. In S. Donadio, S. Railton and O. Seavey (eds), *Emerson and his legacy: Essays in honor of Quentin Anderson*. Carbondale: Southern Illinois University Press.

Forester, J. (ed.) (1985) *Critical theory and public life*. Boston: MIT Press.

Foucault, M. (1970) *The order of things: An archaeology of the human sciences*. London: Tavistock.

Fraser, N. (1989) What's critical about critical theory? The case of Habermas and gender. In N. Fraser, *Unruly practices: Power, discourse and gender in contemporary social theory.* Minneapolis: University of Minnesota Press.

—— (1990) Rethinking the public sphere: a contribution to the critique of actually existing democracy. *Social text, 25/26,* 56–80.

Friedrich, C. J. (1950) *The new image of the common man.* Boston: Beacon Press. Second, enlarged edn.

Garnham, N. (1990) The media and the public sphere. In N. Garnham, *Capitalism and communication: Global culture and the economics of information.* London: Sage.

Garton, G., Montgomery, M. and Tolson, A. (1991) Ideology, scripts and metaphors in the public sphere of a general election. In P. Scannell (ed.), *Broadcast talk.* London: Sage.

Gastil, J. (1992) Undemocratic discourse: a review of theory and research on political discourse. *Discourse and society, 3(4),* 469–500.

Gerbner, G., Gross, L., Morgan, M. and Signorielli, N. (1986) Living with television: the dynamics of the cultivation process. In J. Bryant and D. Zillman (eds), *Perspectives on media effects.* Hillsdale, N.J.: Erlbaum.

Giddens, A. (1985) Time, space and regionalisation. In D. Gregory and J. Urry (eds), *Social relations and spacial structures,* Basingstoke: Macmillan.

—— (1991) *Modernity and self-identity: Self and society in the late modern age.* Cambridge: Polity Press.

—— (1992) *The transformation of intimacy: Sexuality, love and eroticism in modern societies.* Cambridge: Polity Press.

Gilligan, C. (1982) *In a different voice: Psychological theory and women's development.* Cambridge, Mass.: Harvard University Press.

Goffman, E. (1959) *The presentation of self in everyday life.* Harmondsworth: Penguin.

—— (1981) *Forms of talk.* Oxford: Blackwell.

Goodhardt, G. J., Ehrenberg, A. S. C. and Collins, M. A. (1975). *The television audience: Patterns of viewing.* London: Gower.

Goodman, I. R. (1983) Television's role in family interaction: a family systems perspective. *Journal of family issues, 4(2),* 405–24.

Gouldner, A. W. (1976) *The dialectic of ideology and technology.* New York: Seabury Press.

Graham, K. (1986) *The battle of democracy: Conflict, consensus and the individual.* Brighton: Wheatsheaf Books Ltd.

Grant, W. (1989) *Pressure groups, politics, and democracy in Britain.* New York: Philip Allan.

Grice, H. P. (1975) Logic and conversation. In P. Cole and J. Morgan, (eds) *Syntax and semantics, vol 3.* New York: Academic Press.

Habermas, J. (1984) The public sphere: an encyclopedia article (1964) *New German critique, Autumn,* 49–55.

—— (1987a) *The philosophical discourse of modernity: Twelve lectures*. F. Lawrence (Trans.). Cambridge: Polity Press.

—— (1987b) *The theory of communicative action*, vol 2, *Lifeworld and system: A critique of functionalist reason*. T. McCarthy (Trans.). Boston: Beacon Press.

—— (1988) *Legitimation crisis*. Cambridge: Polity Press.

—— (1989) *The structural transformation of the public sphere: An inquiry into a category of bourgeois society*. T. Burger with F. Lawrence (Trans.). Cambridge, Mass.: The MIT Press.

—— (1990) Modernity versus postmodernity. In J. C. Alexander and S. Seidman (eds), *Culture and society: Contemporary debates*. Cambridge: Cambridge University Press.

Hägerstrand, T. (1967) *Innovation diffusion as a spatial process*. Chicago: University of Chicago Press.

Hall, S. (1980) Encoding/Decoding. In S. Hall, D. Hobson, A. Lowe and P. Willis (eds), *Culture, media, language*. London: Hutchinson.

Halloran, J. (ed.) (1970) *The effects of television*. London: Panther.

Harvey, D. (1989) *The condition of postmodernity*. Oxford: Blackwell.

Heath, A. and Topf, R. (1987) Political culture. In R. Jowell, S. Witherspoon and L. Brook (eds), *British social attitudes: The 1987 report*. London: Gower.

Hebdige, D. (1979) *Subculture: The meaning of style*. London: Methuen.

Heider, F. (1958) *The psychology of interpersonal relations*. New York: Wiley.

Held, D. (1980) *Introduction to critical theory*. London: Hutchinson.

—— (1987) *Models of democracy*. Cambridge: Polity Press.

—— (1991) Between state and civil society: citizenship. In G. Andrews (ed.), *Citizenship*. London: Lawrence & Wishart.

Heller, C. (1978) *Broadcasting and accountability*. British Film Institute Television Monograph 7. London: British Film Institute.

Heritage, J. (1991) Retelling media stories: newspapers vs. television. Paper presented at the Popular Culture Symposium: Media-conversation-opinion, Annenberg School of Communications, USC, September.

Heritage, J. C., Clayman, S. and Zimmerman, D. H. (1988) Discourse and message analysis: the micro-structure of mass media messages. In R. P. Hawkins, J. M. Weimann and S. Pingree (eds), *Advancing communication science: Merging mass and interpersonal processes*. Newbury Park, Cal.: Sage.

Himmelweit, H. T., Swift, B. and Jaeger, M. E. (1980) The audience as critic: a conceptual analysis of television entertainment. In P. H. Tannenbaum (ed.), *The entertainment functions of television*. Hillsdale, N.J.: Erlbaum.

Hobson, D. (1982) *Crossroads: The drama of a soap opera*. London: Methuen.

Hoggart, R. (1957) *The uses of literacy*. London: Chatto & Windus.

Holub, R. C. (1991) *Jürgen Habermas: Critic in the public sphere*. London: Routledge.

Horton, D. and Wohl, R. R. (1956) Mass communication and para-social interaction. *Psychiatry*, *19*, 215–29.

Hovland, C., Janis, I. and Kelley, H. H. (1953) *Communication and persuasion*. New Haven: Yale University Press.

Huesmann, L. R., Eron, L. D., Klein, R., Brice, P. and Fischer, P. (1983) Mitigating the imitation of aggressive behaviors by changing children's attitudes about media violence. *Journal of personality and social psychology*, *44*, 899–910.

Huyssen, A. (1986) *After the great divide: Modernism, mass culture, postmodernism*. Basingstoke: Macmillan.

Iyengar, S. and Kinder, D. R. (1987) *News that matters: Television and American opinion*. Chicago: University of Chicago Press.

Jensen, K. B. (1986) *Making sense of the news: Towards a theory and an empirical model of reception for the study of mass communication*. Aarhus C, Denmark: Aarhus University Press.

Jordan, M. (1981) Realism and convention. In R. Dyer, C. Geraghty, M. Jordan, T. Lovell, R. Paterson and J. Stewart, *Coronation street*. British Film Institute Television Monograph no. 13. London: British Film Institute.

Katz, E. (1980) Media events: the sense of occasion. *Studies in Visual Anthropology*, *6*, 84–9.

Keane, J. (1991) *The media and democracy*. Cambridge: Polity Press.

Kellner, D. (1990) *Television and the crisis of democracy*. Boulder: Westview Press.

Kennedy, T. (1990) Beyond the documentary: a participatory approach to community communication. Paper presented at the 40th Annual Conference of the International Communication Association, Dublin.

Klonoff, E. (1983) A star is born: psychologists and the media. *Professional psychology: Research and practice*, *14(6)*, 847–54.

Kluge, A. (1981–2) On film and the public sphere. *New German critique*, *24/25*, 206–20.

Koss, S. (1984) *The rise and fall of the political press in Britain, vol 2: The twentieth century*. London: Hamilton.

Krippendorf, K. (1982) *Content analysis*. Beverly Hills, Cal.: Sage.

Labov, W. and Fanshel, D. (1977) *Therapeutic discourse: Psychotherapy as conversation*. New York: Academic Press.

Lang, G. E. and Lang, K. (1983) *The battle for public opinion: The president, the press and the polls during Watergate*. New York: Columbia University Press.

Lang, K. and Lang, G. E. (1968) *Politics and television*. Chicago: Quadrangle Books.

Lazarsfeld, P. F. and Merton, R. K. (1948) Mass communication, popular taste and organized social action. In L. Bryson (ed.), *The communication of ideas*. New York: Harper.

Leith, D. and Myerson, G. (1989) *The power of address: Explorations in rhetoric*. London: Routledge.

Lentricchia, F. (1983) *Criticism and social change*. Chicago: University of Chicago Press.

Levy, D. (1989) Social support and the media: analysis of responses by radio psychology talk show hosts. *Professional psychology: Research and practice, 20(2)*, 73–8.

Levy, M. R. (1982) Watching TV news as para-social interaction. In G. Gumpert and R. Cathcart (eds), *Inter/Media: Interpersonal communication in a media world* (Second edn) New York: Oxford.

Liebes, T. (1990) Notes on the struggle to define involvement in television viewing. Paper presented to the conference Public et Reception, Paris, December.

Liebes, T. and Katz, E. (1986) Patterns of involvement in television fiction: a comparative analysis. *European journal of communication, 1*, 151–71.

—— (1990) *The export of meaning*. Oxford: Oxford University Press.

Linde, C. (1987) Explanatory systems in oral life stories. In D. Holland, and N. Quinn (eds), *Cultural models in language and thought*. Cambridge: Cambridge University Press.

Livingstone, S. M. (1987) The representation of personal relationships in television drama: realism, convention and morality. In R. Burnett, P. McGhee and D. D. Clarke (eds), *Accounting for relationships: Explanation, representation and knowledge*. London: Methuen.

—— (1990) *Making sense of television: The psychology of audience interpretation*. Oxford: Pergamon.

—— (1991) Audience reception: the role of the viewer in retelling romantic drama. In J. Curran and M. Gurevitch (eds), *Mass media and society*. London: Methuen.

Livingstone, S. M. and Lunt, P. K. (1992) Expert and lay participation in television debates: an analysis of audience discussion programmes. *European journal of communication, 7(1)*, 9–35.

Livingstone, S. M., Lunt, P. K. and Slotover, M. (1992) Debating drunk driving: the construction of causal explanations in television discussion programmes. *Journal of community and applied social psychology, 2*, 131–45.

Livingstone, S. M., Wober, J. M. and Lunt, P. K. (in preparation) Involvement and participation in audience discussion programmes: an analysis of viewers' preferences.

Lunt, P. K. (1988) The perceived causal structure of examination failure. *British journal of social psychology, 27*, 171–9.

Lyotard, J-F. (1984) *The postmodern condition*. Minneapolis: University of Minnesota Press.

—— (1990) The postmodern condition. In J. C. Alexander and S. Seidman (eds), *Culture and society: Contemporary debates*. Cambridge: Cambridge University Press.

McCombs, M. E. and Shaw, D. (1972) The agenda-setting function of the mass media. *Public opinion quarterly*, *36*, 176–87.

McRobbie, A. (ed.) (1989) *Zoot suits and second-hand dresses*. Basingstoke: Macmillan.

—— (1986) Postmodernism and popular culture. *Journal of Communication Inquiry*, *10(2)*, 108–16.

Mann, P. (1990) Unifying discourse: city college as a post-modern public sphere. *Social text*, *25/26*, 81–102.

Martin, G. (1964) The press. In D. Thompson (ed.), *Discrimination and popular culture*. Harmondsworth: Penguin.

Masciarotte, G-J. (1991) C'mon girl: Oprah Winfrey and the discourse of feminine talk. *Genders*, *11*, 81–110.

Meyrowitz, J. (1985) *No sense of place: The impact of electronic media on social behavior*. New York: Oxford University Press.

Mills, C. W. (1959) *The sociological imagination*. Oxford: Oxford University Press.

Morgan, D. L. (1988) *Focus groups as qualitative research*. Newbury Park, Cal.: Sage.

Morley, D. (1980) *The nationwide audience: Structure and decoding*. British Film Institute Television Monograph no. 11. London: British Film Institute.

—— (1981) The nationwide audience: a critical postscript. *Screen Education*, *39*, 3–14.

—— (1986) *Family television: Cultural power and domestic leisure*. London: Comedia.

Moscovici, S. (1981) On social representation. In J. P. Forgas (ed.), *Social cognition: Perspectives on everyday understanding*. London: Academic Press.

—— (1984) The phenomenon of social representations. In R. M. Farr and S. Moscovici (eds), *Social representations*. Cambridge: Cambridge University Press.

Mouffe, C. (1988) Hegemony and new political subjects: towards a new concept of democracy. In C. Nelson and L. Grossberg (eds), *Marxism and the interpretation of culture*. Basingstoke: Macmillan Education.

Mulgan, G. (1991) Citizenship and responsibilities. In G. Andrews (ed.), *Citizenship*. London: Lawrence & Wishart.

Nava, M. (1991) Consumerism reconsidered: buying and power. *Cultural studies*, *5(2)*, 157–73.

Negrine, R. (1989) *Politics and the mass media in Britain*. London: Routledge.

Negt, O. and Kluge, A. (1990). Selections from 'Public opinion and practical knowledge: toward an organisational analysis of proletariat and middle class public opinion'. *Social text, 25/26*, 24–32.

Newcomb, H. M. and Hirsch, P. M. (1984) Television as a cultural forum: implications for research. In W. D. Rowland and B. Watkins (eds), *Interpreting television: Current research perspectives*, 58–73. Beverly Hills, Cal.: Sage.

Nimmo, D. and Combs, J. E. (1990) *Mediated political realities*. New York: Longman.

Oskamp, S. (1977) *Attitudes and opinions*. Englewood Cliffs, N.J.: Prentice-Hall.

Parry, G., Moyser, G. and Day, N. (1992) *Political participation and democracy in Britain*. Cambridge: Cambridge University Press.

Petty, R. E. and Cacioppo, J. T. (1981) *Attitudes and persuasion: Classic and contemporary approaches*. Iowa: W. C. Brown Co.

Petty, R. E., Ostrom, T. M., and Brock, T. C. (1981) *Cognitive responses in persuasive communications: A text in attitude change*. Hillsdale, N.J.: Erlbaum.

Pfau, M. (1990) A channel approach to television influence. *Journal of broadcasting and electronic media, 34(2)*, 195–214.

Phillips, A. (1991) *Engendering democracy*. Cambridge: Polity Press.

Polan, D. (1990) The public's fear, or media as monster in Habermas, Negt, and Kluge. *Social text, 25/26*, 260–6.

Potter, J. and Wetherell, M. (1987) *Discourse and social psychology: Beyond attitudes and behaviour*. London: Sage.

Qualter, T. H. (1991) *Advertising and democracy in the mass age*. Basingstoke: Macmillan.

Quinn, N. and Holland, D. (1987) Culture and cognition. In D. Holland, and N. Quinn, (eds), *Cultural models in language and thought*. Cambridge: Cambridge University Press.

Raboy, M. and Dagenais, B. (1992) *Media, crisis and democracy: Mass communication and the disruption of social order*. London: Sage.

Radway, J. (1984) *Reading the romance: Women, patriarchy and popular literature*. Chapel Hill: University of North Carolina Press.

Raviv, A., Raviv, A. and Yunovitz, R. (1989) Radio psychology and psychotherapy: comparison of client attitudes and expectations. *Professional psychology: Research and practice, 20(2)*, 67–72.

Robbins, B. (1990a) Introduction. *Social text, 25/26*, 3–17.

—— (1990b) Interdisciplinarity in public: the rhetoric of rhetoric. *Social text, 25/26*, 103–18.

Roberts, D. F. and Bachen, C. M. (1981) Mass communication effects. *Annual review of psychology, 32*, 307–56.

Robinson, B. E. (1982) Family experts on television talk shows: facts, values, and half-truths. *Family relations, 31*, 369–78.

Rose, B. G. (1985) The talk show. In B. G. Rose (ed.), *TV genres: A handbook and reference guide*. Westport, Con.: Greenwood Press.

Ross, A. (1989) *No respect: Intellectuals and popular culture*. New York: Routledge.

Rubin, A. M. and Rubin, R. B. (1985) Interface of personal and mediated communication: a research agenda. *Critical studies in mass communication, 2*, 36–53.

Sarbin, T. (ed.) (1986) *The narrative perspective in psychology*. New York: Praeger.

Scannell, P. (1986) Broadcasting and the politics of unemployment 1930–1935. In R. Collins, J. Curran, N. Garnham, P. Scannell, P. Schlesinger and C. Sparks (eds), *Media, culture and society: A critical reader*. London: Sage.

—— (1990) The merely sociable. Presented at ESRC/PICT Workshop on Domestic Consumption and Information and Communication Technologies, Brunel, May, 1990.

—— (1991) Introduction: the relevance of talk. In P. Scannell (ed.), *Broadcast talk*. London: Sage.

Scannell, P. and Cardiff, D. (1991) *A social history of British broadcasting, Vol. 1922–1939: Serving the nation*. Oxford: Blackwell.

Schlesinger, P. (1978) *Putting 'reality' together: BBC news*. London: Constable.

Schudson, M. (1978) The ideal of conversation in the mass media. *Communication research, 5(3)*, 320–9.

Seidman, S. (1990) Substantive debates: moral order and social crises–perspectives on modern culture. In J. C. Alexander and S. Seidman (eds), *Culture and society: Contemporary debates*. Cambridge: Cambridge University Press.

Shields, R. (1991) *Places on the margin: Alternative geographies of modernity*. London: Routlege.

Shotter, J. (1989) Social accountability and the social construction of 'You'. In J. Shotter and K. J. Gergen (eds), *Texts of identity*. London: Sage.

Silj, A. (1988) *East of Dallas: The European challenge to American television*. London: British Film Institute.

Silverstone, R. (1984) Narrative strategies in television science – a case study. *Media, culture and society, 6*, 377–410.

Sontag, S. (1967) Notes on 'camp'. In Sontag, S. (ed.), *Against interpretation*. New York: Farrar, Straus and Giroux.

Spragens, T. A., (1990) *Reason and democracy*. Durham: Duke University Press.

Squire, C. (1991) Is *The Oprah Winfrey Show* feminist television? Paper presented at the International Women's Studies Congress, New York.

Tebbutt, J. (1989) Constructing broadcasting for the public. In H. Wilson (ed.), *Australian communications and the public sphere*. South Melbourne, Aus.: Macmillan.

Thompson, J. B. (1990) *Ideology and modern culture: Critical social theory in the era of mass communication*. Cambridge: Polity Press.

Toulmin, S. (1958) *The uses of argument*. New York: Cambridge University Press.

Tramer, H. and Jeffres, L. W. (1983) Talk radio–forum and companion. *Journal of broadcasting, 27(3)*, 297–300.

Tuchman, G. (1981) Myth and the consciousness industry: a new look at the effects of the mass media. In E. Katz and T. Szcesko (eds), *Mass media and social change*. Beverly Hills, Cal.: Sage.

—— (1988) Mass media institutions. In N. J. Smelser (ed.), *Handbook of sociology*. Newbury Park, Cal.: Sage.

Tulloch, J. and Chapman, S. (1992) Experts in crisis: the framing of radio debate about the risk of AIDS to heterosexuals. *Discourse and society, 3(4)*, 437–67.

Turner, B. S. (ed.) (1990) *Theories of modernity and postmodernity*. London: Sage.

Turow, J. (1974) Talk show radio as interpersonal communication. *Journal of broadcasting, 18(2)*, 171–9.

Verwey, N. E. (1990) *Radio call-ins and covert politics: A verbal unit and role analysis approach*. Aldershot, UK: Avebury.

Walton, D. N. (1989) *Informal logic: A handbook for critical argumentation*. Cambridge: Cambridge University Press.

Weber, R. P. (1985) *Basic content analysis*. Newbury Park, Cal.: Sage.

Wittgenstein, W. (1958) *Philosophical investigations*. Oxford: Blackwell.

Zimmerman, J. F. (1986) *Participatory democracy: Populism revived*. New York: Praeger.

Index